THE HUMANITIES
in general education

BROWN

GENERAL EDUCATION SERIES

EARL J. MCGRATH, *General Editor, Institute of Higher Education, Teachers College, Columbia University*

THE HUMANITIES
in general education

JAMES A. FISHER
Editor

Chairman, Division of Humanities,
Boston University College
of Basic Studies

Wm. C. Brown Company Publishers, *Dubuque, Iowa*

Copyright 1960
by
James A. Fisher

Library of Congress Catalog Card Number: 60-16535

Manufactured by WM. C. BROWN CO. INC., Dubuque, Iowa

Printed in U. S. A.

table of contents

NOTE

The first article in the volume is a reprint of the summary chapter in the original volume published in 1949. It is included to refresh the memories of those already acquainted with the prior study and to serve as background for those present readers who are unfamiliar with the earlier work.

J.A.F.

foreword

Twelve years ago when programs of general education were multiplying rapidly in the colleges and universities of this country, the editor of this series of volumes on the general education in major branches of learning conceived the idea that an interchange of experience among institutions would be advantageous to all. Hence, he asked a group of teachers of general education courses to contribute an article on their own programs to be brought together under one cover with other similar institutional statements in the natural sciences, social sciences, humanities, and communications. The four volumes which resulted, were widely used not only among institutions which had already inaugurated a program of general studies, but also among those attempting to design such a program suitable to the needs of their own students.

The Wm. C. Brown Company Publishers of Dubuque, Iowa, the publishers of the original volumes, has long felt that they should be brought up to date. Several have been out of print for a period of years. In the time since the books originally appeared, many new programs have come into existence, some in the colleges and universities represented in the earlier volumes, and some in institutions which have launched a general program in the past decade. In the main the present volume, therefore, represents a review of the changes that have occurred in a number of the original programs. These statements have been supplemented by others from institutions in which promising new programs are in operation.

In contrast to the earlier works, each of these new volumes has been prepared by a person who is, or has recently been, teaching a general education course in one of the major fields of knowledge. This volume has been prepared by Prof. James A. Fisher of Boston University College of Basic Studies who has for some years been thoroughly familiar with the developments in general education in the humanities. He has brought together an excellent collection of critical essays in this field. He has also prepared a chapter summarizing the trends in the humanities over the past decade. Anyone who wishes to gain an overview of the philosophy and the practice of general education in the humanities will find this volume especially useful. Persons working in the other divisions of knowledge will be interested in the companion volumes also issued by the William C. Brown Company. They are *Science in General Education, Social Sciences in General Education, Communications in General Education, Curriculum Building in General Education, General Education for Personal Maturity, and The Larger Learning.*

The one outstanding generalization gained from a reading of these compendiums is that many faculty members in colleges and universities are convinced that a broader education in the various disciplines is essential if American youth are to understand the complex world in which they live. The recognition of this fact has caused many faculties to launch comprehensive programs of instruction as described in this and the companion volumes. There would be many more such efforts if broadly educated teachers and suitable teaching materials were available. And these preconditions of a suitable general education would exist if the graduate schools would produce teachers prepared for and dedicated to the important work of providing that general education without which the fruits of specialized learning cannot be effectively used in the improvement of American society. These volumes suggest the type of advanced education college teachers must have if this significant mission is to be accomplished. They also stand as eloquent testimony that there is in higher education a sizable group of men and women who have caught the vision of America's most pressing educational need, and are daily devoting a portion of their lives to the better education of this generation of students for their broad responsibilities as citizens in a democratic society.

Earl J. McGrath
Executive Officer
Institute of Higher Education

chapter 1

TRENDS IN THE HUMANITIES IN GENERAL EDUCATION

*Robert F. Davidson**

Several pioneer efforts to revitalize the study of our cultural heritage in the Western world have appreciably influenced the humanities courses now being offered throughout the country. It was becoming increasingly clear thirty years ago that highly specialized and departmentalized work in history, literature, and philosophy was providing university students with little real understanding of the spirit and meaning of their own civilization. This was brought home to the faculty at Columbia University by experiences during the first world war, and two significant efforts were made at Columbia to meet the situation. John Erskine began his "great books" seminar for upperclassmen and the Contemporary Civilization course was introduced as part of the required freshman curriculum. In the one case, students were brought again into direct contact with the great minds and the great literature of our culture; in the other, they were given a well-integrated picture of the historical and intellectual forces that have helped make Western civilization what it is today.

A two-year program motivated by the same spirit was initiated in 1921 at Reed College where President Scholz sought to provide for his students "an examination of the fundamental bases and the historical backgrounds of contemporary civilization as they can be studied in the great representative fields of knowledge." In 1927 Alexander Meikeljohn organized the Experimental Col-

---

*The Author is chairman of the humanities in the University College, University of Florida.

1

lege at Wisconsin, unquestionably the most ambitious of these pioneer ventures. Meikeljohn saw the desirability of a more concentrated study of one great epoch in Western civilization as a foundation for intelligent understanding and effective living in our own society. Consequently, a full year was developed in his experiment to the Athens of Pericles and Plato. The great literature of that age was read; its art and philosophy examined, and its political problems related meaningfully to the issues that face us in America today.

The point of view that dominated these early endeavors is clearly reflected in more recent efforts to develop general education courses in both the humanities and the social sciences. Among the four or five major purposes adopted in humanities courses at present, the concern to provide for the student some broader understanding of his cultural heritage and some enlarged cultural perspective in his own view of life is certainly the most common. Upon this aim there is more agreement than upon any other. It is generally felt that the typical college student needs to be released from slavery to the purely contemporary, and that to accomplish this the limited outlook of our own age and society must be enlarged and broadened by a knowledge of history and by the understanding which such a knowledge provides of man himself and of his creative achievements. Until a student has in some measure at least made the great cultural achievements of the past his own, it is obvious that he cannot live fully and intelligently today.

There is general agreement also that the more traditional courses, whether in the field of history or literature or in the arts, have not provided a broad and well-integrated interpretation of our cultural heritage. New humanities courses that cut across departmental lines, comprehensive in spirit rather than narrowly specialized or analytic, seem essential to almost all concerned if this major aim of general education is to be accomplished. Professor White, of Oklahoma A. and M. College, where this view is accepted, urges in its support that "the disposition to see life whole rather than fragmented by departmental and specialized investigation makes possible saner judgment and more wholesome living in these confused and foreboding days."

Some institutions are committed to the principle that students as a part of their general education should be brought face to face with the great issues of living that man has had to confront in the past and must face today. This is accepted, therefore, as one of the major aims of humanities courses in these institutions. While related to the historical-cultural objective, it is not identical in purpose. Familiarity with great ideas and great books rather than with the major historical patterns of culture is taken to be of primary importance. There is a greater concern here also with the development of intellectual maturity, a sustained interest in the problems with which men have wrestled in trying to find meaning and purpose in life. There is less emphasis, on the other hand, upon the historical forces by which civilization has been shaped; a feeling instead that in the great works of literature and philosophy the enduring insights of the past have been preserved.

This is the point of view, of course, that has dominated the program at St. John's College. As Dr. Kieffer puts it:

> Those who study under the Great Books tradition are able to judge the naiveté of the moderns with great clarity and with an ironic understanding. The question raised by Greek tragedy, the power and limitation of human reason, illustrated in Thucydides and applied by Plato to the cosmos and man's soul, stares us starkly in the face today. These ancients do not answer the question for us. They give us a paradigm and a frame of reference to do our own thinking about the problem. The Biblical treatment of man together with the Medieval wrestling with the reconciliation of revelation and systematic theology confront us with the problem of evil, while Cervantes and Shakespeare superbly illustrate the problem in the light of the actions of men who are very much living beings. Even the great modern problem, the control of nature through natural science, is empty for those who are unaware of what the Cartesian and Baconian revolution implied, of what they were revolting against. Men educated in the tradition thus have a wider perspective and gain deeper insight into the questions that are treated so superficially today.

Many humanities courses accept this point of view. In a few others there is a larger concern with the student's present problems of living and thinking than with his education in the great tradition. Emphasis in these courses is put upon the importance not only of aiding and encouraging "the participating students to build a coherent set of ideals for themselves with which to confront the bewildering present," but also in helping them apply "at a high ethical level a consistent set of values to all situations." The student's ability to consider critically and responsibly his own beliefs, aims, and values is recognized as an important consideration in most courses, and in even more general terms the development of a critical intelligence, the ability to make intelligent choices in life as a free man and a free citizen, is stressed. As thus stated, these are not aims peculiar to courses in the humanities; they are among the dominant concerns of general education. But this whole matter of developing a philosophy of life adequate for the needs of the present has been given particular attention by those responsible for general courses in the humanities and has become one of the major objectives of many such courses.

In recent years, on the other hand, the conviction has been gaining ground in some institutions that the concern of the humanities should be with an understanding of the arts rather than with history or philosophy, and the aim of a number of humanities courses is being stated in such terms. As thus interpreted, it is the purpose of the humanities to acquaint students with the best works in literature, music, and the visual arts, to provide some understanding of the aesthetic principles and techniques in terms of which intelligent appreciation of the arts is possible, and to develop some competence in the use of these principles. The statement of objectives worked out from this point of view at Pennsylvania College for Women throws desirable emphasis upon the practical value of this knowledge to the student. Aims of the course are:

1. To help the student to enjoy and understand the arts as they enter into daily life; to help her become a keen and intelligent reader as well as an enthusiastic yet discriminating member of the audience at plays, concerts, the dance, and art exhibits.
2. To acquaint her with works which have contributed to the development of drama, literature, music, and the visual arts.
3. To show how one art contributes to the understanding of others.

4. To demonstrate the value of being able to think concretely in terms of the arts.

5. To give every student an opportunity to participate actively in one or more of the arts.

6. To give the student an understanding of aesthetic principles.

7. To form a nucleus of society wherein the arts can flourish.

To achieve the objectives that have been mentioned and to provide some general integration of the material included in the humanities area, courses of three rather well-defined types have been developed. It is true that in many institutions two or three, in some cases all, of the broad purposes discussed are accepted. In only a very few courses has there been undeviating commitment to a single objective. But despite minor variations in each case, a dominant aim has served to shape the general character and content of most humanities courses into one or another of these three major patterns.

Without question the most common type of course is that which adopts the historical and cultural approach. Of the institutions discussed in this volume, more than three-fourths have humanities courses which make use of the chronological framework. In some cases these courses originated as historical surveys of Western civilization, and some, as at Michigan State College, have retained such a descriptive title as the History of Civilization. In courses of this type the historical emphasis and point of view naturally has a place of major importance. There is a common assumption that only upon a sound understanding of the nature of the past can one hope to build any true comprehension of the present. The place of the historical method and insight in the humanities is strongly urged by proponents of these courses. Thus Professor Kimber of Michigan State writes:

> To be fully human is not to live restricted to one dimension of space or time. The humanity of man is increased by education that brings about a comprehension and an appreciation of the thoughts, feelings, and ideals of man in all ages. The historical cosmopolite is the truly civilized man. A civilized man is the complete human being.

Gradually the conviction was born of experience, however, that the historical survey attempted too much, was too superficial and too full of undigested detail to achieve its larger purpose. Quite generally courses of this type now select four or five of the great periods in the development of Western civilization for careful study. At Reed College, at Michigan State, at the University of Arizona, among others, the classic Greek civilization, the Roman, the Medieval Christian, the Renaissance, and the Age of Enlightment in Europe — ages that have contributed most directly and significantly to our cultural heritage, that have more direct relationship to contemporary life and thought and so more meaning and appeal for the average student — have found a dominant place in historical-cultural courses.

The three principles that have governed such an organization and selection of material at Michigan State have obviously been at work in all similar cases. First is the principle of *historical economy*. Time is limited; only those facts that are essential to an understanding of the issue under consideration are admissable as part of the course. In particular, ideas are more important than persons or than mere factual information. Second, the principle of *maturity*. A civilization is studied in the period of its highest achievement, its point of prime, its "golden age." It is the inner spirit of the age, not the details of its institutional life, that mean most to us today. Third, the principle of *relevancy*. As the present has meaning only in the light of the past, so the past has meaning only as it is related to the experiences of the present. Every fact that is brought into the course must have meaning not only for the total situation of which it is a part but also for the student to whom it is taught.

This move away from the historical survey to a larger concentration on certain great ages or epochs has gone farthest perhaps at Wisconsin, where the new humanities program is known as the "Culture Epoch" plan. Here only four great periods are treated during the first year; the Greek and Roman during one semester, the Middle Ages and the Renaissance during the other. The end in view, as stated by Professor MacKindrick, is "to emphasize our close relation economically, politically, socially, philosophically, and aesthetically to our classical heritage." "It is hoped that students will emerge from the course with a clearer idea of the responsibilities of international citizenship, derived from an analysis of the factors that make a civilization great, and of some that lead to its decline and disintegration." To this end a series of contracts is introduced between the creative periods and great figures in each culture; a contrast, for example, between the Periclean concept of democracy and the Ciceronian concept of the Republic, between Homer and Virgil, between the philosophy of Plato and Lucretius, between Demosthenes and Cicero.

In several courses of the historical and cultural type a somewhat larger place is given to religion. At Wesleyan University and at Southwestern in particular, much more attention is paid to the Hebrew-Christian scriptures and to their influence upon our cultural heritage than is customary in most courses of this type. The point of view at Southwestern is effectively put by Professor Kelso: "Believing that religion is essentially the inner force creating values, we have tried to show how the religious hopes and faiths of the Western world have directed and influenced the movement of history."

As these courses in one institution after another have moved to the more intensive treatment of a few creative periods, they have also discarded the textbooks and the anthologies with extracts from a number of sources, which were quite common in the early days. In place of these has come the use of a more limited number of "great books," read either in large segments or where possible in their entirety. This indeed has been one of the most pronounced trends in humanities courses of all types. Whatever its objectives, there has been general agreement that the purpose of the course could better be achieved by some direct contact with the great masterpieces of art and literature, with Homer, Plato, Sophocles, the Bible, Chaucer, Dante, Shakespeare, Descartes, and Voltaire, rather than by use of textbooks or other secondary discussions of the works of such men. As Professor Arragon of Reed College points out:

> . . . These cannot all be used as complete works, but they lose much, perhaps all, of their value for us if they are reduced to short and scattered excerpts. They no longer represent what their author thought as much as what the anthologist wishes to illustrate. Torn from content, they offer the student no means of critical

interpretation for himself. He cannot discover relations between ideas in the work or the pattern of the development of its argument. Usually extracts of many pages in length or preferably well-unified sections are used, where the complete work is too long and difficult; but this compromise is inadmissable in the case of most poetry, dramas, and novels. The structure of a work of art is lost if you do not have it all, and with it the meaning.

As a natural outgrowth perhaps of this development in the historical and cultural courses, a second type of course, broadly philosophical in interest and emphasis, has appeared. Indeed these two might almost be seen as variants of one major type. The chronological framework is common to both as well as an interest in our cultural heritage and in the "great books." In the one case, however, it is an historical interest in the great cultural achievements of the past which gives direction to the course, in the other it is a philosophical interest in ideas or great issues. Courses of the former type are more concerned with cultural factors by which all great literature, philosophy, and art is conditioned; courses of the second type examine the philosophical elaboration and validity of certain basic ideas which stand out in the great works selected for study. In the historical and cultural course more attention is given as a rule to architecture, sculpture, painting, and music as vital expressions of the spirit of an age; the philosophical course finds these aspects of culture less significant for its purpose, concentrating instead upon great literature and the ideas contained therein. In the latter type of course as well as the former, however, the cultural context has an appeal and value. Ideas are dealt with in their historical and literary setting. Despite a major concern with ideas, courses of this type are courses in the humanities, not in philosophy.

The course at Haverford College, Interpretations of Life in Western Literature, affords excellent illustration of the more philosophical approach. Its general purpose was that "of finding from the record of past faiths some guide for constructing a workable philosophy for our day." Material for the course, selected with this aim in mind, came in general from the masterpieces of philosophy and literature already mentioned. But a primary concern with the need of the students was not lost in an enthusiasm for the great books of the past.   Because of their timeliness or immediate appeal to student interest as well as their intrinsic merit, Renan's *Life of Jesus* and Koestler's *Darkness at Noon* were included in the course, and proved more effective in developing insight and a lasting concern with the issues raised than did other books of greater literary and philosophical stature.   The underlying spirit of the course at Haverford is aptly described by Professor Gray:

> . . . We made little attempt to be scholarly; no attempt to follow a chronological pattern or to summarize Western intellectual history. We tried to be very serious in the pursuit of a worthy faith. We sought, at the same time, to be appreciative of the masterpieces studied, and we avoided as much as possible ·dreary wastes to be found occasionally in the greatest works.

At Princeton University a somewhat different handling of the philosophical type course is to be found.   One great issue, that of human freedom, has been selected and the course, Man and His Freedom, organized around this central theme.   From the literature of the Bible to that of the present day, great works treating this issue have been chosen for study.   Actually many of the same works used at Haverford are on the Princeton list, but the discussion of each work and the development of the course as a whole at Princeton is unified in terms of one central problem. Although the staff at Princeton is enthusiastic about the merits of such an approach, few other institutions have gone this far in concentration of effort and attention.   A course like that at Wesleyan University which seeks to combine the two approaches, the cultural and the philosophical, is more typical.   Organized at first along topical lines, the Wesleyan course was reorganized in 1946 within a broad historical framework paralleling the development of Western culture.   "We felt that the historical organization gave the course greater unity and provided richer opportunities for appreciating the liberal enterprise as the continuous effort to grapple with recurrent fundamental problems," Professor Brown writes.   Better correlation with the general course in Social Science, just being established that year at Wesleyan, was also provided by this change.   The concern with ideas or great issues is still, however, an important feature of the course:

. . . Free will and necessity is a problem raised by Greek Tragedy, Augustine, Luther's *Essay on Christian Liberty*, and Shakespeare's *Hamlet*. The problem of divine justice is raised by Aeschylus' *Prometheus*, and again by the *Book of Job*. If we study the Socratic doctrine of love in the *Symposium*, we feel we should study the Pauline doctrine of love in I *Corinthians* XIII. Thus the historical organization conceals a thematic organization, designed to enrich classroom discussions.

In institutions where the concern of the humanities is more with an understanding and appreciation of the arts than with cultural or philosophical interests, a third type of course, broadly aesthetic in character, is to be found. Courses of this sort are by no means as frequent as those previously discussed, but at the Univerity of Chicago and at Pennsylvania College for Women in particular carefully developed and articulated courses of the aesthetic type have recently been developed, while this approach has characterized the humanities course at Stephens College since it was begun twenty years ago. In all courses of this type attention is naturally centered upon the art objects themselves, whether drawn from painting, sculpture, architecture, music, poetry, drama, or the dance. There is large use of audio-visual aids of all kinds, prints, projectors and screens, record players, pianos, to familiarize the students with the great art of the past; and much more emphasis is put upon the analysis of particular works of art, and upon the underlying principles and the important techniques to be found in the arts, than is the case in courses that adopt the historical, the cultural, or the philosophical approach.

A number of institutions do, however, include a large emphasis upon the arts and upon aesthetic judgment and appreciation in courses that are primarily historical and cultural. And many teachers insist that such a combination is not only desirable but essential for an understanding and appreciation of the great art of the past or the present. Professor Arragon of Reed College, for example, contends that works of art should neither be swallowed up in their setting nor analyzed without reference to it. In his opinion,

. . . Internal structure and external relations are complementary. To understand the former, we need all the aids to the imagination that we can get through familiarity with the social and intellectual situation from which the work of art sprang and in particular with the deeply rooted meaning of words and other symbols. How should we appreciate the dramatic suspense of the *Agamemnon* of Aeschylus without some grasp of the Greek view of tyranny and *hybris* and of the symbolic meaning of the crimson carpet which is the crucial point in the duel of the king and Cyltemnestra? Such "content" is the very stuff of the structure of the drama of any age, and without an understanding of it there can be no understanding of "form." Verse, symbol, thought, and emotion are fused in the pattern of a poem and in the comprehension of it . . . Art and history collaborate in the interpretation of the particular evidences of human experience.

This point of view is sharply challenged, however, in institutions where the cultivation of aesthetic insight and appreciation is the central concern of the humanities. Those who take such a position insist that the particular works of art themselves should be made the center of interest in the humanities and aesthetic principles used to integrate an interpretation of all the arts. To see great works of art as expressions of any particular cultural epoch or of any particular idea or point of view is, according to those who adopt this approach, to lose sight of the unique and essential significance of the art object itself, which has its own unity and meaning and is complete in itself. Professor Thomas of Chicago states the position unequivocally:

The study of the products of the arts is not the province of the humanist alone. It is obvious that all of the arts are useful to the social and the natural scientists. . . . *Oedipus* is ample testimony of the importance of psychological values which a poetic work may offer to the psychiatrist. The *Areopagitica* is of theoretical as well as historical interest to the political scientists. Folk music, like folk literature and primitive art, provides data to the sociologist. We cannot, therefore, adequately define the humanities in terms of a subject matter, namely the products of men's arts. There are, however, values to be derived from these works of art which are not the professional concern of the scientist. The values of *Oedipus* as a tragic poem, of the *Areopagitica* as an example of the art of rhetoric, of negro folk music as songs are the concern of the humanists, not the scientists. For these are the values which come from understanding the arts, that is, as created or constructed things. . . . Through the study of disciplines appropriate to the interpretation of poetic construction, students may discover those values in drama, fiction, and lyric poetry which are quite distinct from their capacity to express general truths or to inform us about the past. These values lie in the recognition of works of art as complete in themselves and capable of giving their appropriate kinds of pleasure. . . . I would say that a kind of fraud had been perpetrated upon the student who, under the assumption that he is studying lyric poetry, is led to discuss the "Ode to a Grecian Urn" only as a reflection of English romanticism of the nineteenth century or to consider its value only as a universal proposition about Truth and Beauty.

This is not an issue, unfortunately, upon which there seems to be hope of general agreement among humanities teachers. The training, background, and interests of those responsible for handling each course are apt to determine its character and emphasis in accord with one point of view or the other. But the importance of moving in the presentation of the arts beyond the traditional classroom procedure is being stressed in an increasing number of institutions regardless of the particular type of course taught. The large value of audio-visual aids in courses of all types is also widely recognized and a number of institutions are equipping all humanities classrooms with record players, slide projectors, and screens, although not many as yet have gone as far as the University of Chicago or Stephens College in adding a piano to such standard classroom equipment. Listening to music, however, is taking the place of lectures on music; listening hours outside the regular class periods are enabling the student to become more familiar with the music discussed; frequent trips to museums where these are available are providing an acquaintance with good painting; and in institutions where this is not possible, there is more frequent use of travelling exhibitions and of large reprints to do a somewhat less satisfactory job.

Extension of the humanities program beyond the regular class experience is being furthered also by such devices as music-lending libraries and loan collections of good prints. In some cases an ample collection of excellent reproductions, which students may sign out for a semester and use in their dormitory rooms, is available as a regular library service. The selection of one's pictures then becomes a kind of check upon the development of taste and appreciation in the humanities course. The concern with "live art" also, rather than reproductions of any kind, is growing. Attendance at certain concerts, plays, and films is being made a part of the course requirement in many cases, and the work of the course itself is sometimes directed toward enabling the student better to understand and enjoy great music and drama which is brought to the campus. This is especially true in institutions like Pennsylvania College for Women where the emphasis upon student participation and growth is more pronounced.

There is a growing interest also in providing some creative experience in the arts as an integral part of humanities courses that seek to develop aesthetic understanding and appreciation. The University of Chicago has a workshop-studio under the direction of one staff member which is open to any students who wish some experience in working with the materials of the plastic arts (engraving, clay, and stone) or with the various media of painting. Wesleyan University seems to be the only institution which has as yet introduced a "humanities laboratory," staffed by members of the departments of art, music, and theatre, as a regular feature of the general humanities course. Here all students undertake some practical experimentation in one of the arts (the graphic arts, music, theatre). Miss Carpenter of Stephens College has expressed herself on this issue more directly and unequivocally perhaps than anyone else. In her opinion, "it should be one of the acid tests of any humanities course that performance on an instrument, or writing or painting, are stimulated."

Another significant development is the concern to make humanities courses more "functional" by constantly re-examining educational objectives in terms of the life aims and purposes of the student. Instead of emphasizing subject matter and its proper organization, the primary concern in these courses is with the student himself, his present state of development, his capacities, and his needs in the area of the humanities. More and more insistently the question is being raised: What learning experiences will leave the student feeling that he is a more mature and integrated person, with greater powers for creative and effective living? The necessity is being recognized of taking the student where he is and helping him reach a state of greater maturity, rather than of being certain that only literary or artistic master-pieces are selected whose claim to greatness cannot be questioned. Integration is being interpreted as a matter of student experience and growth rather than in terms of course organization.

Such a functional emphasis has been one of the dominant aspects of the general education program at Stephens College for a number of years, and student problems and sense of need in the area of the arts a determining principle used in building the humanities course. The initial question asked was this: What learning experiences will provide the student with the power to understand and enjoy the arts? The choice of examples recog-nized learning experiences of great *immediate* importance to the individual student, eighteen- and nineteen-year-old girls in this case. These girls ask naturally such questions as: Is my evening dress the right line and color for me? Why do I like Debussy's "Clare de Lune" so much? It is around interests and problems of this sort that the discussion of color and line in art, rhythm, harmony, and melody in music has been developed. In architec-ture also the approach has not been made in terms of historic styles or basic principles but rather in terms of the problems which a young woman will face in planning a home today. As Miss Carpenter points out:

> . . . It is not difficult to motivate girls of eighteen to plan a dream home. This is an *immediate* and felt in-terest. With some stimulation, community planning can be taken on as a project in which a group of students face some practical problem connected with the slum areas of a city and try to work out answers.
>
> In the latter case, the need soon becomes apparent for judgment about beauty and its relation to function. Also, it is soon clear that students need help from the consumer education staff and from social studies instruc-tors who can point up the difficulties in connection with budgeting personal and community funds. They will need help in preparing them to meet the obstacles put in the way of good building. They may even want to con-sult the department interested in health education to

determine what factors of public health are involved in community planning. One such project ran squarely up against the consideration of religion, because of the necessity for making a decision about including a community church. In such cases, there is not only integration of the arts, but integration of the entire learning process.

A functional course of this kind, built around specific problems and interests of the student, is certainly the most difficult to work out consistently in the area of the humanities. The integration of literature, philosophy, and the arts in any framework is not easy. Some institutions are still content with several separate courses in these fields, or with one general course which is broken into segments taken from each of the various fields. In most cases the chronological or cultural pattern has provided the simplest and most obvious principle of integration in the humanities course, and this is undoubtedly one reason for its widespread appeal. But the desirability of an increased concern with student problems and need is recognized in courses being developed at a number of institutions. Boston University, the University of Florida, Haverford College, and Pennsylvania College for Women in particular emphasize this fact in the objectives they set for themselves, and progress is being made at these institutions in building courses which, if not completely functional, are certainly in closer touch with student experience and need. A consistently functional course in the humanities, organized and developed directly in terms of the problems and felt needs of the student, has not as yet been attempted, however. The Stephens College seems to have committed itself most definitely to the functional approach in its general course, but even at Stephens it is the aesthetic interest that rather largely determines the pattern of the course. One may well agree here with Miss Carpenter: "No matter what sort of organization is used at the beginning for a general course in the humanities, as long as the objectives are kept in line with student needs, a vital course will develop."

When one examines the teaching methods employed in general humanities courses, he finds a trend comparable to that seen in general education in the natural sciences and the social sciences. In almost all cases specialists in literature, philosophy, and the arts were called in originally to handle their own particular fields and these specialists made large use of the lecture method in presenting their material.   As humanities courses have had time to develop, however, experience has shown more and more clearly that an approach of this sort does not have the desired integration or success in meeting the objectives of general education.   One institution after another has concluded that a better humanities course could be developed when a single instructor took the same group of students through the whole program rather than when specialists were allowed to handle their own fields.   At the University of Florida, where this change in teaching method was made several years ago, the improvement in the course has been particularly marked.   The experience at Florida when one staff member handled sections of his own throughout the year is described as follows:

> . . . This approach has made the course as stimulating for the staff as for the students — perhaps more so, as a matter of fact.   For the creative process of growth and integration has actually been going on in the instructor's own experience.   He has had new insights and convictions to take to his classes from day to day, and has not been tempted simply to repeat to them factual information stored up during his own graduate study or later research.   Likewise, as a learner himself, he is much nearer to the experience and outlook of his students.   He does not loose contact with them nearly so frequently as does the specialist who is preoccupied with problems and distinctions of his own that have little or no meaning for the growth and development of the average student.

One of the major obstacles in the way of this practice, of course, is the lack of adequate training on the part of staff members.   Very few men have had preparation or teaching experience in all the fields included in a general humanities course.   It has taken courage to face the students from day to day when a man was working in a new field, and more courage sometimes to face colleagues who frown upon such practices.   In increasing measure, however, it has become apparent that the aims of general education can best be achieved, not by a dependence upon the narrowly trained specialist but by confidence in the instructor who has broad intellectual sympathies and a genuine concern for the growth of the students with whom he is working.   Eloquent testimony to this fact is given by Professor Gray in describing his experience with the course at Haverford:

> I attribute its success partly to my own ignorance. If I had felt really competent to teach such a course, pride would have prevented me from taking the frank attitude of the learner and sharing with the students fresh discoveries. Evidence of this assertion I found in handling those books which I knew best from my own schooling and which I approached at the beginning with the most confidence. With these it required distinctly more effort to awaken in the students the same kind of stimulating discussion than with those about which I knew little of the secondary material. With the former, they felt, more or less instinctively, that their instructor's opinions were already formed and his competence too far advanced over theirs. It seems to me that this is an important discovery which requires to be accented. Since specialization in such a course is hardly possible in any event, instructors who are faced with the task of teaching a humanities course should find in their relative unpreparedness reason for confidence as well as reason for quaking.

This conviction of Professor Gray's has been further confirmed at the University of Florida, not only in the feeling of the instructors involved but also by testimony of the students to the same effect. At Florida:

> . . . It has amazed us all to see how far and how fast we have been able to go in handling effectively the various fields included in our program.
> Equally encouraging to us in this undertaking have been the results of our initial attempts to evaluate the work of the course. By the use of a student evaluation form we have found that the members of our staff are frequently doing their most effective work with students in areas other than their own speciality. Instructors trained in art have found among their students much greater enthusiasm for their presentation of literature or philosophy than for their treatment of art. Instructors trained in literature have found that they were doing their most successful teaching when handling philosophy or art; the philosopher, that he does a better job when teaching literature than when teaching philosophy.

At Michigan State, at Chicago, at Florida State University, at Wesleyan, at Reed College, the individual instructor has been made responsible for handling the major content of the course with his own group of students, and in many cases some program of "in-service training" has been worked out to increase his competence and give him needed assistance in less familiar assignments. There has been at the same time a marked tendency to move toward the discussion approach in smaller groups instead of depending upon lectures to large sections.   Added informality and group unity has been achieved in a number of institutions by the use of large tables and easy chairs rather than the traditional row on row of tablet arm chairs.   This is an approach which Professor Arragon has been particularly concerned to promote and he points to its values with enthusiasm:

> . . . Here in the give-and-take of discussion across the table, when both students and teacher are active, the most vital instruction goes on.   The group is a small community engaged in a common inquiry, an intellectual enterprise renewed from day to day in the changing guise of different though related problems.   The responsibility rests upon all the members of the group and not upon the instructor alone, who should not bring to the discussion a fixed pattern for the movement of thought and predetermined answers but an expectancy for novel questions and novel ways of putting old questions, fresh points of view and avenues of attack upon these questions.   The flow of ideas is not merely or even mostly between instructor and student but back and forth between students as well. . . . It is a process of exploring among themselves the meaning of the materials under examination, materials which are inert until they come to life in thought that is challenged to discover in them relations that mean something to the students.

The trend at present is clearly in this direction.   In many institutions such group discussions are supplemented by lectures, especially illustrated lectures on the fine arts and lecture-recitals in music; but where lectures formerly came two or even three times a week and provided the backbone of the course, they now as a rule come only once and are recognized as distinctly supplementary. There are a few instances, however, where the opposite viewpoint has prevailed and the lecture method is retained as the chief means of instruction not merely because of necessity but also from conviction.   In dealing with freshmen and sophomores in the humanities courses at Harvard University, for example, the value of the lecture is defended in terms of a philosophy of education opposed to that just stated:

> . . . The use of lectures has been much attacked in recent years, but our experience has not been unfavorable. Education as a whole could perhaps be said to involve two distinct processes: training in ratiocination (that is, disciplined thought on connected material), and growth of sympathy (awareness of things not known before). General education deals on the whole with the second process.   It opens for students periods of history and realms of ideas, of which they had known little.   Its main task is to evoke the reality of these, at first alien, worlds and to suggest, chiefly indirectly, their connection with the familiar.   Without minimizing the weaknesses of lecturing, one could yet argue that the questioning and discussion of small classes are on the whole best adapted for what has been called training in ratiocination, whereas lectures can possess at least the virtue of presenting novelty clearly.

On one other problem of method in humanities courses there is perhaps even less general agreement at presnet; that is the problem raised by examinations.   The inadequacy of the old examination procedures for the purpose of general education in the humanities has become more and more apparent to be sure.   Even in smaller institutions, where courses are not required of all students or the number of sections is not large, and the traditional essay type examination is widely used, there is some dissatisfaction. But in the larger institutions, where a thousand or more students are enrolled in the basic humanities course and many different instructors are involved, the problem of testing and grading is an acute one.   In commenting upon the situation at the University of Arizona, Professor Percy remarks: "Throughout the years since humanities was first established the examinations have proved more difficult to administer than any other part of the course."   To meet difficulties created by large numbers and by the inevitable wide variation in standards of grading on the part of the different instructors, many institutions have moved to an objective examination, common to all sections — and where possible, a machine-scored examination.   This has provided a type of objectivity and uniformity. The students have seen that their grades were not dependent upon the likes or dislikes of a particular instructor and that one section was no harder or easier to pass than another. Also the use of a common examination has produced a concern among students to get "good" instructors, that is, men from whom they learned what the examination required them to know, rather than "easy" instructors who expected little work of their students.

The disadvantages of objective tests and examinations in the humanities are strongly felt, however. Both students and staff members have continued to question the soundness of a judgment based solely upon such evidence. At Arizona, when this practice was followed,

> . . . It frequently happened that a capable student, whose class performance throughout the semester resembled nothing so much as the activity of a sponge, would in his final grade outstrip another, whose contribution to the success of the course far outweighed the small number of points he fell below his competitor in the test. Such cases were numerous; they were resented by the students, and a large proportion of the staff also came to feel that such complete disregard of classwork was a bad thing.

There is a widespread conviction among humanities teachers also that the objective type examination does not really get at the sort of objectives to which the general humanities course is directed. The comment from Harvard on this point is a typical one: "Though we have experimented with 'objective' testing, we have placed comparatively little reliance upon it."

At the University of Chicago, where a common examination largely objective in character has been used for years, these difficulties have been removed in part at least by the more specific objectives adopted for the course. "We are agreed," Professor Thomas writes, "That the proper approach to the study of the humanities is to study the works of art themselves and the skills involved in their understanding and appreciation." At least one-half of the examination at Chicago is based upon materials that have not been discussed in class. The range of the student's knowledge and his skill in interpretation can be rather satisfactorily determined under such circumstances by the use of improved objective testing devices. Until better instruments of evaluation are developed, however, or course objectives in the humanities are limited more narrowly, it looks as if the sort of compromise worked out at the University of Arizona might have greater appeal to most of those who have to deal with large numbers. After quite a bit of experimentation Arizona now uses a common objective examination for all sections at the end of the course, but in computing a final course grade for the student gives weight also to a "teacher's grade" which each instructor supplies for all members of his class. The latter grade is expected to take into account those aspects of student insight and growth which cannot be gotten at by the objective examination.

An equally perplexing and probably more acute problem confronting those responsible for general humanities courses is that of adequate staffing. With the increased pressure of numbers in all institutions, and especially in the larger state universities, it has become almost impossible to find enough men who can teach successfully in an integrated humanities program, to find a place for them in already overtaxed departmental budgets, and to secure the necessary support of departmental heads in making such appointments. At Florida State University, where this problem has been especially acute, Professor Miller writes:

> Perhaps our greatest problem is now an administrative one. There is tremendous pressure on all department heads to meet the needs of the ever-increasing number of students. This increase has intensified the demand for teachers at all instructional levels. New instructors have had no experience with the humanities course, and are not always willing to give the time necessary to prepare for the course when advanced undergraduate and graduate courses beckon more enticingly. Furthermore, new instructors are properly concerned with advancement, and they often feel that promotion can be better secured by faithfully discharging departmental duties than those in a course which has no administrative status.

Institutions which have set up an independent humanities staff, and quite a number have, have solved one aspect of the problem. There is at least no necessity to depend for the appointment of desirable men upon sorely pressed or unsympathetic departmental chairmen. But other problems remain. Good men must be found and kept; and those who teach general courses want, and for their own continued intellectual growth usually need, some opportunity to continue advanced work in areas of specialized interest and training. Where this is not possible, many teachers tend to become dissatisfied, to feel frustrated and lose interest in their work, or seek to find other more appealing positions. Some arrangement for an overlapping in staff appointments, or for dual appointments to general humanities courses and to advanced departmental work seems the most promising arrangement, and several institutions are following this practice at present. But in any such arrangement men must not feel that they will be penalized for giving to general education their wholehearted support in time and energy. Continued contributions to the humanities program must be adequately recognized by advances in both salary and rank, if the success of general education is to be safeguarded.

chapter 2

THE HUMANITIES PROGRAM AT BOSTON UNIVERSITY COLLEGE OF BASIC STUDIES

*Sidney James Black and Peyton Elliot Richter**

Introduction

If a study of the humanities is to fulfill its appropriate functions in general education, students undertaking it must be introduced to the various artistic and philosophic forms; they must be trained to perceive the nature and history of man's creative achievements; they must be encouraged to evaluate critically the contemporary world and to envisage a better world order; and, finally, they must be offered experience in specific creative undertakings. To accomplish these aims in the program at Boston University Junior College, a number of methods are employed, methods which operate as vectors structuring a two-year core curriculum. The *analytic-systematic* vector governs the study of the work of art in itself: its parts, its medium and skills, and its style. The *retrospective-historical* vector focusses the attention of students upon the cultural context in which art objects are created and from which they derive their unique characteristics. The *creative-innovative* vector operates when students are challenged to innovate from what they have learned or to re-synthesize what they have learned, as for example in the creation of short stories, plays, poems, or essays. Finally, the *contemplative-speculative* vector induces the student to consider the ideal ends of the good life and to speculate upon the construction and reconstruction of the older forms of

---

*The Authors are Associate Professors of Humanities at Boston University College of Basic Studies, formerly called Boston University Junior College.

social and esthetic order, thereby widening their own sense of tradition.

These are indeed broad generalizations and lofty methodological ideals. Let us see how the generalizations are particularized and the ideals are put into practice.

Boston University Junior College was founded on a problem and a hope, resulting from admissions policies at the College of General Education. The problem was finding the methodology and administration by which a group of students admitted on the basis of potential rather than past achievement might be profitably educated. If these students were segregated in a Junior Division, could they be taught in such a way as to be able to complete at least a two-year general education? The hope lay in the experimental approaches which might be undertaken with these students. Could such students, with the proper training and help, develop their potentialities to the extent that they might be qualified not only for completion of a two-year program, but also for transfer to a four-year program and earn a bachelor's degree? Fortunately, the answers to both of these questions were found to be in the affirmative; the problem has been solved and the hope realized. Since 1952, when the Junior Division became a separate college, more than 2,500 students have successfully completed the Junior College curriculum and have transferred to four year programs. Such success could not have been accidental. It rests upon a number of features, some of which are unique to the Junior College. Among these are a team system of instruction, emphasis on communication skills, extensive guidance and counseling services, and a curriculum designed to meet the needs and interests of the marginal student.

The administration of the first and last of these aspects is the team and divisional systems, both of prime importance to the Humanities program. The Humanities instructor is a member of a faculty team representing all divisions of the core curriculum: Humanities, Social Relations, Science, Psychology and Guidance, and Communications. Each team member teaches, throughout the academic year, the same four sections composed of approximately twenty-five students each, meets weekly for team meetings, and, at the end of the year, evaluates each student's academic potential and transfer prospects on the basis of his cumulative progress at the Junior College and his ability to handle occasional electives at other colleges of the University.   In a recent article, the assets of the team system of instruction were summarized as permitting

> coordination of faculty effort in curriculum planning; it utilizes informal means to create learning experiences for students outside the classroom; it eliminates waste in the learning situation through integrated instructional effort; it inculcates the democratic ideal of 'learning-through-cooperating'; and, especially important in this context, it permits coordinated faculty evaluation of the student body.   In short, it provides a personalized individual approach to learning that has been instrumental in assisting the student to make full use of his academic potential.[1]

The team system is counterbalanced by the divisional system which is a more conventional aspect of the Junior College organization.   Each Humanities instructor is also a member of a division to which he is responsible and from which he receives his administrative directives.   If the team system insures horizontal integration among divisions, the divisional system insures vertical integration within its discipline.   It is in division meetings, held weekly, that the form, content of the course and the modes of testing are determined; at the same time, since all members of the division, including its chairman, are members of teams, they can see means by which divisional courses may be vertically and horizontally integrated within the entire curriculum.   One scarcely needs to be reminded that the structure of each course in the core curriculum affects and is interrelated to every other course. Through his team and his division each instructor is able to maintain an holistic orientation.

At present eight teams comprise the faculty at the Junior College.   The team can comfortably manage 100-125 students without sacrificing personalized attention to students, the integrity of divisional disciplines, or the ability of faculty members to work at research or teach at higher levels of instruction.

---

[1]LaFauci, H. and Richter, P., "Academic Success Beyond Junior College: The Identification and Selection of The Four Year Student," *Junior College Journal*, November, 1958, XXIX, 124.

The Definition and Content of the Humanities

Humanities at the Junior College might best be defined as those disciplines which are concerned with the imaginative and intellectual experiences qualitatively expressed in symbols. The definition is interpreted as including an introductory study of the patterns of literature, painting, and music, as well as a study of ethical systems and social philosophies.

In the first semester of the two year course, selected works of art from the several genres of literature, music and art are studied in lectures and section meetings with the underlying purpose of introducing the students to esthetic principles fundamental to the Humanities. Short stories by Hawthorne, Poe, Woolf and White; novels by Orwell, Crane, and Porter; poems by Keats, Jarrell, and Donne, plays by Sophocles and Anderson, essays by Swift and Hersey give some idea of the range of works for analysis in literature. In music, folk and art songs, the waltz and minuet, the sonata and fugue, as well as the opera and symphony are listened to and analyzed. In painting examples from the work of Hogarth, Picasso, Dali, and Kandinsky have been chosen. In all three areas, works of art are analyzed with reference to esthetic principles which, abstracted from the context[2] in which they appear, might be expressed in the following manner:

1. All works of art are artificial constructs dependent for understanding upon the fact that they are expressed in a symbolic language.
2. All works of art are enriched in meaning when they are understood as related to the historical, cultural, or traditional context in which they were created.
3. The significance of a work of art is in no way dependent upon the informative data imparted by it, but rather depends for its significance on the artist's ability to transcend the limits of his time and relate to the universal aspects of man's experience.
4. Understanding a work of art is in great meaure a matter of awareness, awareness of the possible choices among the languages, media, skills and technique of a given civilization and its given view of art.

---

[2]Cf. for discussion, Fisher, J., Black, S., and Daugherty, M., *Critical Thinking and the Humanities* (Boston University Press, 1955), 1-13, 57-65, 251-269, 455-466.

Perhaps the major difficulty in orienting students to the basic esthetic principles comes at the outset of the course when they are confronted by the differential media of visual and verbal arts. Reaction to and analysis of particular works of arts, for example, Picasso's *Guernica* and Jarrell's "Loss," serve as the basis for a preliminary discussion.[3] The instructor, with the discussion as a point of departure, may underline the dangers, misunderstandings, and misconceptions that often obscure the relation of the symbol to its referent and that of the symbol to its audience. In these works, the visual and verbal patterns are employed to express different reactions to violence; and the students are asked to conscientiously analyze their own feelings about the symbol constructs in an effort to make them aware of different symbolic languages. Those students who find *Guernica* unsatisfactory because Picasso's use of line, form, and space do not achieve a photographic representation of the effects of a bombing, can be asked to see the distortions, whether they like them or not, as deliberate attempts to convey a point of view — an emotional response to life situations. Different as the poem, "Loss," is in style and expression, students discover that it can evoke through understatement and irony as much, if not more, of an effect than a straightforward emotive attack on war. The limitations and pitfalls of verbal misrepresentation and manipulation of symbols can be illustrated from a study of Orwell's *1984*.

During the introductory sections of the semester, instructors emphasize the development of a sophistication on the part of the students towards different symbolic patterns. Works of art are defined as symbol constructs, derived from self-contained systems of symbols, each having its own disciplines and freedoms. This is carried forward in the weekly lecture where musical constructs are analyzed and related to the central problem of symbol systems and constructs. The distinction is made, for example, between programme music (e.g., *Don Quixote*, *Danse Macabre*) and music divorced from any attempt at literal content (e.g., string quartet or fugue). The failure of music to tell a story except in vague, associational terms is pointed up; and students are asked to listen

---

[3]Cf. Chart, Course Content Humanities, First Semester, for other possible combinations of literature, art, and music.

for rhythm, melodic lines, and harmonies rather than attempt to translate into verbal terms their own emotional reactions.

Each unit of the four comprising the first semester contains selections for viewing, listening, and reading which illustrate the four points of the esthetic offered by the Humanities division of the Junior College. An inspection of the charts which follow will reveal the wide range of works chosen.

COURSE CONTENT HUMANITIES — First Semester

| Unit I The Symbolic Process

4 weeks | On the nature of the symbol and symbolic invention from the spoken word, scratching on stone, and beating of drums to the finished work professionally produced in modern society. Independence, variability, and flexibility of symbols with respect to symbol systems and constructs which are once removed from experience and in cases of some symbol constructs self-contained.

Lectures: Varieties of musical experience, the components of rhythm, melody, and harmony; music as a system of symbols; the waltz and the fugue; the folk song and the art song. | Specific Works for Analysis

"Eve of St. Agnes"
Keats
"Loss"   Jarrell
"The King of Diamonds"
Silone
"Names of Gods Tabooed"   Frazer
"The Invasion from Mars"   Cantril
"The Principles of Newspeak   Orwell
"The Minister's Black Veil"   Hawthorne

1984   Orwell

Guernica   Picasso
Nightwind   Burchfield |
| Unit II Context

4 weeks | Three interrelated components: (1) the historico-cultural context external to the work of art, (2) tradition within the discipline of the art form, (3) internal discipline of the specific work of art. Importance of a critical awareness of all three is needed for broadest understanding of a given work; universality achieved primarily by artistic transcendence of (3) over (1) and (2).

Lectures: Influence of the invention of instruments to musical traditions. The minuet, scherzo, and sonata in context. Dance forms: the ballet. | "Jerusalem"   Blake
"Haunted House" Woolf
"The Door"   White
Candide   Voltaire
Winterset   Anderson
"When Lilacs . . ."
Whitman

Gin Lane   Hogarth
Persistence of Memory
Dali |

Unit III Levels of Language 4 weeks	On the continua between the denotative and connotative, the abstract and the concrete, the general and the particular, the affective and the informative. Art derives its richness and power within these ranges and depends for appreciation upon the degree of sophistication and subtlety of its public or audience and the fabric of traditional forms and media available. Ranges of language illustrated in (1) a recipe or similar expositional material (2) U. S. Constitution: preamble and amendments (3) a parable, "A sower went to sow."	Specific Works for Analysis *The Red Badge of Courage* Crane *Antigone* Sophocles "Dover Beach" Arnold "Ode on a Grecian Urn" Keats "Death Be Not Proud" Donne "The Road Not Taken" "Mending Wall" Frost Ranges in pictorial form *Summer Landscape* Davis: photograph and painting *Daughters of Revolution* Wood *Girl Before a Mirror* Picasso Compositions III, IV Kandinsky
	Lectures: Integration of verbal and visual patterns in the Musical Drama and Grand Opera (*Mme. Butterfly, Porgy*). Forms of Jazz. The concertae.	
Unit IV Selectivity: a Vector in the Creative Process 4 weeks	Words as sound patterns in prose and poetry. Emotive impact of imagery, metaphor and irony. Color, line, texture, form as emotive patterns in painting. Synthesis of the esthetic: symbols, context, levels, and selectivity studied in an epic novel (*The Wall, Fathers and Sons, Lord Jim*).	"The Fall of the House of Usher" Poe "A Modest Proposal" Swift *Hiroshima* Hersey *Noon Wine* Porter *Heart of Darkness* Conrad *Withdrawal from Dunkirk* Eurich
	Lectures: The symphony as interrelated formal patterns found in musical traditions.	*The Eternal City* Blume

The second semester of the freshman year involves the *analytic-systematic* and the *retrospective-historical* vectors mentioned in the Introduction to this essay. Thus, as in the semester preceding, student papers are limited to analytic studies of individual works and the historical traditions from which they spring and to which they give impetus. One is a study of an original painting, usually selected from the galleries of the Boston Museum of Fine Arts. A second is devoted to an analysis of short story technique and its relation to the cultural context in which it was produced; the third may be a thematic study of an epic novel or three novelettes. The classroom discussions center on a series of selected works, verbal and visual, and are interspersed with brief lectures on tradition and history of the period involved. The novel, for example, is treated as a vehicle for bourgeois morals and manners. Its genesis is located in the early eighteenth century, and some of the earlier and later patterns are illustrated and discussed. Concentration is focused on a few works discussed in detail: Dostoievski's *Crime and Punishment*, Hemingway's *A Farewell to Arms*, or Turgeniev's *Fathers and Sons*.

The development of the short story offers somewhat more diversity and can be treated less fragmentarily than the novel as a literary form. Examples from Poe to Salinger can be used to indicate the shifts in context and techniques that the form has undergone. In poetry, the focus is again limited; but drawing from the grounding in the first semester esthetic, instructors concentrate on selected forms of the British-American lyric of the twentieth century.

A retrospective view of the traditions of pictorial art, emphasizing the schools from 1860 to the present, is offered in a series of lectures during the second semester. A two week unit in class generally supplements the lecture material and provides the basis for student-directed discussions of specific paintings. Tours to nearby museums and galleries are arranged by instructors who accompany groups of students and give informal gallery talks.

The creative-innovative vector has been variously directed, often on an individual instructor basis. Reading of novels may be assigned for critical analysis in terms of underlying theme; for example, *The Catcher in the Rye, Member of the Wedding* and *Huckleberry Finn* may be related thematically to problems of maturation and growing responsibility; or, such works as *The Rise of Silas Lapham, Babbitt,* and *Point of No Return* may be related thematically to the problem of moral adjustment in the world of business and finance. Frequently, students offer their own short stories, poems, even an occasional water color, for class criticism and analysis. These are, if found worthy, contributed to the student publication, *Creativity,* sponsored by the Humanities division.

The unit outline on the following page should suggest the scope of the second semester course.

COURSE CONTENTS HUMANITIES — Second Semester

Unit I The Short Story 4 weeks	Definitions: Poe, Chekhov, Mansfield. Components: controlling idea, method of narration; plot; arrangement of events and conflicts; characterization, and setting. 15-20 nineteenth and twentieth century examples from English, French, German, Russian, and American authors.	Art Lectures: What is art: expression, play, utility Elements of art: *Conceptual*: Line, Form, Color, Space, Texture. *Formal*: Balance, Flow, Emphasis. *Media*: Painting: oil, tempera, watercolor. Drawing: pastel, charcoal, etc. Graphic Arts: planographic, relief, intaglio, fresco.
Unit II Poetry 3 weeks	Contemporary British and American forms and poets. Definition of lyric elements and history of contexts in which they appeared. Analysis of 15-20 poems.	Development of modern art. Character and origin of; paint as light-impressionism; light is not enough — Cezanne; Cubism and Decoration — abstraction; Savages and fauves — abstraction; Picasso: history of tapestry; social art. What artists have said.
Unit III The Novel 5 weeks	Definitions and background f r o m eighteenth century. Components: dramatic elements and technical devices. Role of symbol, levels of language, context, and selectivity. Three short novels (varying): *Old Man and the Sea, Ethan Frome, Of Mice and Men*. One epic novel (varying): *Crime and Punishment*.	

(Every attempt is made by instructors to make use of the esthetic developed in the first semester and to apply its principles in the interests of unity.)

In the second year, the first six weeks are devoted to a study of dramatic forms, selections from tragedy, comedy, and problem plays, and their relationship to the cultural context in which they developed. The *analytic-systematic* and the *retrospective-historical* vectors are united whenever it is both necessary and feasible to do so, as in the previously mentioned units on the short story, poetry and the novel. The second unit of the first semester broadens to include the study of basic types of moral philosophy with dramatic works employed as illustrations of moral conflict. The drama is thus seen from two points of view, as the subject of esthetic contemplation, and as the objectification of man's moral and social experience.

The technical elements such as exposition, development, and denouement, are considered in class discussions and lectures. With short plays (Schnitzler's *A Farewell Supper*, Barrie's *The Will*) as points of reference, the student is asked to analyze dialogue, action, and setting in order that he can appreciate the full impact of drama as acted, and that he become aware of the intention, explicit or implicit, underlying the structure of a play. He is urged to attend productions in the local theaters, particularly those of the University itself. Complex plays, such as *Oedipus Rex* and *Major Barbara,* are read and analyzed with specific reference to the *Poetics* and Shaw's *Preface*, respectively. Weekly lectures cover historic cultural patterns of stagecraft, technique, and moral intention. An attempt is made in and out of class to offer dimension and context to the plays assigned. The religious-moral function of Greek drama is compared to the moral implications of serious contemporary drama and the comparison serves both as a unifying theme and as an introduction of the subject of the playwright as a moral arbiter and social critic.

Typical of the questions raised in section during this unit are those which consider the pertinence of the "message play." Does a moral or social theme help or hinder a playwright? What cultural and psychological forces might cause a playwright to dramatize a moral or social problem? References here might be made to *Winterset* and *Antigone* studied in the freshman year as well as to *The Adding Machine* or *The Crucible* studied in the second year. To what extent is setting used symbolically to objectify a social problem in such plays as *Dead End* or *Ghosts*? What kinds of characters triumph or are defeated in plays like *Billy Budd* or *A Streetcar Named Desire*? What questions are raised and answered (or unanswered) concerning right and wrong, truth and falsehood, happiness and unhappiness? In the latter connection how do Aristotle and Miller compare on the function of drama in society? What seems to be the playwright's and critic's view of the role of drama in expressing attitudes regarding the nature of man, the significance of life, and the importance of God or Fate in human affairs?

Discussion of the answers to these questions reveals to the student a relation between the play as objectified experience and his own moral and social problems. The universality and immediacy of these problems are thus made evident. In this frame of reference, the student is introduced to the study of moral philosophy.

The *analytic-systematic* vector employed in the unit on ethics reveals moral philosophy as a form of man's creative experience — as a symbolic ordering of moral data aimed at the clarification of the ends of moral conduct and at the intelligent solution of moral dilemmas. Five or six ethical systems are delineated, and each is illustrated by a play which raises problems relevant to the system under consideration. For example, Kingsley's *Detective Story* makes concrete many of the issues in conflict between Socrates and the Sophists, or between moral absolutism and moral relativism. Individual hedonism (Epicurus) and universal hedonism (Bentham-Mill) are found in conflict in *All My Sons*. Evidence of pessimism and stoicism can be found in *Billy Budd*. Kantian idealism in both the latter play and in *Antigone* becomes comprehensible to the student in terms of the dramatized opposition of the categorical and hypothetical imperatives. Although the systems of ethics are not studied chronologically, the relevant context of each and its contemporary philosophical pertinence is treated in lectures and reading assignments.

An opportunity to utilize the creative innovations of students comes into play during the final weeks of the first semester, when students, in groups of five or six, are assigned the task of writing a one-act play. One member serves as chairman or "director"; another, as secretary or "script-writer"; another as stage manager, etc. The instructor serves as a resource man or guide to any group requiring his services. Many groups have extensive meetings outside of class. If time permits, students are encouraged to perform in their plays before the class; and the class offers its criticism. One of the more important results of this project is that students become actively involved in the process of dramatic invention and seem to gain an unusual appreciation of the synthesis of structural and ideational values inherent in dramatic art. Another effect is that ethics assumes a vitality and appeal for students when they create and evaluate the moral judgments of dramatic characters, when they speculate on the ideal ends of characters in dramatic action, and when they recognize that they, like six characters in search of an author, are searching for the meanings of human existence in fact and imagination.

In the second semester of the sophomore year, students continue their study of ethical systems, widening their perspectives, through a study of social philosophy, to include ideals of a good society as well as of a good individual. Beginning with Plato's idealistic proposals for social reorganization, they then consider Aristotle's realistic view of politics and Dewey's melioristic "reconstructionism". The *analytic-systematic* vector organizes the three philosophic positions as forms of utopian speculation, which leads naturally into several lectures and discussions on similarly imaginative and intellectual schemes.

Such questions as "what is utopia?" "why do men write utopias?" and "of what import is utopian speculation?" are raised. The *retrospective-historical* vector allows by lecture and section a study of the history of utopian speculation, beginning with *The Republic* and concluding with Skinner's *Walden Two*. More's *Utopia*, Bellamy's *Looking Backward*, Butler's *Erewhon*, and Huxley's *Brave New World* are required reading. During the midsemester weeks, the student is required to write a paper in which either he discusses the origin, development and achievements of an actual utopian experiment, such as Brook Farm, Oneida Community, or the Kibbutz, or he analyzes and evaluates a literary utopia, such as France's *Penguin Island* or Wells' *A Modern Utopia*.

In the final unit of the Humanities program, the *creative-innovative* vector directs student work toward social criticism and speculation in the planning and writing of a utopia. Each section of students is divided into five or six planning groups, one member of which is a coordinator, another, a secretary. A syllabus outlining the objectives of the project and the basic categories for consideration (human relations, economics, politics, esthetics, science, etc.) aids the students in structuring their utopias. The instructor encourages the students to be creative and consistent and serves as an arbiter when conflicts in the group emerge. He tells his sections that they may take either a satiric or a constructive view of con-

COURSE CONTENT HUMANITIES — Third Semester

		Specific Works for Analysis
Unit 1 The Drama 6 weeks	On definitions and technical elements: plot, character, staging; structure: exposition, development, climax, and denouement. Concurrent study and analysis of the *Poetics*. Paper: one act play to be written by a student or students in collaboration. Readings in class for discussion and analysis. Lectures: Background and development of drama. Tragic and comic forms. The playwright as social critic. Staging and acting styles.	*Oedipus Rex* *Major Barbara* *Ghosts* *Desire Under the Elms* *The Adding Machine* *Hamlet*
Unit II The Drama and An Introduction to Ethical Systems 6 weeks	Lectures and readings develop into a consideration of the Relativists, pre-Socratic and modern; the hedonists, egoistic, utilitarian and altruistic; pessimism; stoicism, and idealism. Paper: moral analysis of character and situation in a play or plays approved by instructor. Recent selections included: *Death of a Salesman, Glass Menagerie,* and *Miss Julie.*	Reading assignments from texts of Davidson, Durant, and Albert. Selections from Epicurus, Socrates, Epictetus, Marcus Aurelius, Schopenhauer, Bentham and Mill. *Detective Story* *All My Sons* *Billy Budd* *Riders to the Sea*

COURSE CONTENT HUMANITIES — Fourth Semester

Unit I Ethical Systems and Social Philosophies

8 weeks

Lecture and reading assignments deal with naturalism and idealism, naturalistic humanism, and rational idealism. A consideration of literary and fictional utopias from Isaiah to the present. Experimental societies in the nineteenth and twentieth centuries. The constructive and satiric utopias. Visiting lecturers on the Shakers and projective Walden Twos.

Paper: Library research on one of the following: The Shakers, New Harmony, Brook Farm, Koinoinia, Oneida Community, The California Settlements.

Readings from Aristotle, Plato, Dewey

Utopia More
The City of the Sun Campanela
The New Atlantis Bacon
Looking Backward Bellamy
Erewhon Butler
Brave New World Huxley
Walden Two Skinner

Unit II Group Project

7 weeks (overlaps with Unit I)

Paper: A group project (4-7 students) collaborates in the creation of a utopian scheme which they defend in oral examination before a team of instructors representing the Sciences, Social Relations, Communications, and Psychology and Guidance. The Humanities instructor chairs the examination and grades the students on group effectiveness, individual contribution, and oral defense.

temporary society in their projections of a new social order; and, at the end of the semester, he presides over the oral examination during which the students must defend their utopias before their team of instructors representing the various divisions of the college.

The two year program thus concludes with a project designed to promote the synthesis which is a fundamental aim of all programs in general education. The student will have cooperatively attempted to integrate in his utopia the subject matter of the several areas in the curriculum: science, social relations, communication, psychology and guidance, and literature, art and philosophy. He will have had an opportunity to cope with and attempt to work out problems of an ethical nature that are introduced in the sophomore year; he will have tried out his creative and critical powers and tested them against his team of instructors; and finally, he will have had training in the kind of thinking needed for effective citizenship in a dynamic and democratic society.

Methods of Evaluation and Conclusion

Evaluation of the extent to which a Humanities program accomplishes its goals is perhaps the most difficult single problem facing those who are concerned primarily with values rather than facts. To be sure, the students' ability to understand and to retain facts, principles and concepts can be ascertained through objective and essay examinations, both of which are liberally used by the Junior College. But depth of appreciation, increased awareness of esthetic and ethical dimensions of human existence, development of discriminating taste — how can the humanities instructor hope to test and evaluate these? The answer, of course, lies in the minds of the students and could be more clearly evaluated perhaps ten years after the completion of the course rather than while the course is in progress. Tests must, however, be given, data accumulated, grades determined, and decisions made, especially in a college whose basic function is to identify and select students qualified to complete a four year program.

Formerly, in performing its function in the core curriculum, the Humanities Division constructed and administered a series of objective (multiple choice) examinations. Recently, a new approach to testing in the freshman year has been developed. By replacing divisional testing with periodic (usually monthly) "omnibus" examinations, all divisions now offer their tests in one booklet. This examination lasts for three hours, includes approximately seventy items from each area, and assigns thirty minutes to each portion of the test. To date, the Humanities questions have required short essay responses.

Instructors in Humanities are convinced that essay answers allow the student to give evidence of his ability to handle language patterns, and develop fresh lines of critical reasoning in a way that no comprehensive objective test can permit. Individual instructors are left free, of course, to give class quizzes and to assign brief papers according to their inclination and schedule of coverage. In division meetings, however, the instructors usually agree to the number, nature, and length of longer papers to be assigned so that some degree of uniformity of requirements expected of all students can be assured. At the conclusion of each semester of the freshman year a two-hour essay examination is given to all students in a large lecture hall. In order to assist individual instructors in correcting this examination, a guide, containing a list of the expected answers or appropriate lines of discussion, is prepared in division meetings prior to the examination. Instructors use this guide at their discretion and are urged to consider it a helpful compendium rather than an absolute directive At the same time, it helps to give some common basis for subjective evaluation.

At the end of each semester, members of the division meet to determine the relative weight of the evaluative components used throughout the term. During the past academic year (1958-59), the determinants for final grades were as follows:

Section grade includes class quizzes, discussion skills, consistency of effort, attitude, etc. _____10%

Paper grades include composition and research as well as speculative-innovative works _____30%

Intraterm exams _____30%

Final exams _____30%

The policies and procedures used in the freshman year in Humanities are continued through the sophomore year with two exceptions: the omnibus is replaced by two essay intraterms each semester; and the final examination at the end of the second semester is oral rather than written. This examination, which lasts for an hour, is given to each utopia group by their five team members in a semi-formal setting. Part of the time is taken up by the students' panel presentation of their utopia, and the rest by questions from the team, each in his own area. Prior to the examination, students are told that they should be completely familiar with the total utopia and be prepared to discuss any aspect of it; that they should be able to examine the utopia in the light of criticisms which might be made from the points of view of Plato, Aristotle, Schopenhauer, Kant, More, Bellamy, Huxley, Skinner, and other authors read in the course; and finally, that they should be prepared to point out the advantages of their utopia over the contemporary social order.

On the whole, the oral examinations have been enthusiastically received by faculty and students alike. The students seem to derive great satisfaction from articulating the ideas and insights which they have gained through their two years of general education. They are apt to gain additional insights in the course of answering questions asked by team members and from the evaluative comments made on their presentation at the end of the examination. From the faculty point of view, oral examinations can gauge the extent to which students are successful in interrelating concepts and principles from various fields of knowledge and can thus plan their courses better to foster such relationships. The orals also offer a highly subjective, but qualitatively valuable picture of the instructors' success in imparting facts and instilling values.

In the Humanities program at Boston University Junior College, as in any Humanities program in general education, imperfections exist and obstacles remain to challenge faculty effort. Imperfections result in part from the recalcitrance of the student body: student apathy and low morale are often said to be characteristic of the American student today. The morale problem at Junior College is complicated further by the lack of communication between orthodox devotees of "liberal arts" in other colleges of the University and those devoted full time to general education, an aspect of education at the undergraduate level shared by other large universities throughout the country. Another obstacle is that of recruiting faculty members who are broadly and deeply enough trained to teach in an integrated program and sufficiently dedicated to the ends of general education to devote their full time to it. Finally, the most important single obstacle during the seven years of the Junior College's existence has been the lack of appropriate physical facilities. Fortunately, a newer building has now been designated for the relocation of the college on the main campus. Plans for the renovation of this building are now under way. When these plans are completed, the Humanities division expects to have, for the first time, a functional and esthetic environment for its program. Music-listening rooms, an art gallery, a hall for film presentations, and classrooms designed for discussion and complete with audio-visual aids, are among the items planned for the Humanities area in the new building. It is therefore with high hopes that we face the second decade of our service to Boston University and to the cause of general education.

chapter 3

HUMANITIES AT THE FLORIDA STATE UNIVERSITY

*Sarah Herndon**

In the decade 1949-1959 the Florida State University has developed rapidly from a very new coeducational institution with 5500 students and a limited graduate program to an established university with 8000 students and a strong graduate program, especially in the sciences and music. That this phenomenal development has vitally affected the Humanities course is obvious, yet we are perhaps not completely aware of its full significance.

Four important administrative changes have been made. In 1955 the university adopted for the first time an admissions requirement. In 1956 the general education program was revised and the hours required materially changed. Also in 1956 the Humanities Division of the College of Arts and Sciences and the School of Music instituted an interdivisional graduate program leading to the degree Doctor of Philosophy in Humanities. In 1958 a graduate curriculum was set up leading to the degree Master of Arts in Humanities with certification for junior college teaching. This latter is part of another interdivisional program sponsored by the College of Arts and Sciences and the School of Education.

For graduates of accredited high schools entering the university as freshmen, the new admissions policy fixed a minimum score on either the Florida State-Wide Twelfth Grade Testing Program or the Scholastic Aptitude Tests of the College Entrance Examination Board. The results were immediately evident in the im-

---

*Chairman of Humanities in General Education at the Florida State University.

proved quality of the freshman class. Within a year we found that fewer students resented the requirement of humanities, that more were prepared to read intelligently humanities material and discuss the ideas suggested by it. As a result we were able to shift our emphasis in class instruction from content to form and idea. Ten years ago we could not have given the type of essay examination which we now use. We have been amazed at the increased maturity of the students.

The change in general education requirements resulted from a university-wide study of the institution carried on by the faculty between 1952 to 1954. The new program went into effect in September, 1956. In 1950 the university had adopted the semester system and the requirement of 85 quarter hours in general education was changed to 47 semester hours The credit hours in some particular areas had been slightly reduced in making the adjustment, but there was no general revision. For example, the fifteen-quarter-hour humanities course became a nine-semester-hour course. However, in 1956 the program was considerably reduced and the large number of alternative courses previously listed were eliminated. Where alternative courses were allowed in the new program the choice was narrowed. At present the general education requirement includes thirty-five hours prescribed and six elected from the following areas:

1. Communications (9-15 hours)
2. History (6 hours)
3. Social Science (6-12 hours)
4. Humanities (6-12 hours)
5. Natural Science (8-14 hours)
6. Personal Development (0-6 hours)

The six-hour requirement in humanities must be met by taking the integrated course 201-202. It is not open to freshmen unless they have completed the Written Communications 101-102. Additional humanities courses up to six semester hours may be a part of the general education program. These include introductions to literature, art, philosophy, and music. Since these are departmental courses I shall not describe them in my further discussion of our program but shall limit my report to the Humanities 201-202.

In reducing the general education requirement, the faculty may not have intended to deny its commitment to general education or to the objectives of the earlier program. But the development of professional schools and the increase in number of faculty members perhaps not entirely in sympathy with our earlier general education philosophy brought pressure to make in the students' programs more room for specialization. There was at the same time a desire to strengthen general education by the elimination of some ninety alternative courses. We felt there was a distinct advantage in offering to the students a solid unified core.

For the humanities integrated course, the new requirement meant both loss and gain. We regretted that in shifting from nine to six semester hours we needed to reduce the content of the course. On the other hand, we welcomed the opportunity to teach a humanities course prescribed for all students. Since it was to be on the sophomore level we knew we could expect more homogeneity in the classes instead of the previous heretogeneity resulting from a range from freshmen to seniors. It had always been a problem to orient entering freshmen to a course so different from anything they had experienced in high school.

The revised course was first given in 1956-1957. During the preceding winter a committee of six staff members made a complete analysis of aim, content, and method. They worked together for at least two hours a week, discussed thoroughly every aspect of the course, and prepared a mimeographed syllabus of assignments and topics for class discussion. This syllabus has been reprinted each semester with minor changes as the need arises. Such thorough planning and discussion had not been carried on since 1948, when the course was first integrated so that a single instructor taught the entire course. We discovered that after teaching humanities for eight years we had completely lost our departmental biases and were able to consider the course as an integrated whole. "Humanities" to us had come to mean more than simply a combination of literature, art, music, and philosophy. We were not so much concerned with "masterpieces" as with the complex of ideas expressed in enduring forms. Historical periods interested us less than the relationship of ideas in our cultural heritage.

Although we made no arbitrary division of material from literature, art, music, and philosophy, we planned a course in which they were in almost equal ratio. The committee wished to continue the emphasis on our cultural heritage through the study of representative masterpieces, but we had become somewhat dissatisfied with the kind of survey which the course was always in danger of becoming. We realized that in a six-hour course any sort of period study was impossible without superficiality. We recognized the first of our earlier objectives: "To develop understanding and appreciation of the cultural heritage of Western civilization through the study of representative masterpieces," but we abandoned the second: "To present this cultural heritage through the chronological study of the great periods of Western Civilization." There were certain emphases which we had perhaps lost sight of and to which we wished to give more importance. Humanities had come to mean to all of us less a study of cultural history and more an understanding of the ideas and concepts which are important in the world today and which are expressed in works that are still significant and valuable to people in the twentieth century. In the revised course we intended to emphasize humanities today, not only the creative expression of the twentieth century — though we planned to enlarge our section on modern culture — but the ideas and forms of the past which have particular present value and which we believe will be permanently significant. The following statements which appear at the head of each syllabus express our present objective:

> Around a series of "cores" utilizing material from art, music, literature, and philosophy, the course is intended to develop understanding of the diverse ideas and forms of art in our Western Culture today and to discover some of the fundamental principles of the arts as a basis for critical judgment.
> The course is concerned with the meaning of humanities — art, literature, music, and thought — in the world around us and its importance for the individual and society.

Actually the organization is still broadly chronological; but because we leave out far more historical materials than we include, there is no possibility of its becoming a survey. Humanities 201 includes three "cores": The Classical Ideal, The Hebrew-Christian Tradition, The Renaissance Ideal. The rational, logical, and humanistic aspects of Greek classicism are represented by a brief study of the *Illiad,* the Parthenon and its sculpture, *Oedipus Rex,* and Plato's *Republic.* Roman buildings and their decoration show the transition from the ancient city-state to the world empire, with the classical ideal modified by new structural and functional principles. Through the study of these works students become aware of certain continuing problems: the meaning of structure and order, the complexity of human relationships, self-knowledge, destiny and the human lot, justice and the good life, the danger and value of the irrational.

In the second core, "The Hebrew-Christian Ideal," selections from the Old Testament, including the book of Job, furnish an opportunity to examine the nature of religion and its relation to philosophy, the nature of the Bible as a religious book, the Hebrew concept of God and of ethical standards, and the perennial problem of human suffering. The Gospel of Luke in the New Testament shows the ideals of Jesus, upon which the Christian concept of God and Christian ethical principles are based. A comparison is now possible between the Greek and the Hebrew view of life. A study of the problem of suffering in both *Oedipus* and *Job* helps to point up some of these contrasts, and also a comparison between the death of Socrates and the death of Jesus.

The idea of the church at the center of life in the Middle Ages is the basis for the study of two important art forms: the Gothic cathedral and the plainchant. The medieval church is related to Roman building and structural developments are traced from the early western basilica church through the Romanesque to the Gothic type. It is important for students to understand the relation in architecture between structure and function and to appreciate the use of decoration. The function and meaning of liturgy serves to relate the visual arts and music. The Gregorian chant emphasizes the religious origin of our Western musical development, as well as the beauty of melody perfected in the worship of God. The study of Dante's *Divine Comedy* synthesizes the elements in medieval culture and the fusion of classical and religious ideas to be illustrated later in Renaissance art, music, and literature. The cosmology of the poem, its symbolism, its ethical scheme, its visual and auditory aspects, its dramatic qualities — all these aspects lead to the question of its meaning and significance for modern man.

In the third core, "The Renaissance Ideal," the visual arts and music studied in specific works focus upon an understanding of Renaissance Man.   In painting, the new scientific interest in the natural world and in human life, the new understanding of spatial relationships, culminates in the work of Michelangelo.   The synthesis of elements in Renaissance architecture and the new concept of monumentality in sculpture furnish further evidence of the tension between the religious and secular, the classical and medieval, the individual and the institution, in Renaissance Man.   In music this tension is evident in the increasing importance of secular forms, along with religious.   Shakespeare's *Hamlet* also expresses the conflicting ideas of the Renaissance and perennial human problems. Students are able to make important comparisons between Hamlet and Oedipus, Job, Socrates or Jesus and to apply to their own lives what they have discovered.

The emphasis in Humanities 202 is upon the modern world, beginning with the intellectual and scientific revolution of the seventeenth and eighteenth centuries.   In the first unit the ideals of the Enlightment are exemplified in Descartes' *Discourse on Method,* Locke's *Treatise on Civil Government,* Voltaire's *Candide,* the Haydn-Mozart-Beethoven symphony, and David's painting.   Rationalism and empiricism, natural law and its influence upon scientific, political, and social thought are easily observed in the philosophy and literature.   The revival of classical architecture in France and America and the new neo-classical style of David's painting, both influenced by republican ideals, and also the development of the sonata-form in the symphony, show the concern with logical clarity and the ideal of simplicity and order under the growing influence of revolutionary thought.   Students begin to understand something of the complexity of modern culture.

The intensities of the French Revolution and the Napoleonic conflict express a new subjectivity, which in part is a reaction against the classicism of the century before, a return to emotion, intuition, .imagination, violence, shock, mystery, and the supernatural as well as the natural.   This second core, on the Romantic ideal, includes the painting of Delacroix and Daumier, some lyric poetry of the English and German Romantics, the music of Schubert and Berlioz, and the first part of Goethe's *Faust*.

By the middle of the semester we reach the twentieth century. Tradition and Revolt is the theme, which we study through examples of the music, literature, architecture, painting, and philosophy of our time, beginning with the radical departures from tradition in music and painting at the end of the nineteenth century. Wagner serves as a starting point for the distinctively modern movements in music, impressionism, neo-classicism, expressionism, and nationalism. In painting, too, it is necessary to follow a succession of *isms* to understand the revolutionary character of modern culture. The impact of science and a new social consciousness born of industrialism are evident in the philosophy of Whitehead and Dewey and in the architecture of Le Corbusier and Frank Lloyd Wright. A selection of modern poetry, a short story such as Faulkner's *The Bear*, and a play such as *The Death of a Salesman* or *The Glass Menagerie* point up the effect of contemporary problems and tensions upon literature. We do not, of course, attempt to give a complete account of modern culture. We recognize that the twentieth century world shows nothing like the cultural unity of Fifth Century Athens or even of Thirteenth Century Europe. We believe that it is necessary for our students, who belong to this disintegrated modern world, to understand something of the creative life going on around them. Several years ago a student wrote, after looking at examples of modern art, "Now I am ready for the twenty-first century." Many of us on the staff will not see the twenty-first century. We sometimes like to think that we belong more to the past than to the present. But we have a responsibility to prepare these young people for maturity in a world very different from that which most of us have known.

We attempt no thorough exhaustive study of any of the works included in the course. Our aim is to introduce them, to explore leading ideas and to examine artistic form. We try to develop ability to see relationships in the varied content of the course. We hope that students will learn to discuss the humanities intelligently, to see their relation to everyday life, to acquire standards of value, canons of taste, and tolerance for ways of thought, behavior, and expression other than our own. These aims were listed as secondary objectives in 1949, but in our present course they have moved to a primary position.

Such is humanities as it has been given since the fall of 1956. Sophomores do not come into it without a background. The freshman history course is a survey of Western civilization, and emphasizes, particularly in the first semester, the cultural rather than the political aspects of the ancient world, the Middle Ages, and the Renaissance. The approach is descriptive, but it prepares students for an examination of creative works representative of these civilizations. We have tried to achieve some sort of integration between the two courses by asking that history texts be kept and used for review of background in the humanities course. Humanities seems to us so related to the entire general education program that it is the key to any kind of integration of the student's education that he may be able to achieve. Students are continually telling us that humanities opens up a whole new world which they did not know existed and gives a new meaning to their educational experience.

Since most of the sophomore class in 1956 had already taken humanities under the old program as freshmen, we were able to start the new course with only a few sections taught by members of the committee who had worked it out the year before. We anticipated no startling changes in our method of instruction. We found, however, that our new emphasis upon ideas and relationships necessitated some abandonment of the formal lecture in favor of class discussion. We tried to break down student passivity by such class discussion, by the assignment of original essays in which students developed their own ideas, by parallel reading which gave an opportunity for students to explore material of especial interest to them, and by class reports. We have found that a student who enthusiastically presents to the rest of the class, after some investigation of his own, a picture, a poem, a play, or a musical composition, infects his fellow students with his own enthusiasm, whereas the instructor often meets resistance in presenting new forms. Students often become bored with the usual round of reading an assignment and listening to a lecture. A familiar student query at the end of the humanities course has been, "What other courses can I take that are like this? So many courses are arbitrary, but here you can have your own ideas."

An important aspect of the present humanities course is the requirement that students engage in some sort of parallel activity. We not only provide a carefully selected list of books for reading, but we emphasize the importance of looking and listening in the study of the visual arts and music. The excellent collection of fine art books and the prints owned by the library are exhibited during each unit of the course in a special "humanities" room which is informally furnished with easy chairs and couches for relaxed enjoyment, as well as with a table and chairs for notetaking. Students are expected to listen to recordings; the library provides also listening facilities and a collection of records selected by the humanities staff. One member of the staff gives an hour's radio program each week, broadcast from the university station. He uses records appropriate to the current unit and makes helpful comments on them. For a full year these "Humanities Hour" programs have been put on tape, and we expect to make them available to instructors who wish to use any of them in the classroom. In addition to these opportunities for parallel reading, looking, and listening which are provided as a part of the course work, we encourage students to attend the various university sponsored concerts, lectures, plays, and art exhibits available from time to time throughout the year. Almost every week some program relates directly to the course, and students find their appreciation of these events considerably enhanced by their study of humanities. In the classroom, too, we use slides, records, and films as much as possible. Such films as ANCIENT GREECE, CHARTRES AND SALISBURY CATHEDRALS, ROME THE ETERNAL CITY, ART IN THE WESTERN WORLD, THE SHAKESPEARE THEATRE, WHAT IS MODERN ART? are shown in all classes at the appropriate time in the course.

Since 1955 the staff has changed its attitude toward examinations. We had experienced a growing dissatisfaction with the uniform machine-graded test, even though it was combined with an essay for the final, and instructors were free to give tests and quizzes throughout the course. Perhaps we were not sufficiently skilled to devise multiple-choice questions which would test ideas and relationships rather than factual knowledge of content. Perhaps we had not taken sufficient pains. At any rate we felt that students should be able to discuss intelligently the ideas stimulated by the course instead of merely making marks on an answer sheet. Something seemed wrong when the major effort of the examination came from the faculty's struggle to devise questions. The machine-graded test offered little challenge to the students to review carefully, and they took the test with little mental effort.

With the course revision in 1956 we therefore abandoned any kind of machine-graded examination. We provided time for tests at the end of each "core", that is, two each semester in addition to the final. These "core" tests were left to the instructor, but the essay type was recommended. As for the final examination, we have experimented with various types and have been best satisfied with an essay test which includes three types of questions: (1) fifteen or twenty brief identifications; (2) four or five topics for brief discussion of the various works studied in the course, allowing for some choice but distributed so that students must deal with literature, art, music, and philosophy; (3) a general topic for fuller discussion, dealing with ideas and necessitating some integration of material. We have tried this kind of test with uniform questions but recently instructors have been left free to compose their own questions using the uniformly accepted format. Copies of the examination questions are kept on file for study or reference. We have by no means solved the problem of evaluating students' work or achievement. We are still plagued with great variability in grading standards. Studies have been made of the grading practices of the staff and discussion of criteria and standards has been of some value. In the end we must frankly recognize the great diversity of our faculty in background, in interests, in teaching methods, and in grading and testing practices. We believe this diversity is a source of strength. Our staff members are experienced and highly skilled teachers. The study of the humanities is incompatible with regimentation. It accomplishes nothing if it does not foster highly individualized creative gifts, and our staff must needs exemplify these gifts. Many of them are from the professorial ranks and accustomed to teaching their own individual courses in their own way. Each brings his own peculiar gifts and interests to the course, and we feel he should be free to exercise them, provided he accepts the aims and conscientiously tries to cover the content. We have continued to draw staff members from the departments of Art, Classics, English, Modern Languages, Music, and Philosophy, with an occasional experienced graduate assistant and several administrative officers who are qualified and interested in teaching.

The administration of general education has not materially changed since 1949. However, the problem which plagued us then, whether it should continue as a part of the College of Arts and Sciences or whether we should set up a separate administrative unit, has been settled to the satisfaction of at least a majority of the faculty. At the present time the humanities course, along with the rest of the General Education Program, is under the direction of the Arts and Sciences Dean, who appoints a chairman to administer each course. These chairmen form a committee to recommend general policy. The Dean is also advised by a General Education Committee of the Council of Deans. The chairman of humanities is given a full-time secretary and a budget for equipment and supplies but he must bargain with department heads for staff. The system is not as difficult as it sounds, for the various departments strongly support the humanities course and consider it a part of their responsibility. We have continued to maintain a competent staff under this administrative arrangement because we have been free to use only those genuinely interested in teaching the course and because the course itself offers a challenge to broadly trained and alert teachers. In 1949, when it was possible that the general education program might become a separate administrative unit, there was some uneasiness among the various staff members lest loyalties should be divided between general education and their departments. Now there seems no doubt that in the foreseeable future general education will be the responsibility of the departments contributing and of the Dean of Arts and Sciences. Staff members then will be appropriately rewarded for their general education teaching by their own department heads and dean. More and more department heads are considering qualifications for teaching humanities in making new appointments. There is a feeling of satisfaction and security in the present arrangement. The development of our course has always been solidly in the hands of those teaching it, and it seems likely that its greatest strength will continue to be the enthusiasm and devotion of the staff.

Our greatest problem today is the general problem of rapidly increasing enrollments and shortage of qualified teachers. We have felt that with an established humanities course and an experienced faculty we are in a position to do something about training future teachers. Partly for that reason the participating departments set up in 1956 an interdivisional graduate program leading to a PhD in the Humanities. We expect candidates to have or secure a master's degree in one of the humanities fields. Beyond that his program will be highly individual, depending upon his background and his interests. However, all students complete two successive seminars, one in the humanistic tradition, a study of the creative expression of Western man, the other an examination of significent ideas and problems in our tradition. Examinations cut across fields and are both comprehensive and intensive. A research project leading to a dissertation deals with the interrelations of the arts. It must bring together at least two of the areas, though not necessarily all. Without any particular publicity for the program we have several students well along in their research. Within a year we should grant degrees to four candidates, and we have good prospects for an increasing number. We find that graduate students in the conventional humanistic disciplines are often restive under what seems to them an excessively narrow concept of specialization, and they welcome enthusiastically an opportunity to work in a broader field. The program attracts extremely capable students whose major interest lies in teaching, though they are well qualified to contribute to research and criticism. The unusual demands of the program keep out of it those who wish to avoid an arduous academic discipline.

Inasmuch as the graduate program is intended in part to prepare teachers of general education courses, the students in it will inevitably be associated with Humanities 201-202. Already three graduate students have taught sections. In every case they came to us with experience in teaching general education courses either here or elsewhere. All were mature men in the last year of their PhD course work. So far as we could see their success in teaching humanities was no less than that of the regular instructors. We expect to continue to use a few qualified humanities graduate students, although they will probably not often be given full charge of a class. For such graduate students there is a great advantage in being able to teach under careful supervision in the field in which they are studying. In this way teaching as well as research will be a part of the graduate program.

The training of teachers in humanities is also the purpose of a more recent experiment, a cooperative program with the School of Education leading to a master's degree in humanities with certification for junior college teaching. Florida is in the process of creating numerous community junior colleges, and since humanities is required at both state universities these junior colleges will need some kind of humanities course in order that their students may transfer. There is a shortage of teachers qualified to handle an integrated humanities course. Although a single year of graduate study is far too little time for preparation, yet the cooperative program offers us the advantage of supervising internes in our own course and of teaching them methods. Prospective junior college teachers will complete a minimum of 24 semester hours in literature, art, music and philosophy, of which six will be in the seminar in Humanistic Traditions. By a careful selection of courses these students will be able to study in some depth the expression in literature, art, music and philosophy of a particular period, such as the Renaissance or the Twentieth Century. They will, then, have some preparation for a broader kind of study, which they will continue on their own in the institutions where they teach. As for the effect on our own program, if instructors in Humanities 201-202 find themselves working with internes while they are teaching, they will no doubt become much more conscious of their own instructional methods and perhaps more experimental.

Another possibility for meeting the wave of increased enrollment has opened up in the past year through educational television. The university has been granted a high frequency channel and is in process of setting up a station which it is hoped will eventually be part of an all-state educational network. This year the humanities staff has been experimenting with television teaching. We have found among our instructors excellent talent for studio instruction. We have learned some of the advantages of television classes besides the use of superior teachers for more students. Our visual materials can be shown in greater detail than is possible in the conventional classroom. Visual and auditory techniques can be coordinated in new ways. New kinds of graphic aids can be used for literature and philosophy. Even the straight lecture may well seem to students more personal and individual, especially if it comes to him, as it probably will eventually, in his own room or in an informal setting. By bringing in occasional visitors we will be able to use some of the musicians and artists on the campus, whereas it has not been feasible to have them in the classroom.

Television also has its disadvantages, and we are not far along enough in our experiment to say whether it will be successful for humanities classes. One of the chief disadvantages is the necessity of returning to the lecture method. We do not expect, however, to eliminate classroom discussion. No more than two-thirds of the course will be taught from the studio. We expect to provide for the television sections quiz or discussion periods in a conventional classroom atmosphere. We do not expect in the foreseeable future to substitute television teaching for classroom teaching. That would be impossible even if we wanted to do it. We will continue to use our regular faculty for sections taught in the conventional way. We have no illusions about the financial advantages of this new technique. It is considerably more costly than classroom teaching. It remains to be seen whether it will be more effective. It may help in a time of teacher shortage to staff the necessary courses without a sacrifice of quality. We may be able also to help some of the junior colleges in the state who are faced with a more serious staff problem than ours.

chapter 4

THE HUMANITIES IN THE ST. JOHN'S PROGRAM

*John S. Kieffer**

    The St. John's program of liberal arts has done away with departments and subject-matter courses. The college offers to every student the same all-required curriculum. Its Great Books' seminars, supported by language and mathematics tutorials and laboratory exercises in natural science, form a single, unified, and fully required whole. Its faculty are not specialists, not professors of this subject or that, but tutors, teachers who subordinate their special knowledge to general education of their students and who participate in as many parts of the program as their capacities permit and time allows. Therefore, the teaching of the humanities at St. John's is not something to be discussed in isolation from the rest of the program. There is no special course in the humanities and no combination of courses in literature, art, and philosophy exists to make up a humanities major. Nevertheless, the complex of courses and objectives commonly described as the humanities are covered at St. John's.

    The term humanities would no doubt be defined in many ways by those who use it. To some it may signify those studies that cultivate the part of man that distinguishes him from the animals and the material world. To others it may mean the things of the world rather than the supernatural world of theology. The common departmental distinction between the humanities and the social sciences suggests the cultivation of the individual human spirit, while as distinguished from science the term connotes the

    *Formerly president of St. John's College, Annapolis, Md.

freedom of art and imagination as opposed to the iron necessity of natural law. However, these distinctions are accepted, the common practice seems to be to include generally art, literature, and philosophy as humanities.

The whole St. John's program is a humanities program. This assertion reverses the view of the humanities as studies distinguished from naturalistic studies, social studies, or theological studies. It makes the humanties inclusive of all that the human mind has exercised itself upon. If the program were, however, merely inclusive of all this, it would not be a program of education, but a museum. The St. John's program is a humanities program because it has as organizing principle the set of related faculties, sensation, imagination, and intellect, that make up the human mind. Its purpose as education is to develop these faculties in each student to the highest degree his native capacities allow. Although the development of the individual student's powers is the end of his education, this is not incompatible with a social purpose, but is in fact essentially social as well as individual. It is because education proceeds from sense to intellect as the child becomes a man that society can exist at all. To the individual his sensations are unique. It is only because of the generalizing power of the intellect that communication and community are possible. Furthermore, the dependence of modern industrial society on the exercise of reason, in its manufacturing processes, its engineering techniques, and its complex problems of urban living underscores the relation of the fullest intellectual development of every individual to the well-being of society. In short, the St. John's program adopts the principle that a man's vocation and his citizenship are essential ingredients of his humanity.

It is apparent from what has been said that a discussion of the humanities at St. John's entails description of the whole St. John's program. So far I have said that the organizing principle of the program is the faculties of the human mind and that this end includes, essentially and not just as a consequence, vocation in life and education for citizenship. We may now turn to look at the curriculum itself to see how it is organized under these principles, what it is that takes the place of departmentalized subject matters.

The heart and substance of the St. John's program is reading and talking about the Great Books of the Western tradition. The program is articulated by having the twice-weekly discussions of the Great Books (read in chronological sequence) supported by daily classes in language and mathematics, and twice-weekly laboratory periods for the natural sciences. A weekly formal lecture on some topic of the tradtion supplies a thread of authoritative commentary, its authoritativeness tempered by requiring the lecturer to submit to questioning by the students at the conclusion of his formal presentation.

The list of Great Books begins with Homer, carries through the Greek, Roman, and Medieval periods, and continues through Renaissance and modern writings up to the present day. The criteria for the inclusion of books on the list are: that they should be classics, that is to say, be fundamental and enduring treatments of the questions the world propounds to anyone who has to live in it; that they should cover all aspects of man's questions about the world and hence include the classics of poetry, history, mathematics, science, and the various branches of philosophy. A final criterion is that they must belong to the complex tradition of Western civilization, since the world our students will live in is the world of that civilization.

A first comment on the humanities aspect of this program is that the Great Books tradition is in a sense all humanities. Books are the highest use of man's distinguishing characteristics of language. Books speak to their audience in the familiar language of their experience to lead them up to unfamiliar levels on which they can transcend the immediacy of their world of personal observation. This happens on the level of plain information, on the level of imaginative sympathy with unknown persons, and on perhaps the higher level, that of flashes of insight into the reasons of things. Books do not do this by telling the truth to a passive recipient. The process of reading requires the active participation of the mind of the reader. Great Books are those that do what books do with the greatest artistry and about the greatest questions, those that keep recurring to men no matter how often they think they have them answered. To go to school is to withdraw from the world. To go to school to the Great Books is a fruitful withdrawal from the world because the student learns both to build his own world and hence to live in the great world that is the, as yet, unfinished building of the greatest teachers, the great books. The world itself, the cosmos of God's creation, is of course the ultimate teacher. Great Books are a proximate teacher, in that they are more immediately intelligible and better ordered than the world as it appears to the child.

The importance of tradition as the basis of the Great Books curriculum is that it prevents the withdrawal from the world from becoming a retreat to sterile scholasticism. Though the student must be relieved from the distractions of raw experience, his curriculum must possess the reality of the world in which the educated man will live. The tradition accomplishes this first because the books of different authors, different subects and different times, read in succession, continually enlarge the student's insight and force him not to rest content with authority, but to question, to seek to resolve contradiction, to discover analogies between apparently divergent views and subect matters. In the second place tradition is open. New discoveries and new points of view may change it. Thus the student who has fully entered into the tradition is freed to operate as a thinking being and achieves the only human reality, that of finding himself as the builder of his own life.

To emphasize the tradition out of which Western civilized society has grown is not to fix one's eyes on the past. St. John's has begun a revolution against tendencies in modern education, not a counter-revolution. The tendencies we are in revolt against are tendencies toward the denial of man's humanity. Under the name of adustment to society they pave the way for the fascist state. When they deny "eternal verities," they furnish a rationalization for power politics, for the courts to say the law means whatever the strongest pressure group would like it to mean. The semanticists naively contribute to this same chaos by undermining the meaning of meaning. Philosophy has been reconstructed out of existence. The persons who hold any of these positions would indignantly deny my implications, but an examination of their utterances will confirm what I say. The men of good will among them assume such things as human decency and even rationality, but are unaware that these assumptions are undermined by their premises. The cry for revival of the humanities to control the monster of science is evidence both of their touching faith in human reason to get us out of the anarchy we are in and of their lack of understanding on the problem. There is a school of educational thinkers who appeal to "scientific method" as a means of escape. They seem unaware that as far as their appeal is valid they are simply talking about rationality, while they make the absurd assumption that ways of understanding the laws governing matter are appropriate to understanding the human predicament.

Those who study under the Great Books tradition are able to judge the naivete of the moderns with great clarity and with an ironic understanding. The question raised by Greek tragedy, the power and limitation of human reason, illustrated in Thucydides and applied by Plato to the cosmos and man's soul, stares us starkly in the face today. These ancients do not answer the question for us. They give us a paradigm and a frame of reference to do our own thinking about the problem. The Biblical treatment of man together with the Medieval wrestling with the reconciliation of revelation and systematic theology confront us with the problem of evil, while Cervantes and Shakespeare superbly illustrate the problem in the light of the actions of men who are very much living beings. Even the great modern problem, the control of nature through natural science, is empty for those who are unaware of what the Cartesian and Baconian revolution implied, of what they were revolting against. Men educated in the tradition thus have a wider perspective and gain deeper insight into the questions that are treated so superficially today. The St. John's program, therefore, gives St. John's students the cumulative effect of the thought of all the builders of our civilization.

One salient fact emerges from experience in teaching the Great Books tradition at St. John's College. When you abandon departments and the teaching of "authorities in their fields," you can get the students to study with a new kind of attention. They do not study the book or the author's background, but they listen to what the book is saying. Reading books from different fields in close conjunction, the student discovers that they often have something to say on a common topic. For instance, when Hippocrates is read soon after Sophocles and Aristophanes, the tragic and comic patterns of the playwrights are seen surprisingly reflected in some of the patterns of Hippocrates' pronouncements on disease and ill people. Much that is obscure to many readers of Plato is lighted up by Euclid. The seminars in which successive assignments in the books are discussed exploit this kind of reading. The results of one reading are not salted away for examination day, but appear the next time and the next. In the course of four years of seminar discussion each student has found his opinions about man's conduct, his nature, his achievements and the bright and dark faces of the world he lives in, constantly refined by refutation of much folly, by confirmation of bright insights. He learns to live in a world of ideas that become ever more sure illuminators of his world of experience. The Great Books seminars, in brief, make possible the formation of a knowing mind, the development of a critical intelligence.

The seminars in the Great Books bring the student into the vigorous current of human achievement through the tradition of Western civilization. In so doing, they make up a humanities program by giving the student the background and challenge of what men have said and done that has significance for civilization, or more properly, humanization of the human animal. The other side of the objectives of what are called the humanities is in the development of the powers peculiar to the human animal, by which he is able to enter the stream of tradition and stay afloat, whether he swims with the current, as a traditionalist, or breasts it, as a revolutionary. At St. John's therefore, the reading of the Great Books, and their discussion in seminar conversation is prepared for by required tutorials in language, mathematics, and laboratories in natural science. On this level of instruction, too, it is impossible to differentiate between a humanities task and another, whether social, or technical, or scientific.

Since language is the time-honored differentia of the human species, the study of language has an obvious place in the humanities from any point of view. The language tutorials at St. John's have both a general purpose and several specific objectives. The general purpose is development of understanding and technical skill in language, first in its grammatical aspect as an ordered set of symbols for knowing the world and sharing the knowledge with others; secondly, in the rhetorical aspect of literary expression by which the grammatical skills are put to use in giving form to matters that have come under the student's observation and into his understanding. The third part of the general purpose is the study of the forms of logic, which govern both the ordering of symbols for the understnding and the forms of communication by literary expression. The ancient trivium of grammar, rhetoric, and logic is thus the pedagogical framework of language instruction. On the one hand, through specific languages — Greek for the first two years, German, and French — the student is exercised in the traditional disciplines of signification, getting off to a distance for an application of these disciplines to his mother tongue. On the other hand, the theory of signification is approached through langauge study. Habits of readings and close analytical thinking are established which bring the student's mind to bear on the Great Books he is reading for seminar. The more specific objectives of the language tutorials follow from this general purpose: improvement of the student's knowledge of his mother tongue through exercise in translation and writing, close reading of some of the crucial books on the reading list, tighter analysis of some of the questions raised in seminar discussion.

Paralleling the language tutorials are the mathemaics tutorials required also five times a week for all students for four years. In the ancient terms the matter of the mathematics tutorials is the quadrivium. As conducted at St. John's the first year consists of the Greek mathematicians, Euclid, Apollonius, and Ptolemy. The second year continues Ptolemy and goes on to Copernicus, Kepler, and Descartes, with time given to algebra and analytic geometry. The third year covers Newton, and the calculus, and the fourth year, differential equations, non-Euclidean geometry, and modern number theory.

The parallel with the language tutorials is more than a matter of class schedules. The mathematics tutorial is taught as a language study. Greek geometry gives to the study of modern mathematics the same kind of distance and the gracing effort of translation that the Greek language gives to the study of the mother tongue. The return to analytic symbols later in the program is made with a deeper feeling for what the freedom of modern mathematics has cost in intellectual capital. There is likewise opportunity for close reading and analysis of crucial books, with the same reference to questions that are raised in the seminars.

If, however, the mathematics tutorials are a parallel to the language tutorials, they are also a contrast. While the language tutorials are conducted in three different languages, requiring a repetition of grammatical work in successive years and while the books read are often on contrasting subjects, the mathematics tutorials represent a tighter progress, each year's work depending on the year before. The contrast of the two types of tutorial reflects two aspects of the Great Books tradition: the continuity, on the one hand, of book building on book to form a grand progression, while, on the other, the discontinuity of the discoveries of genius and the new things introduced. Each tutorial has some of each of these aspects, but by and large in the language tutorial the aspect of frequent renewal and fresh starts predominates, while the continuity of progress marks the mathematics. In any event, the mathematics taught at St. John's in intent and effect belongs in the category of humanities.

If this is true of the mathematics tutorial, it is also true of the laboratory. This can be said in spite of the fact that in the prevailing opinion science is the very antithesis of the humanities. In this prevailing opinion an inhuman and materialistic science must be counteracted by the softening and humanizing effect of art, literature, and philosophy. I submit that such an opinion mistakes an effect for a cause. The founders of modern science made no such mistake. They were educated men who found in the new discoveries about the physical world the highest challenge to their human powers of observation, hypothesizing, and reduction to principles. It is this point of view that we are trying to recover in the laboratory, in order that our students may enter into the currently most vital part of the tradition. It is the most difficult teaching problem we face at St. John's. The steps we have taken to solve it involve the required participation of all students in four years of laboratory work in physics, chemistry, and biology.

One way of stating our aims is that we are trying to find how the liberal arts are practiced through scientific experiment. We begin with a series of experiments on the instruments of measurement and observation in the natural sciences, so that the student may know what he is doing with them, may have the intellectual right to their use. Then in each of the sciences the crucial experiments on the basic hypotheses are performed. In a series of laboratory reports the student is expected to develop his powers of recognizing hypotheses, understanding the techniques of verification, and discovering the implicit and rarely perceived analogies that go into the development of scientific theories. A close connection is maintained between the work in the laboratory and the mathematics tutorials. Through the latter, the gap between science and philosophy is bridged. The Great Books of science are read in seminar and focus the discussion on problems discovered in the laboratory.

It will be noticed that the St. John's program contains no survey courses, no courses in the history of science, of art, of philosophy. The educational theory underlying the program is anti-instructional. The most real way for a college program to be human is for it to eliminate the devices that prevent the students from behaving like human beings. The work at St. John's requires the student to use his mind like a man, not a school boy. So in every part of the program his mind is brought into direct contact with what I dare to call ideas. He is responsible, ultimately to himself for his own ideas. I mean, that he is not given someone else's opinions, and tested on how well he retains them, but is expected to form his own opinions and the tests he is subjected to are meant to let him show how near the truth he has been able to bring his opinions. The seminar discussions are a continual testing of opinion by all resources common to humanity, logic, imagination, absurdity, insight. He is made to feel that no easy source of truth exists for him to appeal to and that he must always in the end decide himself. The Great Books present cogent arguments for one opinion or another, reveal the emptiness of many accepted opinions, by their agreement or disagreement illuminate one or another perennial question, and finally compel the student to make up his own mind. The function of the teacher is to give the student every possible assistance by directing his attention to the relevant questions, by helping him master the necessary conventions of communication, and by keeping him, where he can, from making a fool of himself. It is never to be instructive or to tell him the truth. Learning of this sort is primarily intellectual, but its end is not to make "intellectuals" of the students. It is not primarily character-building, but in emphasizing the responsibility of the student for making up his own mind, it is making it possible for him to be a man and a free man, one who is able to make intelligent choices in his life as a free man and a citizen.

There are two elements in most humanities programs that I have not touched on. These are the fine arts and religion. The fine arts, as well as the manual arts, are undoubtedly an accompaniment of liberal education. Insofar as they are means of disciplining the body and the senses, the hand and eye and ear in relation to the material world, they act in some sort of reciprocity with the liberal arts and are neglected with peril to the freeing of the mind. Nevertheless, because they are concerned with matter, they have a kind of darkness in them, which is only made the more manifest by the illumination of the work of genius, that makes them more appropriate to the fringe of liberal education. This is where they are at St. John's. A manual arts shop gives students the opportunity to acquire manual skills; an artist-in-residence provides instruction in the graphic arts and helps arrange exhibits. Music, however, is integrated into the program. A weekly choral sing is required of all students and experimental tutorials and seminars in great scores are being tried out to learn how musical classics may be read.

As for religion, for the opposite reason it is not a part of the program. The Bible and great works of theology are read in seminar, and the college thereby recognizes its intellectual responsibility to religion. The religious life of the student is an interior matter that demands an ultimate freedom even beyond the freedom of thought that is the basic of the student's work in seminars and tutorials. The college stops short of faith, though for the student faith may be the beginning of his college work.

The St. John's program, therefore, is designed to accomplish the ends that most humanities programs set themselves. In contrast, however, to a college in which a special course or group of courses in the humanities are set over against other courses in other subjects, at St. John's the usual humanities subjects are blended into a single whole with the other intellectual disciplines. The arrangement of studies is such that every part of the program is conducted with a view to an essential human purpose. Finally, the program as a whole puts the students into the stream of human tradition and encourages him to work so that everything he does contributes to his growth into manhood and civilized responsibility.

The statement of the place of the humanities in the St. John's College curriculum published in the 1949 edition of *The Humanities in General Education* is valid today, a decade later, as far as the fundamental structure and aims of the curriculum is concerned, and in respect to most of the content of the curriculum. There have been some changes of significant detail in certain parts of the program. These changes are the result of the continual study of the program and annual review of its working made by the Instruction Committee of the Faculty. The description of these changes will bring the account up to date.

The most far reaching change was made in the Seminar of the fourth year. There the books, nineteenth century and contemporary classics, have been grouped into units of study, with research seminars, in which written reports by students are given, alternating with discussion seminars. Research reports require individual students to read collateral material related to the book under discussion and develop special themes in connection with the subject of the principal reading. These reports frequently are pre-preparatory to the writing of the dissertation required of all students for graduation. This plan may be extended into the third year seminar.

The trend towards more practice in writing is further marked in changes in the second year language tutorial. Here, although the study of Greek is continued there is more emphasis on English, both in formal study of rhetoric, with practice in writing and with a term's work devoted to poetic analysis of a play of Shakespeare.

The music tutorials have been further developed and extended through the first half of the second year, giving more time for a thorough attention to the technical language of great works of music.

The fourth year mathematics tutorial has been changed to include the study of Einstein, thus better fulfilling the responsibility of making the curriculum properly humanistic, in the sense of giving the student the intellectual equipment a man must have to understand the sinews of the world he will live in. Furthermore, the fourth year laboratory has approached the study of physics through the method of individual research projects, — or rather small goup research — thus paralleling the new emphasis in the senior seminar.

In 1955 the Instruction Committee undertook a self-study project, under a grant from the Ford Foundation's Fund for the Advancement of Education.   A questionaire was sent to all graduates under the present program asking for the alumnus's evaluation of his education at St. John's in the light of his later experience. In addition, a conference of educators from other colleges and universities was held during the year at which the aims of the program were discussed and criticized by these men.   The results of these programs of selfstudy tended to confirm the college in its opinion of the rightness of its fundamental purposes and some of the criticism assisted the Faculty in reaching the decisions it made in making the changes listed above.   Perhaps the most significant result of the study was the weight given to the necessity of more attention to the art of writing.   In general, however, St. John's is well satisfied that its decision in 1937 to require a single program of all the liberal arts, linguistic and scientific if the goal of a true program of Humanities was to be pursued was the right decision.

A LIST OF GREAT BOOKS IN CHRONOLOGICAL ORDER

This list is subject to constant revision. Books read only in part are indicated by an asterisk.

Homer:	*Iliad, Odyssey*
Herodotus:	*History*
Aeschylus:	*Agamemnon, Choephoroe, Eumenides, Prometheus Bound*
Sophocles:	*Oedipus Rex, Oedipus at Colonus, Antigone*
Euripides:	*Hippolytus, Medea*
Aristophanes:	*Clouds, Birds*
Hippocrates:	*Airs, Waters, and Places, Ancient Medicine, Oath, Sacred Disease*
Plato:	*Ion, Gorgias, Meno, Republic, Apology, Crito, Phaedo, Symposium, Parmenides,* Theaetetus, Sophist, Timaeus, Phaedrus*
Thucydides:	*History of the Peloponnesian War*
Aristotle:	*Generation of Animals,* On the Soul* Physics II, III, IV, VIII, Metaphysics I,* V,* VI, VII,* XII, Nicomachean Ethics,* Politics,* Poetics, Organon*
Euclid:	*Elements*
Archimedes:	*Selected Works*
Apollonius:	*Conics I-III*
Lucretius:	*On the Nature of Things*
Virgil:	*Aeneid*
The Bible*	
Epictetus:	*Discourses,* Manual*
Tacitus:	*Annals*
Plutarch:	*Lives*
Nicomachus:	*Arithmetic*

Ptolemy:	*Almagest**
Galen:	*On the Natural Faculties*
Plotinus:	*Fifth Ennead*
Augustine:	*Confessions, The City of God**
Thomas Aquinas:	*Summa Theologica**
Dante:	*The Divine Comedy*
Chaucer:	*Canterbury Tales*, Troilus and Cressida*
Pico della Mirandola:	*On the Dignity of Man*
Rabelais:	*Gargantua and Pantagruel**
Machiavelli:	*The Prince, Discourses**
Luther:	*Commentary on the Epistle to the Galatians**
Calvin:	*Institutes**
Copernicus:	*On the Revolution of the Spheres**
Montaigne:	*Essays**
Bacon:	*Novum Organum*
Gilbert:	*On the Magnet**
Kepler:	*Epitome of Copernican Astronomy IV, V*
Donne:	*Poems**
Shakespeare:	*Richard II, Henry IV, parts 1 and 2, As You Like It, Twelfth Night, Othello, Hamlet, Macbeth, King Lear, Tempest*
Cervantes:	*Don Quixote*
Harvey:	*Motion of the Heart and Blood*
Galileo:	*The Two New Sciences**
Descartes:	*Rules for the Direction of the Mind,* Discourse on Method, Geometry,* Meditations*
Hobbes:	*Leviathan**
Spinoza:	*Theological-Political Treatise*
Milton:	*Paradise Lost* Samson Agonistes*
Bunyan:	*The Pilgrim's Progress*
Pascal:	*Pensées**
Racine:	*Phédre*
La Fontaine:	*Fables**
Newton:	*Principia,* Optics**
Huygens:	*Treatise on Light**
Locke:	*Essay Concerning Human Understanding,* Second Essay on Civil Government*
Berkeley:	*Principles of Human Knowledge*
Leibniz:	*Essay on Dynamics, Discourse on Metaphysics, Monadology, Correspondence with Arnauld*
Swift:	*Gulliver's Travels, The Battle of the Books*
Vico:	*The New Science**
Fielding:	*Tom Jones*
Montesquieu:	*The Spirit of the Laws**
Hume:	*Enquiry Concerning Human Understanding, Dialogues Concerning Natural Religion*
Voltaire:	*Candide, Micromegas*
Gibbon:	*Decline and Fall of the Roman Empire**
Rousseau:	*Essay on the Origin of Inequality, Social Contract*
Lessing:	*Education of Mankind*
Schiller:	*Poems**
Adam Smith:	*Wealth of Nations**
Kant:	*Critique of Pure Reason,* Critique of Practical Reason,* Critique of Judgment,**
Lavoisier:	*Treatise on Chemistry**

United States Constitution
*Federalist Papers**

Goethe:	*Faust,* Sorrows of Young Werther*
	*Poems**
Hoelderlin:	*Poems**
Hegel:	*Philosophy of History*
de Tocqueville:	*Democracy in America* (abridged)
Kierkegaard:	*Philosophical Fragments, Fear and Trembling*
Faraday:	*Experimental Researches in Electricity**
Lobachevski:	*Theory of Parallels*
Balzac:	*Father Goriot*
Stendhal:	*Red and Black*
Flaubert:	*Madame Bovary*
Boole:	*Laws of Thought**
Darwin	*Origin of Species,* Descent of Man**
Marx:	*Capital,* Communist Manifesto, Preface to Critique of Political Economy**
Mendel:	*Experiments in Plant Hybridization**
Tolstoi:	*War and Peace*
Nietzsche:	*Birth of Tragedy, Beyond Good and Evil*
Dostoevski:	*Crime and Punishment, The Possessed*
George Cantor:	*Transfinite Numbers**
Dedekind:	*Essays on Numbers**
Baudelaire:	*Poems**
William James:	*Psychology—Briefer Course**
Poincaré:	*Science and Hypothesis*
Freud:	*A general Introduction to Psychoanalysis*
Thomas Mann:	*Death in Venice*
Valéry:	*Poems**
de Broglie:	*Matter and Light*

Documents from American History
Charter of the United Nations

chapter 5

THE HUMANITIES AT SOUTHWESTERN

*John H. Davis**

In looking back over the history of university education prior to the nineteenth century, one might be tempted to formulate a "law of academic inertia" based on the tendency of curricula to harden. It would also seem that new developments were usually generated outside the cloistered halls and had to struggle to gain admittance to them. Thus the "new learning," or Renaissance humanism, had to force its entry into the scholastic stronghold. Later, seventeenth century science fought the *litterae humaniores* for admission, and the two then combined to hold the line against the newer disciplines, the biological and social sciences.

Since the late nineteenth century this situation seems to have been reversed. The academic community has admitted so many disciplines that we detect now a "law of constant change." And these changes instead of originating from without the academic fold, have mostly been generated from within. The following are a few of the factors which brought this about. First, a veritable "explosion of knowledge" in the past century led to a proliferation of courses and of subdivisions within the older accepted branches of learning and to over-specialization and to over-departmentalization, this creating a multiversity within the university. Next, outside pressures for practical subjects led universities to provide more and more vocational and technical courses. Finally, the spread of the free elective system destroyed the student's hope of attaining a

---

*Professor of history, Southwestern at Memphis, Tenn.

common core of learning, while the increasing use of textbooks isolated him more and more from the "great documents."

These and other factors led to the soul searchings indulged in by so many colleges and universities during the second quarter of this century. This was a time when serious concern was felt lest the "humanities" (a term newly in use) be completely lost. In its early usage this term seems not to have had the connotations it later acquired. In the twenties it was mostly emloyed as a designation for subjects which were not social or physical sciences; that is, it was one of the three (or sometimes more) new "Divisions" into which — for the sake of convenience — the numerous departments of an institution were grouped.

During the period of self-examination (the nineteen thirties and forties), the term acquired much greater weight. These were the days when colleges and even secondary schools sought a "core curriculum" of certain basic "humanities" which would allow the specialized or vocationalized to gain at least the basis for a common meeting of minds. This was the plea of the *Harvard Report on General Education* (1945). Other institutions tended to search for a panacea by constructing a special "general education course in the humanities" which, it was hoped, would synthesize knowledge, cut across department lines, and prepare the student for the fuller life and for the understanding of human emotions. Commissioner McGrath's book, *The Humanities in General Education* (1949) listed and described many attempts to create such courses.

My own institution, Southwestern at Memphis, made one of these efforts in 1945 by constructing a course, "Man in the Light of History and Religion," which was described in Dr. McGrath's volume. Perhaps by quoting some lines (written by Professor A. P. Kelso) from the prefatory statement of our first syllabus, I can indicate something of the concept of the humanities and of the rather sanguine hopes for the course we then held. He wrote:

> Essentially the course rests on the faith that from the beginning of an academic career one must learn the art of synthesis. . . . For an instructor some specialization is a necessity, at least academically; for the student who is not a prospective instructor it leads to his becoming the unhappy possessor of *disjecta membra* of historical, literary, artistic and religious information. If this ends, as

it often has, in a loss of the sense of cohesion and purpose in life, it can be tragic.

One unifying principle is history. We believed as we planned this course, that the framework of the course must be history. This has been reduced to the history of the western world. . . . Selection and emphasis of material has been inevitable, but we have kept steadily in view the aim that whatever value or meaning literature, art, philosophy, and religion have had, it has been carried forward on the great current of history.

At the same time, believing that religion is essentially the inner force creating values, we have tried to show how the religious hopes and faiths of the western world have directed and influenced the movement of history. . . .

We have even attempted to use our knowledge of history and understanding of religion to estimate the character and destiny of America.

We believe such a course is the soundest type of orientation. A feeling for history, based on the experience of using historical documents, the truly humanistic method, is a necessity to the scholar. . . . We have no apology for directing the students' view to the great and startling personalities of the past. Certainly not for the greatest. Unless man knows God, can he know man? That is why we have used some of the great books, for behind great books are great minds. They made the world we live in. Again we have made no apology for the time and effort spent on the greatest of books, the Bible. . . .

Ultimately this course was born of a hope that the American college student, given a chance, is willing and able to become an American scholar, not forever a postgraduate kindergartner, but an independent mind, willing to pay the price of sacrificial studying to become a leader in thought and life. . . . The humanities, we believe, are the heart of a liberal education. The emancipative power of religion as seen in history can and should aid in the emancipating of the American. Such education can create true citizens of democracy.

Critics soon arose, however, to point out that many of these unique courses (including our own) could be avoided; that they were often given to immature first year students with no "follow-up;" and that no two institutions ever seemed to agree on the contents of "the humanities." Some — for example our own statement quoted above — interpreted them as basically an enlarged and interdepartmentalized history of western civilization; some used the "Great Books" or the "Great Ideas" approach; whereas others interpreted the humanities as almost synonymous with the fine arts.

As we have moved into the fifties, "the humanities" have acquired an even greater *mystique*. Some enthusiasts, and these extend even to editors of newspapers and popular magazines, now proclaim them America's "road to salvation." Thus the effect of the cold war with Russia has been ambivalent. It has led our government and the foundations to pour billions into science and scientific research — and so distract many from the humanities — yet it has led us also to proclaim that the "Free World's" superiority to communism lies in our adherence to individualism and to the eternal verities best attained through the cultivation of religion and the humanities. We have a paradoxical situation in that much time and effort is spent in most colleges in the effort to interest and indoctrinate our students in "humane learning," while at the same time "humane scholarship" (the ultimate source of learning) is neglected because the giant share of governmental and foundational largesse is being poured into scientific work. Concern for these factors is responsible for the recent studies by Jaques Barzun, and by Howard Mumford Jones for the American Council of Learned Societies. Concern for arousing the interest of the student in the manifold "tasks of the humanities" (and Professor Jones in *One Great Society* has listed twenty) has engaged the attention of our faculty for the past decade. The "Man Course" has continued but newer aims and objectives have been discussed and tried out in the realm of general education.

General education is itself a term almost as difficult of definition as "democracy" or "the humanities." Southwestern in the mid-forties appointed a Committee on General Education, yet after many meetings it produced only a host of conflicting definitions arranged in the fashion of Abelard's *Sic et Non*. However there are two ordinary, though discrepant, uses of the term. The first makes "General Education" almost synonymous with a general survey course in one of the divisions; in the second, the term is almost the equivalent of the liberal or humane education by which the student should gain a better understanding of himself and the world before he enters the more limited sphere of his "major" or of some professional skill. I would say that during the past decade Southwestern, along with many other institutions, has moved from a primary concern with the first of these usages to a greater interest in the second.

Though our course "Man in the Light of History and Religion" still flourishes — and has perhaps furnished some new techniques and ideas to the faculty and administration — the efforts we made in the 1940's to create similar courses for social or natural sciences proved abortive. Now in the 1950's our expressed aims have become: to deepen "the motivation of the student for the general education program of the liberal arts college," to try to create the feeling of "a community of learning," to convince the student somehow that even social and natural sciences have human implications, and that a study of the humanities is a lifetime job, "a continuing education," and not one that ceases the moment of graduation.

One way to observe these newer emphases is to note curriculum changes which have been made (or even contemplated) during the past few years. Our "general degree requirements" (in some cases as high as seventy-two hours) have remained formidable in spite of efforts to reduce them. The only modifications have been, 1) permission to substitute a Greek or Roman civilization course (based on literature in translation) for the second year of an ancient language, 2) the addition of a year of social science, and 3) the requirement of general comprehensive examinations in the major field. We have added two new departments, one in Fine Arts, the other in International Studies, and we have launched a flourishing Adult Education division. The more significant changes in attitude to general education have been in the direction of extending the content of existing courses, creating new courses which cut across departmental lines, and experimenting with new teaching techniques.

Thus in addition to our original interdepartmental course, "Man in the Light of History and Religion," (taught by members of the history, Bible, and philosophy departments), we now have courses in Art taught jointly by members of the philosophy and art departments, courses in Religion taught jointly by philosophers and Bible professors, and an American Studies course which is taught by one man but includes materials from several fields. In fact as I contemplate our local treatment of the "cross-fertilization idea," I discover more cases in which one professor attempts to synthesize materials from several fields (e.g., in Freshman English, American Studies, and Modern Novel, Great Books, Mythology, Social Problems, etc.) than those in which representatives of several departments collaborate in a single course.

Among newer techniques, we have experimented with language teaching by tape recorder (and our International Language Center has made available to students and public, dictionaries and tape recordings of at least thirty languages from Arabic to Urdu). We have employed the discussion method widely with undergraduates — many professors having praticed this technique by working with the Adult Center. An interesting by-product of this idea is the fact that this year the student council chose a small group of student leaders who during the fall Orientation Week discussed certain selected books with incoming freshmen. For a long time we have used tutorials and seminars and, since the students of our college are required to attend chapel, we have employed lectures and films in attempting to educate this captive audience in "Free World Issues" (a series of lectures by distinguished outside speakers on world problems), and in the Fine Arts. Among some of the many ideas discussed in faculty committees, but which have yet to be accepted, have been: the formulation of an "ideal integrated curriculum," the placing of reproductions of great art in all student dormitory rooms, and the creation of an "Educational Evaluation Week" (to parallel an existing Religious Evaluation Week) in which during the assembly period, a scientist would explain some great scientific idea, and its implications would be discussed by a panel of social scientists and humanists. A group of faculty members have for several years been meeting regularly for the discussion of great books taken from different fields of knowledge. This year we will inaugurate some Sophomore Seminars in which groups of three professors from different fields and a dozen students will discuss such topics as, The Individual and the Community, Myths and Realities in Contemporary Life, and The American Scene, as these are reflected in certain selected contemporary writings.

When a group here at Southwestern in the mid-forties began to construct a syllabus and work out details of the "Man Course," some pioneers were already in the field. There was also a general feeling in the academic atmosphere, that "something was wrong," but few knew what to do, and attempts at change were often met by opposition or indifference. Many products of specialization and departmentalization opposed the idea of interdisciplinary graduate work, and though some universities set up committees which would permit the graduate student to cross departmental lines, many students who attempted to do so found obstacles in the way, and at first few survived. The supply of trained interdepartmentalists was therefore limited. Besides this lack of trained personnel, the small college also confronted other difficulties: the lack of adequate texts, of collected readings, of obtaining a large lecture room with the necessary equipment (maps, slides, projectors), and of finding a convenient spot on the schedule for a large course. Time, patience, a sympathetic administration, and friendly cooperation between the members of the staff enabled us to survive. One habit we developed early was the policy of having lunch together once a week. This enabled us to plan tests, make suggested revisions in the syllabus, absorb new personnel, and to discuss other problems connected with the course.

Our "Man in the Light of History and Religion" was launched as a six semester hour course for freshmen, and was originally taught by a staff of five. We gave three lectures each week, on successive days, to the assembled class of about a hundred. On the remaining three days of the week the class was divided into five sections, one for each teacher; and sections were rotated so that every student was exposed to each teacher for about a six week period in the course of the year. Though in the main we lectured only on subjects in which we had some competence, each member of the staff was expected to conduct all the discussions. As these centered around Biblical selections, literary works, and readings in philosophy and political science, the staff, at least, acquired a general education. For the first few years we attended all lectures, which proved an excellent stimulant to better preparation.

During the fifteen years of the Man Course's existence there have been numerous changes, and — we hope — improvements. But the organic structure has remained much the same. Enrollment began with about a hundred, dropped to about eighty when it was found to be tough, but has gradually increased to a hundred and fifty as its reputation has spread from graduates to incoming freshmen. Only two of the original staff remain, though we have increased the teaching staff from five to six. We are now on the sixth edition of our syllabus and are preparing for the seventh.

Our first syllabus divided the year's work into thirty weekly units and contained mainly the lecture topics and reading assignments for each week. We soon developed longer units, and now have ten units of three weeks each. These are centered more directly on the concept of man (Origin of Man, Religion and Civilization; Man's Discovery of man — Helenism; Man's Domination of Man — Rome and Imperialism; Christianity in Human History — Its Concept of Man and God; Hierarchy of Man and Society — the Middle Ages; etc.). To each unit in the syllabus we have added a prefatory essay, a chronological chart, outlines for each lecture and a number of discussion topics for each discusion meeting. It can be seen, therefore, that as we change lecture topics and revise readings, new outlines and topics become necessary and syllabi soon bcome obsolete.

Most of our problems have been minor ones. Routine difficulties have arisen over such things as finding a time in the schedule, or a lecture room large enough for our full group. Thus after outgrowing our original room we found we were relegated to the college chapel which had no desks, no way to darken the room for projecting slides, and no blackboard or maps. This was a year of great trial to the staff. We now have the science lecture room, but are threatened with eviction as that department's need for space increases. As stated above we started the course by having three consecutive days of lecture, then three days of discussions (on the theory that the student, needing no preparation for the lecture, would be free to read more intently for the ensuing discussion). Because of scheduling difficulties we had to change the lectures and discussions to alternate days. By shifting some of the topics so that the lecture in a sense prepared for the ensuing discussion, we now feel the new system works more smoothly than the old.

The problem of testing a student in a course in which six different people lecture and in which each of the six discussion sections may go off on entirely different tangents, has been a difficult one. Since dividing the course into units of approximately three weeks each, we have given a "collection" or quiz at the end of each unit. Then we divided the final examination into sections which have corresponded to the units and have made the student's final grade an average of the two (the test grade is sometimes modified by the teacher on the basis of the student's attendance, participation in discussion, preparation of outside work, etc.). Both quizzes and final examinations have usually been constructed at our luncheon conferences, by general agreement. The same tests and final examination are given to all. At first, most of us, accustomed to the "essay," "identification," or "recognition of quotation" type tests, used these methods; but as student numbers increased we have experimented more with the objective types, matching, and multiple choice. We have done this especially on the examination, which is a six hour affair with each professor responsible for giving and correcting one of the six units for the entire class.

The above refers to evaluating the student's grade in the course. On the larger issue of evaluating the impact of the course on the student's subsequent academic career, or on his life, we have made little progress. We have given some opinion questionnaires and we have received some flattering statements from alumni, but we have never made a really adequate study of the subsequent academic records of those exposed to the Man Course in comparison with those who chose an alternate route.

The much publicized fact of the pressure of the increasing student population has been recognized by Southwestern. In general the policy of the college has been, almost of physical necessity, to keep down any large increase in enrollment, to make admission more difficult by more searching tests and by elimiinating more and more applicants from the lower percentiles. This policy is already reflected by the increasing number of students on the honor roll or dean's list, and by the occasional complaint of the president in faculty meeting that "we are not having enough failures." This is not to say that as yet we have created the spirit of emulation noted in Russian and European universities, or that we do not continue to take in inadequately prepared, maladjusted, or purposeless students. We are certainly spending more time in trying to wake them up.

The dangers now confronting a truly liberal or humane education are so many and so complex that it is impossible even to summarize them. Some are actual, some potential. The rising tide of student population is expected to create an acute shortage of adequately prepared teachers which in turn is expected to drain teachers from the smaller colleges to the larger (or better paid) institutions. Many small colleges will have to abandon certain individualized or personalized instruction practices, for already many of the larger universities are tending toward larger classes and mechanized methods. The recruitment of teachers is further handicapped by the highly paid competition of industry and science. Mr. Barzun has pointed out that even the many foundations, supposedly created for the advancement of education, often add to its problems. Think of the time spent by deans and professors in concocting schemes which might attract grants; and of the many conferences — local and national — which draw the teacher away from teaching and research; or of the projects which are started by the foundations but which the institution is then left to shoulder. Meanwhile the government with its "world responsibilities" sends professors and students around the earth. Many of these present day developments may produce good, some may produce evil results. It is too early to "run a balance." Meanwhile the academic community is in a ferment, though it is a different sort of ferment from the one fifteen years ago. The solutions of the "problem of the humanities" are also different. Then most colleges sought a kind of "one-dose panacea;" now there is danger in being swamped by the multiplicity of nostrums.

chapter 6

THE HUMANITIES PROGRAM AT STEPHENS COLLEGE

*Marjorie Carpenter**

1. THE TERM, HUMANITIES

At Stephens College, we consider the term, "Humanities," to include all the forms of learning which have to do with beauty as man creates it in music, literature, painting, sculpture, architecture or the combined arts.   This involves, necessarily, background consideration of history as well as some aspects of philosophy and religion.   Since the course was initiated in response to the Charters Study of the needs of women, it attempts to answer their felt need for some approach to the arts which would give them a sense that they could enter into the various arts with intelligent enjoyment. The purely theoretical approach of aesthetics, the historical approach which surveys great works of art as evidence of the culture of a period have been avoided.

In other words, the principles underlying the arts, and exposure to experience with music, painting, literature and other arts form the basis for the course.   The objective of giving the student practice in exercising judgment based on these principles has remained the central purpose, since we, as a staff and as a college, are still concerned with general education.   The staff of seven who teach the course in General Humanities still have an enthusiastic interest in the education of young women who may or may not have a specialist's desire to perform or create.   We feel that these women will help to make the cultural climate in the United States.

*Professor of Humanities, Stephens College, Columbia, Missouri.

Not only do our students and alumnae continue to express themselves as pleased with an approach to the process of making judgments in the arts, but we have evidence to support the fact that they grow in the development of this ability.

If anything, we are more than ever convinced that the layman needs the arts. We are more than ever aware that the layman has need of experience in judging the arts and in finding in them genuine release from tension. Facts about shifts in our culture are relevant at this point: there is an increase in the amount of leisure time for the average man and woman; there is in the 'mass arts' a challenge and a danger unless we educate intelligent viewers and listeners; the increase of science and the emphasis on it as the solution for all of humanity's problems is in itself a problem which needs an antidote; the trend towards "the organization man" tends to de-humanize the individual. Also, the proliferation of courses, the pressure to teach more and more details about what has been learned, points up the necessity for supplying the undergraduate with some streamlined courses which are *thorough* in their integration of important principles, and *more than surface deep* in their provision for education in the process of making judgments.

2. CONTINUING NEED OF GENERAL EDUCATION

It was this very proliferation of courses which started the emphasis on general education;* it has not decreased. For that matter, these changes in education have been observed by humorists as well as by educators for many years. Stephen Leacock, former professor of Economics at the University of Toronto, commented that plain people have noticed that formal education is getting

---

*The term itself, we are told by many administrators, is not now in good repute; they say that we cannot distinguish it in *practise* from the term, 'liberal education'. This may well be true. It is difficult to influence faculty members to teach material in any other way than that in which they themselves learned it. Especially in the ivy-league colleges there has always been a tendency to consider the efforts of general education beneath their notice, even after the publication of the Harvard Report. There are, however, certain tendencies which separate the two terms 'liberal' and 'general' as they are applied to higher education. A summary of these distinctions should be considered:

General education is that approach to continuing education which stresses the materials and the methods which increase the layman's ability to enter into all the aspects of life with satisfaction, irrespective of his vocation. This includes especially: understanding of the basis for relationships with friends and family; understanding of scientific developments; preparation for responsibilities in local and world community; and an approach to health, recreation and enjoyment of the creative arts which promises full enjoyment of life.

The difference between liberal education and general education

First, let us grant that many people use the terms without relation to practises. Let us grant that both "general education" and "liberal education" can be good or bad.

LIBERAL EDUCATION:

1. *Tends* to use traditional materials in the hopes that they will "liberate the mind."
2. *Tends* to emphasize mental training in an assumption that everything else is going to get done somewhere.
3. *Tends* to education the elite, the students whose intellectual capacity is greatest, without too much consideration of the student who has average ability (ability *tends* to be identified with verbal ability);
4. *Tends* to ignore methods of teaching (even, at times, to scorn them), or to choose those methods which are convenient for faculty and administration, regardless of consideration of methods which best suit the student.

Willingness to use the term, GENERAL EDUCATION, has the following implications (regardless of words used in the definition):

Institutions which use the term and try to follow through on its implications:

1. *Tend* to explore the needs and interests of students — both immediate and future needs, in so far as studies reveal trends which are significant.
2. *Tend* to sift all *materials* AND *methods* through considerations of #1, rather than adopting materials which have traditionally been presented in the way in which they have been traditionally presented. This selection of materials and methods may or may not result in curriculum and course changes. It should do that in many cases.
3. *Tend* to consider students with average ability as important as brilliant intellectuals.
4. *Tend* to offer guidance to students to a greater degree than is the case with liberal education.
5. *Tend* to consider the student's total development — emotionally and socially, in and out of the classroom — as a part of good education.

It will be unfortunate if we ignore the differences and concentrate on the similarities because we do not wish to come to grips with the challenge in developing general education courses, because it is not now popular to do more than make our higher education courses, as difficult in traditional respectability as the Russian courses in science.

longer and longer. He defines plain people as "those who shudder at mathematics, go no further in Latin than 'e pluribus unum', and take electricity as they find it." He reminds us that in the early twentieth century, "people learned to read out of a spelling book at six years of age, went to high school at twelve, taught school on a third class certificate at sixteen; then two years in a sawmill and two at medical school made them doctors, and one year in a sawmill and one in divinity school fitted them for the church." Now, he adds, it is all changed: "children at school at six years cut up paper dolls — they are still in high school at eighteen learning civics and social statistics — studies for old men. They enter college at nineteen, take prerequisites and post requisites in various faculties for nearly ten years; then they become demonstrators, invigilators, researchers, or cling to a graduate scholarship like a man on a raft." This satire on the increased amount of time spent in college is not without point, even though we wish to give "the plain man" more and different education than formerly. It must differ in quality as well as quantity; it is forced to be more selective.

It is, indeed, possible that in our system of degrees and certificates, we have defeated the real ends of education. It has become imperative that we lead youth out (e-duco) from ignorance into a lifelong pursuit of truth and wisdom. We must face the fact that we have to counteract the prevailing idea that a college degree is "a good thing to get," and that you "get a degree" so that you can "get a job," "get adjusted to others," or "get ahead," not get a good HEAD but "get ahead of the other fellow".

Ten years ago we blamed highly specialized training, and professional schools. It is still true that some engineers, doctors, and research men have lost a sense of a common heritage and find it difficult even to carry on a conversation with one another, the situation is rapidly changing. Business, labor, industry unite in

stating that they will train in an apprentice fashion the young
graduates whom they employ; but they would ask of higher education, people who can make critical judgments, and mature people
who recognize the significance of values in their own lives.

These are facts in the national picture. They have been
considered by our staff in evaluating the rationale for our present
course. The special applicability of these truths to our present
concept of the humanities course centers around our belief that in
this country we shall suffer a dangerous dying back of the mind
if we ignore man's creative expression in the arts. The more complicated the truth — and there are plenty of very complicated ones
today — the more chance there is that it can be grasped by an
experience with one of the poems or paintings or compositions
of music which speak through ear, eye, mind, heart to strike responsive chords in us. Marianne Moore puts this poetic truth about
poetry into very suggestive phrases:

"I, too, dislike it: there are things that are important
        beyond this fiddle.
    Reading it, however, with a perfect contempt for it,
        one discovers in
    it, after all, a place for the genuine.
        Hands that can grasp, eyes
        that can dilate, hair that can rise
        if it must, these things are important not because
a high-sounding interpretation can be put upon them but
        because they are

        useful _____
    nor till the poets among us can be
        'literalists of
        the imagination' — above
        insolence and trivialty and can present
for inspection, imaginary gardens with real toads in them,
        shall we have
    it."

Thinking about the "imaginary gardens with real toads in
them," having the experiences which genuinely "make the hair
stand on end," coming to grips with the shock of a painting like
Guernica, hearing the dissonances and the disturbing rhythms of
Strauss' Elektra or Orff's Antigone against a background of familiarity with the plays of Sophocles — these experiences are not

only a part of our heritage, they provide opportunity for articulating the individual's values and for arriving at critical judgments.

In an age when exposure to mass arts without the antidote of immediate public response to good and bad may well deaden intelligent response, some sort of education which gets at the roots of selectivity in art experiences is an imperative. It is only in the arts that Americans do not demand the best. We sweep past the real re-creation which can take place in the conscious exercise of the mind. We know that we are going to live longer (especially women); we know that working hours are now being shortened. Is this just time to be killed? As Chesterton says, "There is a great deal of difference between the eager man who wants to read a book and the tired man who wants a book to read." The unfortunate result of this use of the arts is that time is not the only dead matter left lying around.

There is another concept of the use of leisure of which librarians are well aware. A growing number of adults use their leisure hours to defeat the high cost of living and get revenge on an inefficient plumber by "doing it themselves." There is a real danger that our newly found hours, days, and years of leisure will be used up in more labor for more physical comforts. If so, the housewife who asks the librarian for a book on the kind of paint to keep her basement dry may indeed live in a painted basement as the jet planes sweep by. It is an understatement that we must have new thinking on a backlog of unsolved issues; we need fresh creative expressions from artists who can arouse in us the desire to live and respond to the challenge, "Think It Yourself."

3. COLLEGE SELF-STUDY

It is true that as we go on with our present extensive college selfstudy, various dissatisfactions are expressed with our treatment of the basic course in humanities. These are of various kinds: the younger members of the staff, fresh out of graduate school, are naturally better informed about the traditional approaches of liberal education than they are about the philosophy which initiated our program of general education. They tend to think, ironically enough, that general education is the tradition, and liberal education the new answer to the challenge of Russia! On the other hand, there are several members of the staff who feel that we should require the course as one of several basic courses, rather than trust to the advising system to "encourage" entering students to take this course. Just what will finally be decided is not clear.

Other approaches have been suggested by the present curriculum committee; namely, a survey of western civilization which concentrates on ideas which have influenced us in the United States. This has been generally viewed with disapproval because of the need for more knowledge about the East and less concentration on the West, and also because there is a pronounced feeling that the arts for our students need to be understood for themselves. We view the arts as living experience, as parts of life. We try very hard not to attach labels to a work of art and then dismiss it.

4. NEW METODS OF INSTRUCTIONY CAUSES OF MAJOR CHANGES

Our major objective has remained the same; much of the course content has remained. The new editions of the text show more and more examples of contemporary art; and we supplement the text with more and more slides and records of recent artists and composers. Since we hope to provide our students with experiences in the arts, we use more and more exposure to live performances; and since we wish to provide opportunity for practise in making judgments, there is a tendency to teach with pairs of examples. To illustrate the first of these points, a list of campus-wide cultural events will demonstrate the extent to which it is possible for students to use programs on campus as a sort of laboratory:

Music
        Donald Gramm, Baritone
        Sylvia Zaremba, Pianist
        Henri Tamianka, Violinist with Paganini Quartet
        Carl Weinrich, Organist
        Roberta Peters, Soprano
        Budapest String Quartet
        Bach Aria Group
        Walter Hendl, Pianist
        Lucia di Lammermoor, with Marjorie Gordon, guest artist
        Don Giovanni, with Hugh Thompson, guest artist

        Faculty recitals for Organ; piano; organ and strings; cello; oboe; flute, cello, piano; harp; voice
        Chamber Music Concert by faculty members
        Chapel Choir Concerts
        Advent Music Concert, Chapel Choir
        American Guild of Organists Recitals (students)

Opera Workshop
   "Hansel and Gretel"
   "Game of Chance"
   "The Bandit"
College Concert Chorus — Christmas program and annual spring
                                                                                   concert
   Senior recitals by students from voice and instrumental classes

Drama
   Plays presented by students in Theater Arts, and faculty
      "The Tender Trap"
      "The Flies"
      "The Rivalry"
      "Anastasia"
      "Teahouse of the August Moon"
      "The Wild Duck"
      "Everyman"
      "Thieves Carnival"
      "The Reluctant Debutante"

Dance
   Orchesis recital (Orchesis is the departmental club of students of the
      dance.)

Art
   Exhibits in Stephens College Art Center
      Original Hiroshige Prints
      Retrospective exhibit by A. H. Maurer
      Objects from the Far East
      National Association of Women Artists exhibition of oil paintings
      Dr. Konrad Prothmann exhibit of color reproductions
      Original works by Stephens College faculty members
      Gallery lecture on art objects in the Art Center

Lectures and Discussion Groups for Humanities students
   The Electra Story and Existentialism
   Primitive Art
   Sartre's "The Flies"
   The Growing Faith in Hemingway
   The Quiddities of Scenic Symbolism
   Everyman

a.   Adult Education Program

   The development of an adult education program in the humanities has increased our tendency to discuss several examples
of art as a way of arriving at critical judgments which result from
accurate observation.   This adult education experiment began with
requests from some older alumnae to have the benefit of the sort
of course which was not in existence in their day.   The Fund for
Adult Education, established by the Ford Foundation, made possible a grant by which we were enabled to prepare materials and
to try them out in alumnae groups in different centers.   The first
multilithed materials were then revised and the present printed

manual and supplementary materials is self-supporting. This development has proved what we already suspected: many adults feel at a loss in judging art — especially contemporary art. Many people would like to discuss books, music and painting with their friends but they need materials which are difficult to assemble, and they would like some guidance.

We have sent the set of materials* to every kind of group in every part of the United States and even to South America. There are ten units, closely interrelated, but with a special emphasis for each unit. At the end of each unit there are suggestions for further exploration at varying levels of difficulty. There have been an impressive number of voluntary letters expressing appreciation of the opportunity to *discuss* the arts. Poetry reading groups prove to be very popular and we have been asked to supply various groups with supplementary material, since they found that following a reading recorded on a disc with group participation was more satisfying than reading a poem to onself. One member wrote to us: "There is no doubt in my mind that for the average person, learning to understanding the various aspects of the arts seems to be better accomplished in a group of people — rather like corporate worship."

These statements from adults have been responsible for some shifts in our methods of instruction. We tend to emphasize discussion more than we did; we have the students work in groups,

---

*For each member of a group of from fifteen to twenty, we provide a manual which can be kept. It contains small reproductions of paintings which can be kept, and it also has self-tests, bibliographies, and copies of the literature used. For the group there are large mounted reproductions of paintings, record albums, discs with recordings and poems, folio size paintings and pocket books. The group materials must be returned. For the leader, there is a Leader's Guide which must also be sent back to us.
The ten units consist of the following:

    I.   Relation of art to the world around us. The emphasis is on painting.
    II. New levels of satisfaction other than subject matter. Observation on the elements of which visual arts are composed.
    III. Sound and Sense: The two essentials of poetry.
    IV. Idea and Story: Two Aspects of prose.
    V. Tension and Release: Two Aspects of Ordering the Arts.
    VI. Styles and Isms: Differences of Approach.
    VII. Long Vocal Forms: Sacred and Secular.
    VIII. Long Instrumental Forms: Symphony and Concerto.
    IX. Two Considerations in Making Choices: Your Attitude and the Artist's Effectiveness.
    X. The Role of a Discriminating Audience in the Mass Arts.

make judgments and take self-tests to establish their own confidence in articulating opinions and to force a defense of opinions by specific observations.

Also, we have increased our emphasis on the value of trying to create something. We do not make this a required part of the course because we feel that creativity in the arts cannot be forced in that way. It can, however, be stimulated by providing opportunities in the art laboratory, and in the music department. It is stimulated by display of the work of beginners and discussion of it by their peers. For example, if students attempt to use visual and non-verbal methods of summarizing the main impact of a play such as *Othello* — especially if line and color are used without reference to visual representation — the other students can interpret and ask their fellow students if they are right in their reading of the abstraction. More can be learned in this way than merely by an analysis of a painting by Mondrian, although some of this needs to be done first, as preparation for individual creative efforts.

b.   TV Instruction

Another development has changed our method of instruction. The opportunities of closed-circuit television have influenced us in two ways. First of all, we developed a course called "Ideas and Living Today" which is given over a closed-circuit television and required of every beginning student. Each student sits with a group of some seventeen or eighteen other students and hears a presentation for about twenty minutes on some topic which she then discusses with her fellow students for thirty minutes, while the impression of the lecturer is fresh in its impact. This year, we have used such disputable points as "Freedom and Authority," "Principle and Expedience." Such topics are discussed by a group of representative teachers in the various disciplines so that the student in any one series begins to realize how many subject matter areas need to be known before decisions can be reached. Also, experience in handling new ideas can stimulate mature discussion. Naturally, some material presented over television has concerned the arts; for example, What constitutes freedom for an artist? What should be the principle which governs our attitude towards the Mass Arts? These discussions have freed us in the Humanities course for more detailed study of some of the same principles in class.

In the second place, the opportunities afforded by television to make available to all students in the general course the talents of the specialist, and the possibility of live performances proved irresistible; as a result, we have been offering, for this last year, a series of programs which provide a common experience for all of our students. We have not thought it advisable to dispense with the discussion sections which still meet three times a week, with each teacher carrying his class through from the beginning of the course to the end; but the fourth hour, the television hour, is a sort of laboratory session and attendance at it replaces an assignment hour. Some of the programs have been better than others; we are beginning to realize that whereas it is an enormous advantage to have a good professional artist draw, as he talks about the elements of the visual arts, it is not as valuable to hear a symphony over television, since that form can be taught better in class, with skeleton scores available and with the possibility of immediate answers for the student who gets lost. In music, on the other hand, it was advantageous to have the vocal forms illustrated by college students singing folk songs, madrigals, arias, recitatives while those forms are explained. The difference between the appeal of the opera, *Otello,* and the play, *Othello,* can be made clear by using students from the drama department to act out the scene between Emilia and Desdemona, while students from the music department sing the Willow Song and Ave Maria. In addition, the lecturer points up other differences in the organization of the two media and gives students material which presents in parallel columns the words of the play and the words of the libretto, in such a passage as the love duet.

5. OBSTACLES WHICH REMAIN AND SOME WHICH HAVE EMERGED

As a by-product of the television method of teaching one hour of the course, we feel that we have overcome one of the original difficulties. For some time we have recognized that students who take the course with one teacher have quite a different course from the students who elects the same course with another teacher. We have always felt that each teacher should choose for himself significant material and aim at the common objective. It is clearly more difficult to do this if all students hear the same lecture once a week. The advantage of having a more uniform approach to the material of the general course is offset by the disadvantage of forcing all teachers to do the same thing. This both complicates the use of classroom materials when several sections meet at the same hour, and it also leaves the instructor feeling pressed for time and dissatisfied at having to push on whether or not his students are ready, in his opinion, to leave the topic under discussion. Another advantage of great importance emerges as the staff discusses the programs. For example, the new member of the staff who teaches visual arts, and feels uncertain of music, developed a wonderful device for teaching the form of the passacaglia. Instead of using works to emphasize the constant repetition of the theme in the bass while the treble plays variations, he draws a series of large boots which never change, while the figure of the man above changes in his drawings. Such a device, developed for television, suggests other imaginative approaches for the classroom.

6. METHODS OF EVALUATION USED IN THE COURSE

We still feel it important to evaluate the course as well as the student. For the television presentations, we used interviews with a sampling of students for the series offered the first semester. The students made many valuable suggestions — chiefly they wanted the material more structured and they pointed out that there was too much repetition of class material. For this last semester, we had them evaluate each program. In addition, we wish to evaluate the class sessions, and at the middle of the first term and at the end of the first and second semesters we supply blanks which enable a student to indicate the units which have been most significant for her and those which have had the least meaning. In the early part of the year, we also ask for points of difficulty and encourage individual conferences. At the end of the year, we encourage individual conferences, also at the end of year, we encourage the student to indicate what steps she intends to take next in order to further her growth in mature and intelligent enjoyment of the arts. This underlines the fact that it is one of our major objectives to encourage the student to realize that this course is supposed to offer her an approach which she can use the rest of her life; it does not intend to be a terminal experience.

In trying to make our evaluation materials match what we say we set out to teach, several of us use the entire last month for a summary in class of ways of comparing two pieces of music, two poems or novels or plays, and two paintings or two pieces of sculpture. The student is then responsible for three comparative analyses — one in the visual arts, one in music, one in literature. The value of her observations and conclusions in these three papers is used as the basis for evaluating her work. At mid-year, on the other hand, the test is frankly one of vocabulary so that discussions can be based on common use of terms for the second semester.

We have set up for honor students a system of extra reading and papers which we call The Humanities Award. No prize money is given, but the student is presented at a final awards convocation with a certificate which indicates that she has, in a period of two years, completed extra work in the interrelated arts to the satisfaction of her supervisor and an examiner with whom she must discuss the books she has read, the music she has heard, and the paintings which she has studied.

Another type of evaluation is used by some teachers who give a two day test early in the year on vocabulary and analysis of painting, literature and music. This same test is given again at the end of the year to allow the student and teacher to evaluate her progress. This test is being revised every year.

The most persistent difficulty is, of course, the sense that there is not enough time to get done all of the important things which need to be done, not enough time to take each student as fast as she can go, not enough time to open up to worlds which will enable her, for the rest of her life, to have a really creative leisure, and an understanding of herself and the world around her, which is deepened because of the insights she has gained into the way artists present their subject. If she leaves the course wanting more and more arts which present life to her in a significant way, that is what we want.

chapter 7

THE HUMANITIES PROGRAM AT THE UNIVERSITY OF LOUISVILLE

Ernest C. Hassold*

Towards a New Concept of General Education

After thirty years of experience with the humanities in general education, I have come to the conclusion that the concept of general education needs a radical revision.

The Louisville Humanities program in general education was officially organized in 1932 and the intellectual outlook on which it was based has had a powerful impact in three directions. It has increased the average student's awareness of the world he lives in and of human greatness in all cultural fields. It has facilitated the rapid rise of departments of Art and Music, and the reorientation of the existing departments of English, Modern Languages and Philosophy towards a common cultural background; and it has helped to establish a better understanding between the university and the community by educating a public responsive to the best in art, music, literature and thought. Despite these achievements, there are indications that the program is now no longer an adequate platform for the advancement of the humanities.

In reviewing the Louisville Humanities program as it developed since 1949, one is struck by a startling contrast. The development of advanced departmental and divisional programs has been more or less dynamic. But the humanities program of general education has been practically at a standstill. This situation calls for a closer analysis.

---

*Chairman Division of Humanities, University of Louisville, Louisville, Kentucky.

The most startling phenomenon of the past decade has been the rapid rise of two new departments, Art and Music. These, undoubtedly, would have come into existence regardless of a program of general education, but without a college-wide requirement of at least one hour in both these subjects, their development would doubtless not have been so rapid or broad-based. The Art Department, or rather the Allen R. Hite Institute, has grown almost overnight into a model of its kind, aided by three essential conditions: a readiness in the public, benefactors of remarkable generosity, and wise leadership in planning the program. It has laid a deep and strong foundation in a multilingual library, supplemented by a large collection of slides, reproductions, and prints. It has attracted gifted students from a wide circuit and stimulated them to productivity by constant exhibits of their work. It has assembled a staff of resident artists and art historians, on terms conducive to the greatest productivity. And it has established a network of community relations through the years of affiliation with the Art Center School, an art column in the Sunday *Courier-Journal,* and cooperation with the leaders in teacher education. The result has been an impact on the artistic culture at all levels.

The function of the Music department has been more circumscribed. Since there is a School of Music in the university, the task of the department of music in the college essentially is building an audience for serious music. Without the requirement of music in general education, this department would hardly have come into existence. Now it has become autonomous and has added breadth and depth to the musical culture of the community. Its staff consists of a music historian and a composer. It collaborates with the School of Music in its program of teacher education and specializes in making educated listeners out of musical illiterates. For this purpose it has built a strong library of recorded music, and cooperates in ways that are unique with the Audio-Visual department and radio station of the Louisville Free Public Library, which broadcasts programs related to the courses offered by the department; students are supplied with FM sets. Once a year the department organizes a "Humanities" concert, when some leading artist plays a program of pieces rarely heard because of their difficulty; audience and critics regard these as the best concerts of the year.

The new developments in the older departments may be summarized more briefly. The departments of English and the Modern Languages have supported and developed the divisional program from the beginning. They have provided staff for the humanities courses in World Literature, in Great Books of all periods, in period courses in cultural history, and in senior coordinating courses in Linguistics, in Principles of Cultural History, and in the Advancement of Culture. During the past decade they have been preoccupied largely with other interests than general education. Thus the English department has developed its own program of leaves of absence for research, a study of Job Possibilities for English Majors, and a course in English Fundamentals, designed to relieve the pressure of the English Laboratory for aid in remedial English. It has expanded its program in Creative Writing to the graduate level, and it has finally established a program of Dramatic Art and thus enabled the University Players to provide ancient, Elizabethan, and modern plays for general education in the humanities. The department has always taken special interest in developing superior students and in teacher education. Recently it has expanded its advanced pro-seminars, which are perennially productive of honor students. For the graduate seminars in English and the Humanities it has now established the Fowler Room, in memory of the founder of graduate studies in English at the University of Louisville.

In the Modern Languages, the chief innovations are a language laboratory with twenty booths, a four year program in Russian developed in cooperation with an International Studies Program, a two year program in Italian preparatory to a third year in Rome; and cultural area studies offered in French, German, and Spanish. A one-man Philosophy department is hardly equal to the demands made upon it not only by the humanities division but also by the other divisions for aid in coordinating their courses in the history of ideas. Since the newly appointed dean of the College of Arts and Sciences is a professor of Philosophy and intends to continue teaching, a dynamic development in that department is to be expected.

The division of the Humanities coordinates the departmental offerings and promotes interdisciplinary studies. In the past its chief function has been to integrate the programs in general education, to synchronize departmental courses in all periods of cultural history, and to provide a coordinating course in each period, one in Linguistics, and another in Principles of Cultural History.   Recently it has developed both undergraduate and graduate programs for majors in the Humanities.   The Undergraduate program is based on interdisciplinary studies in either one cultural area, or in one period of cultural history, or in a combination of two of the subjects offered: History of Art, Music and Literature and Thought.   Each program is topped with twelve semester hours of advanced pro-seminars.   The graduate program is based on the History of Modern Thought since the Enlightment.

In contrast to these more or less dynamic developments, the humanities program in general education has remained essentially unchanged.   The college requirement of a one-year introduction of six semester hours remains the same, and so has the option to meet the requirement by examination.   The breakdown into three semester hours for World Literature and a choice of two one-and-one-half hour courses in Art, Music and Philosophy, has remained the same, and likewise the expansion of the offerings in Art, Music into separate introductions to Architecture and Painting, Cultural History and Styles of Music.   In content and method, the courses have changed slightly, allowing for individual preferences of new instructors.   Only in Philosophy has there been a constant experimentation until the shift from Plato to Aristotle was completed. In World Literature there has been some experimentation with antholoiges of short novels and modern plays, but at length the staff has returned to reading in depth *Anna Karenina* and plays by Ibsen, Strindberg, and Shaw now available in paperbound editions. The only elements that have decidedly changed are the students, who seem to have less intellectual background and less time for cultural activities, and the reaction of most of the instructors to the task of teaching the short (1½ hour) courses.

The unchanging character of this program for the past ten years is to be attributed only in part to preoccupation with other interests.   In large part, it comes from lack of focus on viable new directions.   The desire for change is there, especially in the instructors of the short courses with their constant repetitions, frequent change of students, frustrating lack of time to permit new experiences of seeing, listening, thinking to develop. But if these courses are expanded, without enlarging the total requirement, the principle of exposing the students to as many cultural experiences as possible is abandoned. Those instructors who have them giving larger allotments of time to the humanities in general education. But even if the time allotment were enlarged, the question would remain: would the best interests of general education be served by simply expanding short courses designed as eye-openers in 1932 into standard departmental introductory courses? The cultural situation has completely changed since 1932; the advanced programs in all the humanities have outgrown the premises from which they started. A candid appraisal of the present performance of our program and a review of its entire development in search for latent possibilities may help us grope towards a new concept of general education.

In the 1930's when the University of Louisville engaged the architect to draw up a plan for its physical developments, he submitted a sketch for a Humanities Building, with two wings, one for English and the other for Modern Languages. When he was asked whether he had taken into account the way the humanities were being taught here, he said, "No. How are the humanities taught here?" He was told, "All together — Art, Music, Literature and Philosophy — all, as it were, under the same roof." Then he said, "Oh, I didn't know that. From my point of view as an architect that is ideal." He began to project a plan for a building with four wings. By now the architect's plan has been abandoned, and the university has built some new buildings and rehabilitated some old ones. The Humanities Building houses the departments of English, Modern Languages and Philosophy, with miscellaneous other things. The Hite Institute has gotten its foot in the big tent reserved for the Administration, and the Music department shares a renovated building with the Band. The point is not to suggest stuffing all the Humanities back into one building, in order to keep them from falling apart. It is to suggest that they have completely outgrown not only the physical plan but also the intellectual platform devised for their development in the 1930's. What they need now to work them together is a new idea and a new direction.

II Four Basic Questions

1. DOES THE HUMANITIES PROGRAM AFFORD AN ADEQUATE CULTURAL PERSPECTIVE?

The cultural perspective of the humanities program is subject to pulls in opposite directions: to meet the need for an expanding cultural horizon and to adjust this to the limited cultural background and capacity of its students. The Louisville Humanities program has always aspired to the horizon of Western culture rather than that of Anglo-American culture. But its staff is not always adequately equipped to enlarge its horizons to the worldwide perspective unfolded by World War II. A first step would be a basic course in twentieth century geography, which would serve as a backdrop for the history of civilization and provide the entire program with the basis for an axis formed between the historical long section and the contemporary cross section of the cultural development.

2. DOES IT AFFORD AN ADEQUATE ACQUAINTANCE WITH THE BASIC MEDIA?

Basic media of cultural expression are those which: (1) have a great "literature" susceptible to systematic (scientific) treatment; (2) are requisite to the enrichment and rounding out of the individual person; (3) are needed as background for the new technology — film, radio, video. The Louisville Humanities program meets the first two of these tests. The media it has chosen to represent are Art, Music, Literature and Thought. Religion is treated as a spiritual energy expressing itself in all these media. The new technology is explored only in relation to these basic media, largely with the aid of the facilities of the Louisville Free Public Library.

3. DOES IT PROVIDE AN ADEQUATE EXPERIENCE OF CULTURAL LIFE?

Experience of art and music, literature and thought must be direct and deepened by an education in seeing, listening, feeling and reflective thinking along lines developed in the long history of culture. The Louisville Humanities tries to emphasize reading in depth. This takes time, especially in unfamiliar media. The program also encourages participation in the current cultural activities, at least for the duration of the course. The chief objection to the eye-openers in Art, Music and Philosophy is that they do not allow for either intensive or extensive experience.

4. DOES IT ENGENDER AN ADEQUATE INTEREST IN THE ADVANCEMENT OF CULTURE?

A scale of interest might show (1) toleration, (2) respect, (3) interest, (4) participation, (5) creative contribution. The higher levels of response depend on higher levels of experience — creative participation, perception of the absolute need of continuous creativity. The response to the brief exposure in the short courses can hardly be more than rudimentary. But the ultimate goal of general education must be to engender a sense of responsibility for the advancement of culture. This takes time and thoughtful experience. All things excellent are as difficult as they are rare.

III   A Background Glance: Three Challenges Unanswered

The College of Liberal Arts was organized in 1932, on the model of the then new program of the University of Chicago, with two levels — junior and senior college — and three divisions — natural sciences, social sciences, and humanities. It is interesting to speculate on what the college might be like today, had the advice of the then president been followed. His advice was to make a sharper break between the junior and the senior college than between the senior college and the graduate program, and to be highly selective in admitting students to the senior college and graduate program. It is possible that Louisville was not ready in 1932, only twenty-five years after the College was founded to support a first rate college. The development of a strong senior college would have prevented overemphasis on general education in the thirties, and the explosive reaction against it in the late forties. It would also have kept the graduate program balanced.

From the beginning, the University of Louisville program in general education, has depended largely on the Humanities. Whereas the University of Chicago has set up one-year courses in both the Biological and Physical Sciences, Louisville reduced these to two semesters (from which the majors were excused as were the majors in the Social Sciences from their divisional "survey") and. whereas the University of Chicago made a one-year History of Civilization serve also for the Humanities, the University of Louisville added a one-year Introduction to the Humanities, which must include Art, Music and Philosophy along with Literature. This decision proved most beneficial to the rapid development of Art and Music, especially after emigrees from Europe headed these programs. But the Humanities division not only developed an introduction "good enough for its own majors" but also worked out the implications of the new program at the senior college level, by setting up a four-semester program to coordinate the several branches of culture in four periods of their historical development. The Natural and the Social Sciences, after experimenting with a senior coordinating course in the history and philosophy of their subjects, now propose that the Humanities help them develop a one-year course in great documents representative of all three divisions, in order to fill the gap between the History of Civilization and the divisional introductions. This proposal was not accepted because the addition seemed more than traffic could bear. Had it been developed, it would have integrated the entire program of general education and started the staff on a stimulating search for noetic integrators.

Finally, after the collision in 1947 had reestablished the vocational-minded B.S. degree (dropped in 1932), the central problem of the college was to find a rationale for harmonizing these two antipodal but thoroughly indigenous educational philosophies. This problem has not yet been solved.

IV An Enlarged Concept of General Education

Education is the encounter of the rising generation with the advancement of culture.

General education and specialized education are only modifications of a process which must be integrated to be effective. The process of education must be continuous, lifelong and dynamic. The function of general education is to furnish a basic design and define the possibilities of that process at three distinct levels.

To be educated today, one must be able to view one's experience of the world through the eyes of the biologist and the physicist, the anthropologist and the historian, the artist, composer, creative writer and thinker, and to know at least one foreign language and culture. This multiple view of the world, with or without the foreign language, has been achieved more or less well in programs of general education developed during the past generation. But this is obviously not enough.

45526

We do not think of that person as educated who does not also have an insight into that groping and struggle for a new idea, a new form, a new organization of relations, a new vision, that goes by the name of the creative process, an insider's view of how knowledge is achieved in the workshop, the laboratory, in field work, studio, or study, not merely in one field, but in several fields of the major areas of knowledge. This is the real rationale of all departmental specializations. What is proposed here is that creative experience in all divisions be incorporated as an essential element in the basic design of general education. But even this is not enough.

We do not think of a person as educated, who does not know and understand in his own experience that even the basic concepts of nature, culture, society and man are constantly changing and that this mutability constitutes not only the limit of possible knowledge, but also the basic challenge to continuous creative activity. The fuller implications of this problem are or ought to be, developed in our graduate program, but this level of insight into the basic condition of the advancement of education, science and culture must also be embodied in and pervade the basic design of general education.

If we accept some such enlargement of the concept of general education, we cannot, of course, hope to crowd it into the first two years of college. Such an education will take time and need to continue through several levels of intellectual maturity. It will have to begin in high school, be fully developed in college, but also be continued marginally in graduate and professional schools, to provide an educated awareness of how the state of knowledge in general is related to one's own special field. And it will have to involve both more immediate and direct experience and more intellectual or philosophical background and capacity to reflect than we have hitherto demanded.

Such an enlarged concept of general education would guarantee a vast improvement of our specialized education, and of teacher education, and enlarge considerably the scope of our research, especially in the humanities.

Conclusion

During the past three decades the Louisville Humanities Program has developed through three stages — experimentation, consolidation, and working out the implications of a new perspective. Despite its failure to develop certain possibilities and to meet certain challenges presented by a shifting situation, this program has been conspiciously successful in releasing creative energies in new directions. Its highest achievement has been, in the words of an alumnus unconsciously quoting Whitehead, awareness of simultaneous greatness in many fields. Now this program is entering a change of phase. What the new phase will bring depends on many factors, some of them altogether unpredictable. But one important factor at least submits to isolation, the concept of general education can be reconsidered in the light of many developments that have occurred since it was formulated. To stimulate this reconsideration, not only in the University of Louisville, I have sought to derive from our experience an enlarged concept of general education, which is consciously framed to do three things: to assimilate the values of the traditional concept of liberal education; to provide a basic design adequate to embrace the several varieties of education now current and to meet the intellectual needs of all kinds of professional men and women; and to be susceptible to that dynamic development which the world has a right to expect from American colleges and universities today.

chapter 8

THE GENERAL COURSE IN THE HUMANITIES AT HAVERFORD COLLEGE

*Marcel Gutwirth**

In the decade since its experimental beginnings as one single section, described by its founder, Professor Gray, in *The Humanities in General Education* (1949), the General Course in the Humanities at Haverford College has grown to a peak of five sections in 1955, and leveled since to an average of three sections a year. With a maximum of twenty-five students in a section, and an average of twenty, the population of the course has fluctuated between sixty and a hundred in the last few years, against a total enrollment of 450 at Haverford (these figures include a dozen Bryn Mawr girls at most). The course is offered for Sophomores primarily, but it includes a generous sprinkling of upperclassmen. The staff, hitherto, has been drawn exclusively from the French and English departments, but will be joined next year by a member of the German department.

The change in the course has not been one of growth and stability merely. The reading list itself has expanded notably, bringing with it a change in the orientation and the aims of the course. Where the readings originally were rigorously selected to help the students "build a coherent set of ideals for themselves with which to confront the bewildering present"[1] the course nowadays reflects rather the abundance and the variety of the tradition from

---

*Chairman of Department of Romance Languages.

[1] J. Glenn Gray, "The Humanities at Haverford College," in *The Humanities in General Education*, Earl J. McGrath, ed. (Dubuque, Iowa: Wm. C. Brown & Co., 1949), p. 1.

which such ideals may be culled. The earlier stress on moral utility exclusively (*Don Quixote* was left out for not embodying "any particular ideal of life relevant to today, not better treated elsewhere"[2]) has given way to the sense that "in my Father's house are many mansions."

Having gone over from a standard three-class meetings a week to a single two-hour discussion, the pace of the reading in the course, with some exceptions to be sure, is of a book a week (two weeks are spent on the *Iliad*, three on the *Divine Comedy*.) Next year's reading list is as good a sample as any of the pace and content of the course:

FIRST SEMESTER

1.	Shakespeare	*Julius Caesar*
2.	Homer	*Illiad* I-XII (Lattimore transl.)
3.	Homer	XIII-XXIV
4.	Homer	*Odyssey* (T. E. Shaw transl.)
5.		*Genesis*
6.		*Genesis*
7.		Reading Period
8.	Sophocles,	*Oedipus Rex. Oedipus Coloneus.* PAPER BACK
9.	Saint Matthew	*Gospel*
10.	Vergil	*Aeneid* (Humphries transl.)
11.	Dante	*Inferno*
12.	Dante	*Purgatorio*
13.	Dante	*Paradiso* (Rinehart edit.)

Exam Book: Euripides, *Phaedra* (U. of Chicago Press)

SECOND SEMESTER

1.	Machiavelli,	*The Prince*
2.	Cervantes,	*Don Quixote* Part I (Putnam transl.)
3.	Spinoza	*Ethics* (I, IV-V)
4.	Diderot	*Rameau's Nephew*
5.	Goethe	*Faust* (Oxford Press)
6.	Jane Austen,	*Emma*
7.	Stendhal	*The Charterhouse of Parma*
8.	Browning	*Selected Dramatic Monologues*
9.		Reading Period
10.	James	*The Spoils of Poynton* PAPER BACK
11.	Thomas Mann	*The Tales of Jacob*
12.	Kafka	*The Trial*
13.	Joyce Cary	*The Horse's Mouth*

Exam Book: Camus, *The Stranger.*

---

[2]*Ibid.*, p. 10.

It will be noted that we have come to use Shakespeare as the introductory figure for reasons that seemed sufficient to justify the breach of chronology: the exigencies of time in the that first week demand a shorter work, and the relative familiarity of the material makes it a very good initiation to the method of the course, since it allows the student to measure how far it diverges from the standard academic procedure.

This list by its very nature, refutes the idea of a fixed canon. The inclusion of a contemporary novelist such as Joyce Cary, and the somewhat capricious selection in the latter half of the second term, are part of the effort to keep the course adventurous and alive by varying the readings from year to year (though some fixed stars — Homer, Dante, Shakespeare, Cervantes — remain), and by bringing it into the perilous, uncharted seas of the present.

As may be seen, one of the aims of the course is to give the student a sense of the sweep of the tradition: hence the somewhat breathless pace. Deliberately we have exchanged the more leisurely but perhaps dangerously selective method for a painfully hurried but more comprehensive view. The students themselves do not miss the fact, and the lesson is brought home to them thereby (as their comments sometimes bear out) that this can be but a *first* reading of books that demand far more time and thought to yield all that lies buried in them.

While there has been no fundamental revision of content (it is still a course in literature and philosophy, with music and the fine arts — regretfully — absent), secondary material (biographies, information *about* the works used in course) has been firmly ruled out. The 1949 statement asserts "the value of approaching ideas through the medium of personalities" and hence argues that changes in the course ought to be "in the direction of introducing more biography — as a stimulus and way of approach to the ideals and ideas the great writers incorporate" (p.13). Though such a method has its own merits, it clashes head on with what has come to be the central business of the course: direct and un-mediated contact with the works themselves — establishing, in other words, the student as a reader. Much stands between the college student and those very works the study of which should constitute the core of his education: a sense of their chill remoteness, of their inaccessibility to the untrained mind, of their ponderousness, their fuitility perhaps. To dispel such a misunderstanding in the simplest way conceivable, one has only to bring them together, the fearful youth and the hoary classic! For to let him read Homer and learn for himself — with no preaching or blandishment — that no better company could ever be devised; this, transposed for us moderns, is the very heart of the Humanists' creed, and the only fitting task for a course boasting kinship, if in name only, with that great movement. To read the books that before had been names only to him, such is the whole occupation of the student in this course, and little enough of that can he get done in the compass of twenty-eight weeks! Having once tasted manna, let him then go read prefaces and introductions, treatises and biographies: his appetite is whetted, his interest awakened, not by the glamor or the mystery of an author's life, but by what makes the author's life worth inquiring about in the first place.

Reading, then, constitutes the first, the capital half, of the diptych. Then comes the discussion. Variaions in temper and interests among instructors, to say nothing of the students, render any fixed scheme to govern discussions inadvisable. A general *Gestalt*, however, can be suggested for all class discussions, constituting as it does the heart of the method in the course:

1. The discussion is not non-directive. It ought not to consist solely of an airing of student views, a kind of democratic assemblage of unreconciled but mutually tolerant asseverations. It is the instructor's task to direct the discussion by his questions and comments in such a way that the class may be made aware of elements in the general scheme of the book, or in the issues it raises, which might otherwise have escaped them.

2. As the above suggests, the instructor does not act as an authority (which in most areas of the course he is not) lecturing from special knowledge; nor yet is he to be impartial moderator of a forum. Ideally, he ought to function as the experienced reader who helps the class come to a more focussed awareness of what they may themselves have but dimly perceived in their own reading.

3. Finally, the discussion ought to be a coming to grips with the work as a living thing. It must do away with attitudes — either fawning or condescending — by which the student seeks to evade the sharp point of the book's argument. Neither the wor-

ship of greatness nor a misguided sense of the past as radically *other* must be allowed to come between the reader and, say, Pascal's denunciation of him!

As far as the mechanics of the course go, the need to check whether the reading has been done, and so incidentally to protect a discussion course against those who would abuse its freedom and poison its climate, was at first met by the use of identification questions on the examination at semester's end. This method proved too capricious, as it tended mainly to reward a certain kind of memory and penalize good students who did not possess that knack. More recently, the problem has been solved by havng the students hand in a "brief for discussion" on the book they have just read. These briefs, which are due by the beginning of the discussion period, outline the questions raised in the student's mind by his reading of the book, and thus propose some directions for class discussion. The briefs are either graded and returned, or kept in an alphabetical file which, by the end of the term, proves a very valuable index of the quality of the student's thought.

A practice that has also crystallized over the last couple of years has been to grant a week's rest from reading some time during the term, during which the class is assigned an essay to write on the next work in the reading list. Discussion as a rule gains in intensity and fervor at the next meeting, from the sense of commitment that binds an author to his written words, especially when a grade is in prospect!

Finally, at the end of the term a book is assigned which is not discussed in class, with the understanding that some of the questions in the final examination will bear on it, thus testing the student's ability to carry on unaided the method of the course. All examination questions attempt to make the student re-think what he has understood of the works in the course, either by having him establish parallels unhinted at before among several apparently disparate works, or by directing his attention to some aspect that had not been probed when the book was discussed in class, or finally by having him call on all the books he has read as resources to deal with some vast generalization about man.

As may be gathered from these few remarks on the pace, the content, and the method of the course, it aims at bringing the students as close as the best translations available allow to the

major works in the Western tradition in their integrity. By allowing them to enter into contact directly with these works, practically
unescorted, it is hoped that they may learn to grow familiar with
them, and treat them eventually as their own, from which to pick
and choose and take only what is wholesome for *them*. Thus can
they come into their own, and truly call theirs the heirloom that
awaits their claim.

As far as the situation of the course in the College is concerned, since the days of the 1949 report, the following may be
said. In the first place, the course is no longer a tentative one-man
venture representing an unorthodox approach to the subject matter
of the Humanities tolerated for its experimental value. It is now
an established yearly program, which has proved successful in at-
tracting and interesting students — for it is not a required course,
although it can be offered in fulfillment of one part of the limited
elective requirements in the Humanities. As the general course
of the Humanities division, it has succeeded as well in creating a
climate favorable to its aims and method. It has withstood a
strong attack on its very existence several years ago, when influen-
tial members of the Division leveled charges of superficiality and
meretriciousness at it, claiming it "skimmed the cream" off departmental offerings and could give no more than passing acquaintance
with the works read. The quality of the interest that the students
have shown for the course, and the fact that it has proved sufficiently demanding not to act as an easy substitute for courses in
literature and philosophy may have done much to allay these fears.
But the most powerful factor for a favorable change in attitude
has been the rise of courses patterned in part after the General
Course in the Humanities, such as the renovated Freshman English
course and the General Course in English Literature. The former
combines the feature of the tutorial session with the discussion
method, the student writing his weekly theme on a book that has
been the subject of class discussion in a section of twelve, and in
turn reading his theme in a tutorial sub-section of four, where it
is criticized by his fellows under the tutor's guidance. It can readily be seen that such a course, which is taken by every single entering Freshman, and which has become one of the most characteristic
features of Haverford education, constitutes an ideal prerequisite
to the General Humanities Course, which in turn complements it

harmoniously. The task of self-examination initiated by the Freshman course (ominously titled *Reading and Writing on Human Values*) is rounded off for the Sophomore by setting his homely values, much tried in that earlier contest, in the perspective of a wider tradition.

In a changing, more youthful Haverford (two-thirds of the present faculty have been appointed since 1949) the place of the Humanities course seems securely founded in the general esteem of the faculty, the Administration, the students, and of its own alumni. Two glaringly unsolved questions remain, to keep alive the sense that this is not the best of all possible worlds. One is the problem of staffing the course. The French and the English departments alone are duty-bound to supply one instructor each to the course. The recruitment of the third (and sometimes fourth and fifth) staff members is a somewhat haphazard affair, hinging on the good will of department heads, the availability of interested faculty, the possibility of bringing in adequate part-time replacement for them within their departments, and so ultimately the nature and flexibility of their own commitments. I suppose, unless undesirable subpoena powers could be granted the program chairman, it could not be otherwise in a college of small two-and three-men departments loosely federated and jealousy autonomous. The path of progress here lies in the direction of a more general recognition of the excitement and the challenge in teaching such a course, which if it were more keenly felt would pry loose some who now think they cannot be spared in their own bailiwick.

The other thorn in our flesh is the absence of any official followup on the junior and senior level. I say "official," for there exists, for those who have taken the course and wish to read further in the same spirit, an informal gathering one evening a week at my house, where we talk over together the book currently read in the course that week. But there exists at the College a general attitude of mistrust of new courses ("proliferation" is the anxious watchword of the Curriculum Committee) based on the view — all-too-worldly but hard to refute — that a new course which does not replace an old one constitutes an added budgetary encumbrance. This attitude, reinforced by memories of a recent ill-fated experiment in a senior seminar that was to be the General Course for all three Divisions — and did not please any — renders dim the prospects of an advanced seminar in the Humanities on the model of Columbia's Junior and Senior Colloquium. The paucity of our resources in the fine arts and music (a single course in History of Art, and a Music department of less than two full-time members!) make unlikely the emergence of a parallel course in those directions. Finally, the staffing problem for a Junior-Senior seminar would only compound existing difficulties.

To sum up, the General Course in the Humanities at Haverford is a well established feature of the curriculum. For the sophomores and upperclassmen whose interest lies in the other Divisions of the College, it constitutes an excellent way of approach to what the Humanities are all about — and quite frequently those students contribute a very thoughtful and significant note to the discussion. To the literature, music, fine arts, and philosophy majors, the course provides a fresh look at what familiarity may have dulled and departmental blinders obscured. To teacher and students alike it gives a weekly opportunity to converse thoughtfully about some of man's achievements. The problems just mentioned do not seriously threaten such activities: to say more would be to tempt the gods.

chapter 9

THE HUMANITIES AT MICHIGAN STATE UNIVERSITY

*Charles Hirschfeld**

The two courses which constituted the program of studies in the humanities at Michigan State University in 1949 have since been merged into one Humanities course. The introduction of this course in 1952 was part of a general reorganization of the general education curriculum in the Basic College of the University. In order to give all Michigan State University undergraduates a common academic background, the number of basic courses was reduced from seven, some of which were optional, to four — Communication Skills, Natural Science, Social Science and Humanities, all of which became mandatory. All students must now take all four courses which total forty-five hours, or about one-half of all their work in their first two years at the University.

The humanities course which consolidated the field previously divided between the History of Civilization and Literature and Fine Arts is a four-credit course, in which classes meet four times a week in a sequence of three ten-week quarters. Students may not enroll in it until their sophomore year and until they have already taken most of the other basic courses. Some of the students in the humanities course are juniors and even seniors before they finish the sequence. This deferment attests to the fact that only relatively mature students can cope with and benefit from the course to the fullest. Since 1949, the number of students enrolled has fluctuated from about 2,900 to 4,000. At present (1959), some

---

*Professor of Humanities, The Basic College, Michigan State University, East Lansing, Michigan.

3,600 students meet in about 90 sections of which the average size is 41.

The rationale and objectives of Humanities have not essentially changed from those of the two older courses; they differ only in that they have been brought into sharper focus. The fundamental definition guiding the construction and teaching of the new course is that "Humanities is the study of man as a unique, creative being." As such, it includes "his most distinguished and most enduring achievements — intellectual, spiritual, aesthetic, and ethical — together with his social and political heritage." Its primary purpose is "to enlarge and to enrich the student's comprehension of his historical heritage," the common cultural tradition of the Western world. The educational goal, however, goes beyond mechanical exposure and the acquisition of a cultural veneer. The course seeks to involve the student personally and thereby "to deepen the degree of his intellectual maturity, to enhance his sensitivity to humane values in all fields of man's thought and endeavor, to elevate his ethical outlook, and to make him intelligently aware of his own worth and dignity, his obligations and responsibilities, as an individual human being." In short, it tries to awaken each student, to the extent of his capacity, to the underlying creativity of the human spirt and thus arouse and strengthen in him that self-conscious awareness that is the peculiar gift of human beings.[1]

Since the human mind and spirit have not functioned in a vacuum, the course examines man's creative expressions in the context of historical reality. It presents the ideas, beliefs, and aesthetic creations of men as rooted in historical culture. It sees them as interrelated: ideas and men and society and the arts and religion are brought together in a way that brings out the "style" or coherent world view of a given epoch. It stresses the likenesses without effacing the variations of individual expression, refusing to bury the individual act of creation, its universality in form and in substances in the unmarked grave of sociological relativism. It combines the temporal and the universal in a fruitful relationship.

This thread of historical continuity also serves to lift the student's view above the purely contemporary, so that he may see

---

[1] *Humanities*: A Syllabus, Department of Humanities, Basic College, Michigan State University, (East Lansing, 1959), p. iii.

"the nature of man as reflected in the historical process." The course is basically concerned with the persistent problems that man has faced, what Professor Crane Brinton has called "The Big Questions:" the nature of the universe, man's place in it and the meaning of his being, the nature of good and evil, of truth and beauty, the disparity of man's deserts and rewards, the gap between society's ideal imaginative ends and the means used to realize them, and the inadequacy of language to express ideas and feelings which cry for expression. At the same time, the student is brought to see that each age offers solutions to these constant problems in its own terms. This paradox of permanence amidst change is particularly challenging to the complacent acquiescence in the overwhelming impact of the merely contemporary. Finally this dynamic historical approach provides the basis for the organization of the content of the course.

The result is not a superficial survey of the totality of Western Man's achievements. The course selects for study the high points in the history of Western Civilization and concentrates on the significant and representative contributions to the mainstream of the Western tradition. The rationalist humanism of the Greeks as expressed in fifth and fourth century Athens, the political and legal genius of the Roman Empire at its height, the Christian view of man's relationship to God and its institutional expression in the Roman and medieval worlds, as well as the adaptation of Christianity to the changed conditions of the modern world in the Reformation, the liberal-scientific cosmology which sees man as the agent of his own destiny in an orderly physical universe and as the searcher in a world he never made — these are the broad basic subjects chosen for study. Selections from history, philosophy, religion, literature, and the arts all contribute to illustrate, underscore, and give substance to these master ideas.

These primary sources constitute the heart of the course. No idea, no work of literature or of art is discussed unless the students can read or see the best original expression of it (or a reproduction on slides, in the case of painting, sculpture, or architecture). Lectures, explication, and discussions revolve around these original works. The students thus grapple, perhaps for the first, perhaps for the only time, with whole or partial selections from Homer, Plato, Sophocles, the Scriptures, St. Augustine, St. Thomas Aquinas, Dante, Chaucer, Shakespeare, Locke, Voltaire, Marx,

Hemingway, and Reinhold Niebuhr, to mention a few examples. Among other works of art, they see and study slides of the work of Praxiteles, Da Vinci, Michelangelo, El Greco, Rembrandt, Rubens, Goya, Delacroix, Renoir, and Picasso. These selections and slides afford the opportunity for an intensive study of the idea in its original form and set against its cultural context. The universal aspects and meanings are thus related to the historical conditions from which they arose and in which they flourished.

A single compact volume, George H. Knoles and R. K. Snyder, *Readings in Western Civilization* (Revised edition, 1954) provides most of the selections of original works. This is augmented by separate paperback editions in which students read the whole of an epic, play, or novel. The historical background and analysis of works of art and architecture are covered in another required text, E. H. Gombrich, *The Story of Art* (1952). The social setting of each great culture is presented in lectures of a general and introductory nature supplemented by carefully selected appropriate portions of a general text of European civilization, the first volume of Brinton, Christopher, and Wolff's *A History of Civilization*, (1955). This text gives the students a running account of the historical background and allows the instructor in his lectures to dwell on the significant trends and relationships. A syllabus prepared by the department organizes all the readings, lectures, and slides into a unified whole with helpful outlines, subject-headings, and analyses for the students' guidance. It also creates a common course for all the numerous sections, providing general guidance within with each instructor may teach according to his own understanding.

The course is divided into three parts, each comprising one term of ten weeks or forty hours. The work of the first term, called "Roots of the Western Tradition," covers the ancient world from about 500 B.C., to 500 A.D. The first five weeks are devoted to Greek religion, philosophy, literature, and art. In this time, the students are required to read a major portion of the *Iliad*, the Platonic dialogues, *The Crito* and *The Phaedo*, and Aristotle's *Nichomachaean Ethics* and *Politics*. One complete Greek tragedy is studied — either the *Oedipus Rex* or *Antigone* of Sophocles, or Euripides' *Medea*. The students view slides of the Parthenon and other Greek temples, and of Greek sculpture from the Archaic through the Hellenistic period with special emphasis on the work of Myron and Praxiteles. All these varied expressions of the Greek mind are considered against the background of the unique form of Greek social organization, the city-state, in general, and the experience of Athens in the Golden Age, in particular.

The next ten hours or two-and-one-half weeks of the first term are devoted to the consideration of the role of the Romans in creating and organizing an imperial order in the Mediterranean world and in Europe. This imperial organization reflecting the political, legal, and engineering genius of the Romans, is both studied for itself, and, in a broader scope, viewed as a magnificent instrument for the transmission of Hellenic culture to Western Europe. In this portion of the course, the students read selections from Polybius' *Histories, The Thoughts of Marcus Aurelius,* Cicero's *The Laws,* and Tacitus' *Annals,* and study slides of the Pantheon, Colosseum, and some imperial monuments and portrait busts.

The final ten hours of the first term are devoted to the beginnings of Christianity, its Jewish background, the life and teachings of Jesus, the spread of Christianity in the Roman world, and the development of ritual, the doctrines, and the organization of the Church. Required readings include selections from *Exodus, Isaiah, The Gospel of Matthew,* Paul's *First Epistle to the Corinthians, The Acts of the Apostles,* St. Augustine's *The City of God* and *Confessions.*

The work of the second term, called "Medieval Culture and the Dawn of Modern Times," is divided into two parts. Four weeks are given to the study of the Christian culture of the Middle Ages under the heading, "The Medieval Unity." After a brief review of the feudal setting, close attention is given to the Christian faith and its embodiment in the medieval Church and its expressions in art and architecture, literature, education, and philosophy. Substantial readings are taken from *The Song of Roland, The Canterbury Tales,* Dante's *De Monarchia,* Abelard's *Sic et Non,* and Aquinas' *On Cheating.* The slides offer for study examples of Romanesque and Gothic architecture and sculpture, with particular attention to the abbey church at Vezelay and the cathedrals of Notre Dame of Paris and Chartres. The last six weeks of the term are devoted to the different transformations of the medieval world-view created by the Renaissance and the Reformation. The development of humanism in art and literature and the main currents of Protestant thought and action are considered against the background of the rise and expansion of capitalism and of the nation-state. Readings include selections from Machiavelli's *The Prince*, Cellini's *Autobiography*, Rabelais' *Gargantua and Pantagruel*, Erasmus' *The Praise of Folly*, and Calvin's *Institutes*, as well as one whole Shakespearean tragedy, *Othello* or *Hamlet*. The slides show the works of Giotto, Van Eyck, Donatello, Da Vinci, Michelangelo, Raphael, El Greco, Holbein, Breughel, Rubens, Rembrandt, and Bernini, and examples of Renaissance and Baroque architecture.

"The Modern World" from 1650 to the twentieth century is the subject of the third term's work. This too is divided into two parts, of which the first takes up "The Establishment of the Modern Cosmology and the Liberal Order" (1650-1850) in five weeks. The topics considered are: the intellectual foundations of the modern world, science and rationalism, the main currents of the liberal and democratic ideologies and their differing historical realizations in France and the United States, and the expression of the times in literature and art. For the first time, the American experience is brought into view. Readings include large portions of Newton's *Mathematical Principles of Natural Philosophy*, Locke's *Essay Concerning Human Understanding* and *Second Treatise on Government*, Tocqueville's *Democracy in America*, Burke's *Reflections on the Revolution in France*, Pope's *Essay on Man*, Voltaire's *Candide*, Franklin's *Autobiography*, and Goethe's *Faust*. The slides present American and English examples of Greek Revival and Gothic Revival buildings, and the paintings of David, Goya, Constable, Turner, Delacroix and of the Americans, Cole and Bingham.

The last five weeks of the course cover the contemporary world from 1850 on. The main ideas and institutions of the Western world in the last century are considered in such subjects as the industrialization of society and its impact on the human personality, nationalism as one of the governing ideas of modern democracies and its extension into imperialism, the ideology of collectivism, and the expressions of the twentieth century mind in the novel and the modern drama, and in painting and architecture. The students read selections from such authors as Mazzini, Marx, Mussolini, Carl Becker, Julian Huxley, Reinhold Niebuhr, and

Sherwood Anderson. One whole novel is read, Hemingway's *A Farewell to Arms* or F. Scott Fitzgerald's *The Great Gatsby*, as well as a complete modern drama, Arthur Miller's *Death of a Salesman* or Tennessee Williams' *The Glass Menagerie*. The slides show the work of Monet, Renoir, Cezanne, Matisse, Picasso, and Frank Lloyd Wright.

Realizing that the objectives of the course ideally extend far beyond the classroom experience, the department has arranged cooperative ventures with other departments of the University which offer the students direct experience in the drama, art, and music. With the Department of Speech, plays on the Humanities' reading list have been produced at the time they come up for classroom discussion so that the direct visual experience of the drama may buttress the reading of the text. The student attendance at performances of *The Death of a Salesman* and *The Glass Menagerie* has confirmed both departments in their enthusiasm for this cross-campus cooperation. In addition, the Humanities Department has worked with the University Lecture-Concert Bureau to bring to the campus professional performances of *Othello, Hamlet, Oedipus Rex* on the stage and on film. In every case the attendance and enhanced class discussion have been most gratifying. The Department, although not giving any time to music in the course, has worked with the Music Department to arrange concerts with the needs of the course in mind and has encouraged attendance and understanding by distributing program notes in all its classes. Similar efforts have been made with regard to art exhibitions on the campus and at nearby museums.

The Humanities Department has also organized a Humanities Reading Center in the University Library, where may be found the complete editions of all selections read in the course as well as other appropriate secondary accounts, historical novels, and plays. A guide to this collection has been printed in the syllabus of the course, and all students are encouraged to make use of it. Students are also directed to inexpensive paperbound editions of these works which may be purchased at the local bookstores, one of which has given them a special display and has reported a substantial number of sales. This extra-mural interest has produced a request by the students for an occasional symposium on vital issues in the history of ideas, and the department has agreed to give the necessary guidance to these sessions if the students will take upon themselves the necessary organization problems.   The measurable successes in all these activities give a strong indication of the impact of the Humanities course on its student and indeed on the intellectual life of the university community.

The department does not consider the present choice of contents and methods of instruction as final and perfect in any degree or form, nor does it anticipate achieving such a perfection.   It accepts no definition of the humanities as an ineluctable prescription to be followed, basing its conception rather on the overall expressed function of the Basic College, the needs of its students, and the experience of other similar departments as well as its own. The whole course is under constant scrutiny and evaluation by standing departmental committees on literature, philosophy, and religion, and the arts and by a general curriculum committee.   New reading selections, new slides, new texts, and new methods of instruction are always being considered by these committees and by the department as a whole.   In line with its ideal objectives, the department is constantly facing up to the problem of offering a challenge to its members and to the increasing number of students with a great range of interests and perceptiveness.

For the better students, it has organized pro-seminars and honors sections which permit the prescribed subject matter to be taken up more intensively and with a higher degree of sophistication. The trying problems inherent in such classes have by no means been solved and more study and adaptation are necessary before they can be considered generally successful.   The Department also makes it possible, under Basic College regulations, for some superior students to earn credit for the course on the basis of examination only. It has also conducted an experiment on a substantial scale to encourage independent work on the part of the students.   Students in some sections of the course have met in class only three times a week and have been assigned the work of the remaining hour to be done independently.   The results showed that the better students profited most from this procedure.

With regard to content, the feeling of satisfaction of the department has not been allowed to degenerate into complacency. The broad, generous coverage of material, the task of trying to teach so much in so little time, and the inevitable effects of such dispersion of effort and impact are weighed carefully against what is prudently feasible and against the realization that for most students this will be the only time, however brief, they will be brought into contact with these varied expressions of the cultural heritage of the Western world. The department has also been concerned with the fact that the course now slights some of the ways in which non-Western cultures have influenced the development of Western thought and ideals. It has considered the possibility of introducing this subject in an additional fourth quarter. Some thought has also been given to the possibility of using such an extension of allotted time to discussion of the great current issues of politics, the term being taken in the broadest sense of the word to include those problems that affect the very marrow of our lives as Americans in 1959.

The evaluation of the students' work is based on achievement in the classroom and on a common examination at the end of each quarter. The instructors assign a grade to each student at the end of each quarter, basing it on classroom examinations, quizzes, oral participation, and attitudes. All students then take a common examination, designed to test their mastery of all materials presented in class. The two grades are then combined equally to give the student his final grade for the quarter.

These common term-end examinations are constructed by the Humanities Department with the cooperation of the Office of Evaluation Services of the Basic College. They are composed of questions submitted by the staff of the department to the specially assigned and trained Humanities examiner who, then edits them and adds more questions to form a balanced examination. The complete test is reviewed by a Humanities Department committee to insure that it samples adequately the materials and reflects the aims of the course.

These common examinations at the end of each quarter compensate, it is believed, for the variations in grading practices which are inevitable in required courses having many sections and many teachers. It discourages too much attention by instructors to limited phases of the course to the neglect of others. By including materials from the preceding terms in the examination for the second and third terms, these common tests reinforce for the students the view of the course as a unit.

The key to success in all the above-mentioned enterprises lies in the hands of the staff. The new course has been taught by a nucleus of instructors who had taught the old History of Civilization course and had been trained primarily in the academic discipline of history. The challenge of the new materials in philosophy, art, religion, and literature was met by instituting a series of in-service seminars conducted by members of the staff and by such distinguished scholars as Sir Richard Livingston and Professor John S. Whale. Under firm administrative guidance, the necessary general reorientation has been successfully effected. The new orientation has also been reflected in the appointment of new staff members as such has become necessary in the ordinary course of events. New appointments have included men with broad training, background, and interests in the fields of literature, art, religion, philosophy, as well as history. It has been fully realized by the administration that very few men can come to the course effectively and precisely trained for it beforehand: polymaths who are effective teachers are rarities, indeed. The new men appointed to the staff have thus been specialists in one or another field and have not been expected to abandon their specialties. They have been selected rather with an eye to their ability and will to enlarge their viewpoints in the direction of a cogent and meaningful conception of general education as applied to the humanities. All staff members, old and new, are expected to teach the whole course; no specialists are assigned to teach this or that part of the course. Much more, it is believed, has been gained than lost by this procedure.

The problem of staff has not been completely solved. Accommodation to the new orientation has been and still is going on. No flattering unanimity has been imposed, nor could it be, by administrative fiat. Differences of opinion and emphasis remain and may be said to make for a healthy tension as to the best means to achieve the common general ideal. The result is again a constant salutary evaluation of purpose and methods that keeps the program on a challenging and realistic course.

Administratively, the new Humanities course has received the fullest support on the basis of its objectives, methods, and achievements. Critics have not been lacking on the university campus. But the administration of Michigan State University and the Basic

College have recognized the program as an outstanding one and given it effective encouragement in its aim of bringing to the students, through interested and superior teaching, a knowledge of Western man's creative achievements that will challenge them to make them a part of their own lives.

chapter 10

THE SEQUENCE OF GENERAL COURSES IN THE HUMANITIES IN THE COLLEGE OF THE UNIVERSITY OF CHICAGO

*Russell Thomas**

Since the publication of the first edition of THE HUMANI-TIES IN GENERAL EDUCATION ten years ago, there has been no significant change in the principles which determined the definition and organization of the subject matter of the three courses which were described in that volume. Nevertheless recent changes of major importance in the definition and structure of the College of the University of Chicago and in the entire undergraduate curriculum will have consequences of great significance for the role which the courses will play in the new curriculum.

General courses in the humanities have been planned, since 1931, as a part of a comprehensive program of general education, and the whole program has always been adopted upon approval by the Faculty of the University. As the Faculty has found reason to alter the structure of the entire program, the scope and content of the humanities courses have been expanded or modified to adjust to the design of the whole. Thus in 1931, when the University adopted its first program of general education, provision was made for one required general humanities course. This course, a one-year introduction to the history of Western civilization, was one of seven course requirements in general education. Other general courses in social science, biological science, and physical

---

*Professor of Humanities, The College, The University of Chicago, Chicago, Illinois.

science were developed at the same time, each a one-year course; and one year of study of English composition and a foreign language were included in the requirements. To complete the curriculum of seven course requirements, each student was required to take a second year of work in either the humanities, the social science or the natural sciences. No general course in humanities was created to meet this latter requirement. Instead students were permitted to choose any one of certain specified three-quarter sequences recommended by the various departments of the Humanities Division. Although the instructional staffs of the four general courses were free to decide upon the proper content of the courses, no staff could, at its pleasure, withdraw its course from the curriculum.

In adopting this curriculum the Faculty gave approval to other innovations. Class attendance was not required, but all students were required to pass comprehensive examinations based on the subect matter of the courses, and grades on these examinations were the sole determinant of the student's final standing. An independent examining body, the Board of Examiners, was established whose duties were the supervision of preparing examinations and administering them. Members of the instructional staff were assigned to work on the Board of Examiners. The College was at this time officially defined as the academic unit of the University responsible for general education, and the discharge of that responsibility, its sole academic function, was vested in the Faculty of the College under the direction of the Dean of the College. This definition of the College continued until 1958; and it is the departure from this definition, attended by far-reaching curricular and administrative changes, which will significantly affect the character of the entire program of general education in the future.

The program adopted in 1931 remained essentially unaltered until 1942. It required slightly less than two of the four undergraduate years, and it was usually, though not necessarily completed during the first two years of residence. One of the major arguments in support of programs of general education held that it was an important preparation for specialization in any field. During this period the College did not award the Bachelor of Arts degree; but students might, upon application receive a certificate of Associate in Arts. Completion of the baccalaureate degrees was achieved by two years of study in a departmental program of concentration.

In 1942 a revision of the College curriculum of major significance was approved by the Faculty of the University. The College was expanded to a four-year unit with the adoption of a plan which admitted students to the College after they had completed two or more years of high school. High school graduates continued to be admitted, and at first were permitted to take an abridged program of general studies which could be completed in two years. For students who entered prior to high school graduation the new curriculum was expanded to fourteen courses, three of which were in humanities. The system of comprehensive examinations was continued, and a few years later a system of placement tests was introduced. These tests, which were based on the subject matters of the fourteen courses, were taken by all students when they entered the College; and their scores determined the number of comprehensive examinations each student would be required to take in fullfillment of the requirements of the College. With the expansion of the general curriculum, the Faculty also gave approval to the awarding of the Bachelor of Arts degree upon completion of the required examinations in the general education program.

The system of placement tests allowed the best prepared students to complete the requirements for graduation at an accelerated pace. Many students were excused from the comprehensive examination on the first of the three humanities courses, and a few were excused from the first two examinations. It was apparent, however, that high school graduates fared little better on the placement tests than students who had completed only two or three years of high school. Later, when all students were held for all requirements established by their placement test scores, regardless of the number of years of high school preparation they had, it was evident that the average high school graduate could not complete the College in less than three years. Since it was impossible to complete a Master of Arts degree in less than three additional ye 's' of concentration, the general education program proved cost_y in time and money to a considerable number of students.

This was one of the reasons why the Faculty of the University rescinded in 1954 its previous action and restored the Bachelor of Arts degree to the position which it had held prior to 1942. Simultaneously with this action a plan for awarding the degree jointly by the College and the Divisional Faculties was approved. Under this action the College retained its status as the official academic body responsible for general education, but it was now necessary for the College faculty and the departmental faculties to work out degree programs for all areas of concentration. The Graduate Professional Schools (Law, Business and the Graduate Library School) agreed that students should complete three years or a maximum of twelve of the fourteen comprehensive examinations and one year of profssional study, after which the College would, as in the past, award the B.A. degree. Approval was also given to a plan for a general B.A. for such students as did not wish to concentrate in any departmental field. For these students, the general course requirements were a maximum of twelve courses in the College and one year of tutorial studies under the direction of a faculty committee called the Council on Tutorial Studies. All other students, and this was the great majority, were enrolled in one of the joint-degree programs.

The system proved to be administratively so complex and the variations in the degree requirements, both of general studies and of concentration, so extreme that almost no one was satisfied. In most programs the number of general courses required was eight, but there were numerous differences about which eight courses of the available fourteen the students should be required to complete. Some of the programs allowed room for the free election of two or three quarter-courses; others allowed room for no election. The science programs, particularly the physical sciences, were so cowded that some students could not complete them in less that four and a half years. The dissatisfaction culminated in the action of the Faculty of the University in 1958, which once again defined the College and its responsibilities and gave approval to a new curricular program of undergraduate education which unites under the administration of one Faculty (the College) a program of general studies and programs of concentration in the numerous areas of study offered by the University. Both the Bachelor of Arts and the Bachelor of Science degrees will be awarded upon completion of this curriculum.

The new curriculum, which becomes effective in the Autumn Quarter of 1959-60 provides for approximately two years of general courses, one year of area concentration, and one year divided between guided electives related to the student's area of concentration and free electives. Since the principle of the placement tests will be retained, it is possible that the number of general course requirements may be less than eight, the normal number of courses and examinations required for a two-year program. The University continues to admit students who have not graduated from high school, though the number is greatly reduced and the admission standards are, in terms of aptitude, the same as they are for high school graduates. Early entrants will take the same program as high school graduates. The Faculty of the newly defined College will consist of members of the old College faculty and members of departmental faculties assigned to it on the basis of their interest and experience in undergraduate teaching. It is an independent ruling body of the University under the administration of the Dean of the College. The action of 1958 is the most significant from the standpoint of defining the functions of a college since the action of 1931.

The decisions which the Faculty of the newly defined College was compelled to make concerning the content of the revised program of general studies have been extremely difficult. Although there was not universal approval of all of the fourteen courses which had been developed between 1942 and 1954, there was general consent that in themselves they were excellent courses. Certainly there was little desire to abandon any of the disciplines represented in these courses. There was general agreement that the requirements in humanities, social sciences and natural sciences might be reduced from three to two courses, but there remained the problem of requirements in English composition, a foreign language, mathematics and two terminal integration courses — one in the history of Western civilization and one in philosophy devoted to a study of the organization, methods, and principles of knowledge. Since each of these was a one-year course, it was impossible to add these to the requirements in the humanities and the sciences and keep within the two-year maximum alloted to general studies.

Experience with the placement tests, however, had shown that many students would enter the College with a knowledge of one or more of these subject matters sufficient to warrant exemption from one or more comprehensive examinations. For many of these the problem of prescribing a satisfactory program would not be difficult. The serious problem would lie with those who were less well prepared in all of the desired subjects. After much deliberation the Faculty adopted a plan which it is hoped will prove sufficiently flexible to permit all students to have a reasonable experience of those subject matters in which there is a demonstrated need of further study. The staffs of the humanities, the social sciences and the natural sciences were instructed to develop three course-sequences: one of three quarters, one of five quarters, and one of six quarters. Only those students whose placement test scores indicate superior training will be required to take the three-quarter course. Other students will be required to take the five or the six quarter course, the decision between the two to be decided by relative competence the students show in the several subject matters on the placement tests. It was decided to omit the philosophy course from the program on the assumption that no student would be likely to complete the undergraduate requirements in any area without some experience with philosophy. The staffs of the one-year courses were instructed to prepare two and three-quarter plans for their subject matters. Decisions about the content of the revised programs were assigned to the instructional staffs of the various subject matter fields.

It has been necessary to give this account of the reorganization of the College and of the undergraduate curriculum because it would be impossible otherwise to explain the circumstances which have made necessary some recent changes in the general requirements in the humanities and impossible for the reader to understand the problems which the staff of the general humanities courses have faced. The record may, moreover, be of interest historically as an account of nearly thirty years of experience in planning humanities programs as part of a general program which has been subject to frequent changes.

The decision in 1942 to abandon the historical approach to the study of the humanities was not taken lightly, and not without an appreciation of the place of history in the total program of general education. The three courses which were introduced at that time were planned as a sequence, and such changes as have been made during the fifteen years of their history were intended to strengthen and clarify the basic concepts which guided the staff from the beginning. The courses have been successful, and the staff has been reluctant to abandon any of the three as a part of the required curriculum. Nevertheless it seemed clear to the majority of the staff that the objectives of the sequence would not be well served by a compression of three years of work into two.

The first of the three courses was planned as an introduction to the arts: music, visual arts, and the poetic or, as they are sometimes called, the imaginative forms of literature. The second course, though restricted entirely to literature, is concerned with the major modes of literary expression and interpretation. It extends the study of the poetic foms begun in the first course, and enlarges the scope of the students' experience through the study of historical, philosophical, and rhetoric works. The third course is an introduction to the principles and practice of criticism of the arts; it has been developed and taught cooperatively by the humanities staff, the English staff, and the foreign language staffs of the College (1942-58).

When the staff began the planning of these courses in 1942 we accepted the view that, while the *materials* for study in all of our courses were rightly the great achievements in the arts, these materials were not exclusively within the domain of humanistic study. Our colleagues in the social sciences would have made this clear to us had we not accepted the view, because their reading lists not infrequently contained titles of works which appeared in ours. It seemed important to us, therefore, to define the humanities, not merely as the study of the arts of mankind, but with enough precision about the subject matter of the humanities to enable our students to understand the differences between our approach to art, music, and especially literature, and that of the social sciences. We could not deny that the *Republic*, the *Federalist*, or *Darkness at Noon* were useful as documents in the scientific study of human behavior and social institutions; but we were confident that there were values in each of them that were not likely to emerge in such a study. Admittedly a curriculum might be devised which ignored formal distinctions between the humanities and the social sciences; but the curriculum of the College was based on a three-fold distinction of the problems of knowledge and their related disciplines: the humanities, the natural sciences, and the social sciences. Our aim, therefore, was to develop as large an experience of products of the various arts of mankind as time allowed us and to cultivate the understanding and the exercise of the disciplines which lead to an intelligent and cultivated appreciation of works of art, as *works of art*, and not as documentary evidence of political and social theory or of natural history.

We were conscious, too, of the fact that we were planning courses for several hundred students, the majority of whom would not continue formal study of the humanities beyond our courses. It was therefore necessary to consider what, of all the activities which we might legitimately pursue within the sphere of humanistic study, would be most profitable as a comprehensive experience and most useful to these students in the future. We agreed that we could not do justice to the artistic achievements of men if we neglected any one of the three great media of creative expression: music, the visual forms, and literature. We agreed, too, that in each course and at all times the particular work of art ought to be the principal object of study. Each work of any kind should therefore be chosen not merely because it was representative of a type, of a historical period, or of any of the great ideas that have stirred the minds and emotions of men, but because it possessed values which were its own unique achievement.

This is one reason why it was decided not to organize the sequence in a historical framework or around themes and ideas, since there seemed to us to be a tendency to reduce the study of works of art to only one of their many dimensions. The decision was in no way a rejection of the importance of historical knowledge in the appreciation of the arts nor of the contribution of the arts to cultural history. We recognized that where history would enlighten understanding, historical knowledge should be given, and this was one of the uses which we made of lectures (one each week) in the first two courses. We believed that it would be impossible to read the *Protagoras, Crime and Punishment, King Lear,* or the *Decline and Fall of the Roman Empire* without considering significant ideas about public and private virtue; but it seemed better that students should understand how each author treated these ideas in his own way and for his own artistic ends whether as philosopher, as dramatist, as novelist, or as historian. We knew that in other courses these same ideas would be encountered in other ways.

Hence the staff chose to develop a sequence of courses which gave prior importance to teaching the students the arts of listening, seeing, and reading thoughtfully and analytically: to hear what the music is saying in a symphony by Beethoven; to see with eyes trained to see something akin to the visual experiences of artists so different as Botticelli and Cezanne; to read Thucydides, Shakespeare, Conrad, Plato, and T. S. Eliot in ways appropriate to the artistic form and purposes of each author. The basic arts of interpretation were the first task of the first two courses in the sequence. To complete the sequence we developed the third course which introduced students to various criteria in terms of which judgments about the nature and values of the arts have traditionally been made. Of course judgments of the values of particular work could not nor should not be excluded from discussions in the first two courses; but no systematic approach to critical principles was made prior to the third course.

Faced in 1958, sixteen years after the initial planning of these courses, with the necessity of reducing the scope of the required content of the curriculum, the staff agreed that the subject matter of the first two courses have a prior claim, since these are the courses which give an extensive experience with works in all media and of the major genres of each, and which develop the habits of careful analysis. This experience is a necessary condition for an effective study of critical principles and their application. Our first decision therefore has been to retain the subject matter of the first two courses (formerly Humanities I and II) as the basic content of the required general humanities program in the new curriculum of the College. We shall retain the course in criticism (formerly Humanities III) as an elective. We have reason to expect that it will appeal to many students as a free elective and that it may be included in some of the degree programs as a guided elective.[1]

Although the substance of the first two courses in the old sequence will be retained, this period of transition is one that gives opportunity for a thorough review of the internal organization of their content. Because we are committed to developing a five-quarter sequence which will be parallel to but in some manner an abridgment or variation of the old six-quarter program, a committee of the staff have been appointed to develop recommendations within the year 1959-60 for this and other desirable changes.

Since the objectives and the general procedures of the three courses will remain very much as they have been in the past, a brief summary of these courses as they are being given at the present time will be the most useful way of describing the general program of humanities.

1. *The first course*:   Formerly Humanities I A, B, C, and now 111, 112, 113.

This course has been subtitled An Introduction to the Arts. Its materials are representative works in the three great media, music, visual arts, and literature, though the literature is limited to the so-called imaginative or "poetic" forms. The course meets five times each week, one hour devoted to a lecture and four to discussions in class sections of approximately twenty-five students. The content is organized in terms of problems which have their peculiar applications in each of the media. At the beginning of the year the elements of musical, visual, and literary forms are studied intensively. In the first approach to music, students are introduced to the elements of tonal organizations: metric organizations, phrase, structure, tempo, dynamics, melody, and tonal range, and to the effects of these in various kinds of compositions. This is followed

---

[1]The College as now organized will consist of four Sections: Humanities, Social Science, Physical Science, and Biological Science, the whole under the direction of the Dean of the College. The Humanities Section is composed of the General Humanities Staff (which will be responsible for the general courses and the program of concentration leading to the Bachelor's degree in General Humanities), the English Staff, the Foreign Language Staff, the Philosophy Staff, and the Fine Arts Staff (music and art). These Staffs will plan degree programs in their respective areas, direct the courses in English composition and foreign language which are required in the general education program, and supervise undergraduate courses in the various departments which form the several Sections.

by an introduction to the elements of color, line, volume, mass, etc., in the organization of painting, sculpture, and architectural works, and to the differences in visual expression achieved through different uses of these elements.   The analogous problem in literature concerns the power of language to achieve its poetic effects through the uses of sound, imagery, figures of speech, and statement.   Following this elementary beginning, the cycle is repeated, this time with the study directed to more complex problems of organization, as for example, part-whole relationships.   In the study of music three compositions having superficially the same formal structure (A B A) may be studied with the purpose of understanding through careful listening the different ways in which each realizes this formal organization.   In the study of literary works, problems of plot structure and the relation of plot, character, and diction to the whole structure are the center of interest. In the visual arts, where the organization of parts is not dependent on a temporal sequence of statements, there are problems in the relation of points of view in the organization of three-dimensional works — for example, the relation of the interior to the exterior of a building or the integrity of a sculptural work perceived through viewing it on all sides.   The works selected for study in each media are more complex than those chosen in the first problem. After the middle of the year, each of the arts is approached in a quite different way.   Thus far works have been studied individually and comparatively but without regard to their historical context except insofar as it might be necessary to explain some details of content.   To complete the course, the arts are now considered within the context of historical problems.   According to the Instructor's Manual,

> the aim of this study is not to explore the context *per se* — to be able to characterize or label 19th century music or "Romantic" painting — but to note the existence of such contexts and how they illuminate further the individual work of art.   A different aspect of the problem of historical context is treated in each of the arts.

This unit of the year's work has been particularly useful in bringing modern, even contemporary, problems of style and subject matter into intelligent relationship with the past.   Yet even within this consideration of the temporal continuity of the arts, the work of the course does not allow the students to lose sight of the individuality of the artist or his works, i.e., "how artists of a given time or movement may seem to resemble each other closely in respect to past art or a general historical development, yet differ radically from each other when individually considered."

The course has always made use of the rich resources of the city as a part of the subject matter. The Art Institute of Chicago has cooperated in making original works available for classroom study, and study of particular works in the galleries of the Institute under guidance of a staff member is regularly assigned. The staff maintains a studio and small gallery, under the direction of a staff member who is a painter and sculptor. Exhibits in the gallery are on display at all times, and studio assignments give the students familiarity with the materials of the visual artist and of his problems of technique and organization. The studio is open at all times to students in the College who wish help in drawing, painting, printmaking and sculpture. Listening rooms are available for individual and group study of musical works. Some of the weekly lecture hours are concerts or recitals of music and poetry by guest lecturers and staff members.

One of the curricular problems under review at present, however, arises from the opinion of staff members that there is considerable difference in the previous experience with visual art and music among the student body, as well as with the rate of progress which students make during the year. For many students the experience is entirely new. The staff feels that it might be well to recognize these differences and has proposed a change affecting the Spring Quarter. For those who make the most rapid progress in the first two quarters, work might be suspended while the remainder of the class, needing to move at a slower pace and needing intensive review, would continue through the third quarter, with more attention to fundamentals of listening. A new one-quarter course has been proposed for the more advanced students, but it would be deferred until after students had completed the three quarters of literature which follow the first course. This plan, it is argued, would have the advantage of returning to an integration of the major arts after the study of historical texts and after completing the course in the history of Western civilization. The study of the arts in relation to problems of history, coming at a later point in the sequence would, it is thought, prove more effective. If the plan is approved next year, it will be the first major change in this course since 1942.

2. *The second course*:   Formerly Humanities II A, B, C, and now Humanities 121, 122, 123.

This course, devoted entirely to the study of four major literary forms, has undergone less internal change than either Humanities I or III in the sixteen years of their existence. The course meets four hours per week, one lecture and three discussion periods in sections of about twenty-five students each.

The four forms studied are: history, "poetic" narrative (drama, fiction, and epic), rhetoric, and philosophy. The course is not, however, a conventional "types" course. The purpose of the course is to inform the student of four modes of literary expression and to develop the skills and habits of reading proper for the appreciation of each. The continuation of the study of dramatic and fictional works, begun in the first course, is deliberate. Analysis is more intensive, and the differences in the problems of interpretation between the poetic arts and the other forms are clarified in the course of the year. The selections of works representative of each form are chosen with a view to presenting different kinds of problems of form and subject matter. Although the order in which the forms are studied has changed occasionally, in recent years the first quarter has been devoted to the study of historical works, followed by drama, fiction and epic poetry. This continues through most of the Winter Quarter, which concludes with three weeks' study of rhetorical works. The whole of the Spring Quarter is given to the reading of philosophy.

Two kinds of questions, therefore, are paramount. The first is: What is the nature of a history, a novel, a philosophic demonstration, and a rhetorical argument? The second: What kinds of questions does one raise which will guide him in understanding the structure and purposes of each of these forms? In addition to these logically prior questions, there is a third which is no less important. What are the characteristics — in subject matter, point of view, style, modes of argument, etc., which give any work of any kind a distinction that makes it unique among its kind?

Students are expected to discover that there is a kind of truth characteristic of works of each form and that the standards of assessing the truth differ according to its kind. Yet, though the course is not likely to leave any student in doubt that Gibbon wrote the *Decline and Fall of the Roman Empire* for historical purposes and was guided by the formal principles of the historian's art, it does not ignore the fact that Gibbon uses the arts of the rhetorician in frequent defense of his historical theses. Similarly the students should understand, after reading *Emma,* something of the form of the novel as it emerged from the genius of Jane Austen. We would expect them to recognize the differences in a novel and a social history, but we would not ignore the fact that *Emma* has its historical values as a representation of life in an English village near the beginning of the 19th century. The poetic uses of the social record, however, are the chief concern. By the end of the year's work, we hope that students will have perceived that great works of art may be interpreted in more than one way and that the most complete appreciation requires the exercise of all of the arts of interpretation. In this course, as in the other two, students are assigned some works for study which are not discussed in class. These are important, not merely for extending the reading experience beyond the limits of time available for adequate discussion, but also because they provide means of testing the extent to which students are able to read intelligently without direct supervision.

The principal changes in this course will likely affect only those students who are required to take the five-quarter sequence. For this group some abridgement of the content of the first two courses will be necessary.

3. *The third course*:   formerly Humanities III A, B, C, and now Humanities 201, 202, 203,

This course, an introduction to the principles and practice of criticism, will undergo the most radical changes in the future. Formerly required of all students or (as in recent years) required in its entirety in certain degree programs, it will now be an elective. Students may elect the first quarter only, the first and second, or all three. It will be therefore a sequence of three related but independent quarters. It meets three hours per week in sections of about twenty students. Since the course aims at developing some competence in practical criticism, considerably more attention is given to writing than is done in the other courses. It has been taught jointly by members of the Humanities and English and foreign language staffs for several years. Three kinds of activities engage the attention of the students: the study of texts which establish theories of art and principles of criticism, the study of plays, novels, and lyric poetry with discussion directed toward the relation between various theories of art and criticism and the kinds of judgments students make of the works read and the writing of criticism. Themes (about five each in the first two quarters) are expository and critical essays based upon problems in the theoretical texts and the poetic works. One of the interesting achievements of the course has been the development of variant forms in foreign languages and in art and music.

In the Autumn Quarter of the parent (English) version of the course, which will not change greatly, the theoretical texts are selected from Plato and Aristotle. About three weeks are devoted to the study of Aristotle's *Poetics,* followed by the reading of a non-Greek tragedy, e.g. *Othello.* At this point the works read in the two previous courses are extremely useful as references and materials for comparisons. The aim, of course, is to determine the usefulness of the *method* of the *Poetics* in the criticism of litera- ture and the limitations of the method. This unit is followed by an equally careful study of Platonic dialogues, the *Phaedrus* and the *Ion,* and the reading of a short novel, e.g., *Death in Venice* or *Heart of Darkness.* At this point, the differences between the two approaches to art and criticism begin to emerge; and the students take the first steps in comparing the different kinds of assumptions as well as the different kinds of purposes which control critical judgments of plays and novels. The quarter ends with the study of one work, often a comedy or a work which unites the serious and the comic; and the students are asked to consider how one might apply the principles of both a Platonic and Aristotelian sys- tem to the criticism of it.

The procedure in the Winter Quarter is much the same as in the Autumn. The theoretical texts, however, are chosen from modern philosophers. In recent years we have used selections from Benedetto Croce successfully, and we now plan to add a substantial portion of John Dewey's *Art and Experience.* Problems of criti- cism of lyric poetry become the chief concern at this point, and the exercises in practical criticism are based on a wide range of lyric forms.

The procedure anticipated for the third quarter will be a departure from past practice which has been a continuation of the criticism of lyric poetry. Since the students who elect this quarter will have received the experience of the first two, and may be expected to have a special interest in the arts, we plan to allow them more latitude in the subject matter upon which they will concentrate most of their time. The course will be, in effect, a seminar; and the principal work of the quarter will be the writing of a critical essay by each student which will be based on one or two works by an author of the student's choice. Drama, novel, lyric — the whole range of imaginative literature will be available to him in making his choice. Class discussion will probably include analyses of a variety of criticism by recognized critics of works with which the students are aleady familiar.

The procedure for this quarter will be similar to one which the staff has employed for many years as an optional variation of the work of the second and third quarters. Qualified students, might, if they wish, elect a "preceptorial" version of the parent course during these quarters. The preceptorials have been conducted as seminars, and one or two have been offered each year. Any instructor in the course may submit a plan for a preceptorial (e.g., a Critical Study of Shakespeare's Comedies, Theories of the Art of the Novel, Contemporary American Poetry). Upon approval of the plan by the staff, a prospectus is given to the students, and those whose grades make them eligible may take it instead of the regular course. The basic theoretical texts were always included in the readings of any preceptorial. Each student found a problem during the Winter Quarter which became the subject of an extended essay. The greater part of the Spring Quarter, the student worked on his essay independently, with only occasional conferences with his instructor. The essay constituted one third of his comprehensive examination. The success of these essays encouraged the staff to extend this kind of assignment in a somewhat less ambitious form to all regular sections. For the past two years, all students, including those in all variants, have been required to write a long critical essay as the major assignment of the Spring Quarter. Students chose a topic from a list of four or five, each based upon a particular poem (or other work appropriate to the variants) which was not discussed in class. These essays also constituted a third of the comprehensive examination.

Our experience with the variant forms of Humanities III has persuaded us that it is possible to develop a variety of approaches to a common problem which will demand the exercise of common disciplines and enable the students to achieve comparable standards of excellence on examinations.

An account of the general humanities program which was restricted to a description of courses would not do justice to the program. Administrative organization and staff procedures have been important factors in whatever success our program has achieved. Since 1931 the general courses have been staff-planned and staff-taught. There has been at all times the closest cooperation in the deliberations on all matters of policy. Weekly staff meetings, most of which are in fact staff discussion of the instructional problems of the course, have been a necessary part of our work. With rare exceptions the members of the staff have found that the interchange of views about the assigned works has been stimulating and has encouraged rather than restrained the independence of staff members in developing their approaches to any given work. At the same time the staff meetings have enlarged the staff's views of its task through the free interchange of ideas. Because the work of the entire sequence embraces a wide and diversified body of works of art, it has been essential that the staff should have among its members some who have special competence in each of the arts which are included in the sequence. The special knowledge of each staff member has always been available to every other member, as a result the educational activity of the general program has been by no means limited to the students. The *esprit de corps* developed over the years in the general humanities staff has been a source of its greatest strength. It is not expected that any staff member will teach only one course, and indeed we hope that very member will be familiar with each of the courses, though this is not always possible.

The system of comprehensive examinations, a requirement in all general courses, has been one factor which has commanded close staff cooperation. When students are to be prepared for a common examination there must be a clear understanding of common objectives and cooperation in planning the ⌣⌣⌣s.   The system will be retained, though it is likely that examination procedures will be modified.   Some important changes have occurred in the character of these examinations since they were first introduced. At that time they were wholly objective.   Today nearly half of all examinations are essay examinations, and in the case of Humanities III, two-thirds of the grade are on essay assignments. Almost all of these are written under supervised conditions, however.   All essays are read by two instructors, who do not know the identity of the students, and if there is more than one grade point difference in their judgments, a third reader is required to give judgment.

In a period of transition such as the College is now experiencing there will no doubt be changes which at present cannot be foreseen.   There is, however, little reason to suppose that our basic conceptions of the principal needs of the students in humanistic education will be changed or that the approach which we have found successful will be altered in any radical manner.   The importance of a general knowledge of the disciplines of humanistic study for all students in the College has not been challenged by any one in the University.

chapter 11

THE COMPREHENSIVE HUMANITIES COURSE AT THE UNIVERSITY OF FLORIDA

*Robert F. Davidson**

The past ten years (1949-1959) have seen a gradual maturing of the basic philosophy of general education presented in the essay on the Humanities course at Florida in the original edition of this volume. There has been no fundamental change in the major objectives of our program but rather a growing body of evidence to support the soundness of the approach adopted in our particular situation. Since the general education program at the University of Florida was established some twenty-five years ago (in 1935-36), it has been handled by an independent administrative unit, the University College, and has had strong administrative support during this entire period.

Our situation with regard to staff is a comparable one. We have a staff each year of from twenty-five to thirty members. Twenty of these are on our own Humanities budget; four or five staff members are "borrowed" from the departments of English and philosophy, and four or five from other areas in the University College. Consequently the teaching staff as a whole is not only sympathetic to the broad aims of general education but is committed professionally to making a success of the Humanities program. My experience during twelve years as chairman of the program at Florida confirms an unqualified enthusiasm for this type of organization.

*Chairman Humanities, University College.

I

There have been three changes in our program during the past decade, however, of some general significances. The first of these is foreshadowed perhaps in the original (1949) description of the program. As pointed out there, the conflict of values in contemporary life has always been a major concern of ours at the University of Florida. We are committed to the position that a vital Humanities program, if it is to meet adequately the needs of students today, must enable them to deal more intelligently and more constructively with the world in which they live — that is, with the particular problems of the mid-twentieth century. At this point we have not been willing to accept the position, apparently adopted in some Humanities courses, that a study of the great works of the past is sufficient preparation. Even with skillful teaching directed toward interperting the enduring significance of great books and suggesting concrete applications to our age of the insights of the past, it has been our experience that most students still fail to think realistically and constructively about present issues and situations.

Likewise in a large required program such as ours at Florida we have come to see that *motivation* is as important as are the more specific questions of objectives, course structure, evaluation and the like. In our course we have all the sophomores at the University, no matter what their pre-professional interests may be, about 3,000 students at present. They are not here — in large measures at least — because they have an interest in the Humanities or want to take this particular course. They are here because they have to be; and this must becomes a very important factor in course planning if one is concerned to see that as far as possible a required course in the Humanities is of maximum benefit to the students involved.

As a result of the foregoing considerations, we gradually became more and more dissatisfied with the traditional course organization which began with Homer and the Greeks, moved through the various creative periods in the development of Western Civilization, and concluded with a hasty survey of important trends during the past hundred years. After a good deal of soul searching and no little difficulty with deans and registrars, we simply reversed the order of the course. The first semester we now devote to "The

Humanities in Contemporary Life;" the second to a study of "Our Cultural Heritage." This change was made almost ten years ago. At the time there were the usual predictions from colleagues, administrators and text-book publishers that such a change could only be very temporary. In a few years at best, perhaps a few months, we would be back where everyone else was with a good old chronological frame-work in which both staff and students felt comfortably at home.

I am happy to report that on the contrary the change has proved a most successful one. In "The Humanities in Contemporary Life" we include literature, philosophy, art and music of our own age (the past hundred years being a convenient period), selecting material that makes immediate and effective contact with the experience and vital concern of students such as ours. The general student response to this approach to the Humanities has been quite encouraging — we now "lose" during the early weeks of the semester far fewer practical-minded students who had never been reconciled to this requirement, and we find a growing and very genuine enthusiasm among a majority of our group. But this we had expected. What we had not anticipated was the way in which this interest and concern, developed during the first semester, would carry on into the second course dealing with "Our Cultural Heritage." Our students are now far better prepared — that is, far readier psychologically — for a study of "the great books," the great ideas, the great art and music of the past. They now have, in much greater numbers certainly, the needed sense of the relevance of this material to their own interests and the needed desire to enlarge their understanding and appreciation. The uncertainty, the confusion and the anti-intellectualism so widespread in our own age has made them anxious to find in our cultural heritage ideas and values that will give to human life some greater meaning, stability and purpose.

In order to provide in convenient form the kind of materials essential for our study of contemporary literature, philosophy, art and music, we prepared an anthology, entitled *The Humanities in Contemporary Life.* Published for us in 1955 by The Dryden Press, this volume has been revised and is now handled by Henry Holt & Co. For any interested in the more detailed organization, point of view and materials used in the course, that anthology is available. We supplement it each semester with several inexpensive paper backs, usually a novel or two like *Darkness at Noon, 1984,* or *Of Human Bondage* and a book on modern art. In recent years we have used *The French Impressionists,* the *Van Gogh* and the *Picasso* in the Pocket Library of Great Art.

As far as I am able to judge, this concern with contemporary ideas and values is one of the most important features of our Humanities program at Florida and one of the more basic reasons for the success of the program in our situation here.

II

A second major development during the past ten years has been our effort to provide in the Humanities program an educational opportunity for the superior student in keeping with his needs and abilities. In most colleges and universities, general education programs are pitched at the level of the average student. If such programs are to be required of all students and a common core of basic insights and experiences is to be made available to all, this is certainly understandable. But under such circumstances the abler students, as well as those who have been better prepared than the average, will not usually be stimulated to their best effort. Experience has shown that such students are apt to lose interest in the general courses, to waste time, to become bored. In so far as this does happen, programs of general education are open to legitimate and serious criticism.

Broadly speaking, two practices have been followed in the attempt to meet this problem. One can be seen at private institutions such as Columbia University, the University of Chicago, and Harvard. Here the general education program is simply set at the intellectual level of the superior student and only students of superior ability are encouraged to enroll in the university. This, of course, is not a practice that can be followed by large state universities or private colleges with less highly selective admissions policies. The University of Minnesota has gone so far as to set up two independent programs of general education, one for the student of average or below average ability, another for the abler student. But in most institutions the practice has been to work out some scheme by which the superior student, if he chooses to do so, is able to meet the general education requirement by special examination, credit for work previously done, or the substitution of more advanced specialized courses for the general courses. For a good many years the University of Florida along with many other institutions has followed practices of this sort.

Actually, however, this way of dealing with the superior student implies that general education is something he does not need, that it is rather largely a way of making up deficiencies in high school preparation. Neither of these implications seems defensible. Students of superior ability quite often tend to be more highly specialized in their interests and outlook than their less talented fellows; they are frequently more academic in their approach to higher education, more in need of the kind of insights that will enable them to deal intelligently with contemporary social and ethical problems. On the other hand, they are also more capable of integrating broad areas of knowledge, and better able to profit from the predominant concern with ideas and values rather than with facts which one finds in general education at its best.

If this analysis is sound, some way must be provided for students of superior ability to enjoy the benefits of general education without being subjected to the frustration that almost inevitably follows when they are simply put into large sections of general courses. The dimensions of this problem become even more apparent, of course, when one faces the rapidly rising enrollments expected during the next twelve or fifteen years. This great influx of students will demand a maximum effort by university administrators to care for the numbers involved. The plight of the superior student will then become even more acute, for while there will be increasing need that something be done for him, there will be less in the way of facilities, money and faculty time to do it. At Florida we felt it imperative to work out an honors program in Humanities for the superior student while there was still time and opportunity to do so.

About five years ago we set up in our second Humanities course, entitled "Our Cultural Heritage," a number of honors sections open to students who had completed the first semester's work with distinction. The top five per cent of the students in the first course are automatically included in the honors program, and Humanities instructors are asked to recommend from the top quarter of their classes other students who have shown the qualities of mind desired. The chairman of the Humanities staff sends a personal letter to each student thus selected, inviting him to participate in the honors program if he wishes to do so. Thus far about two-thirds of those invited have gone into honors work.

To accomplish the purposes of this program for superior students it was felt that honors sections should be limited to twenty (instead of the thirty to forty enrolled in the regular sections of the course), that more active student participation should be encouraged, and that more opportunity should be provided for individual achievement. More challenging reading has also been introduced in the honors sections; but in most instances, it was not so much the materials used in the course as the level of instruction that failed to demand of the abler student the desired effort and achievement. For such students one of the most serious weaknesses of higher education has been its heavy emphasis on "teaching" and its failure to place much responsibility on the student beyond attending class and making satisfactory grades. We have given even our best students too little chance to discover what has been called "the first law of learning: Whatever a man learns he must learn for himself." No program for superior students can be defended if it fails in this. One of our chief concerns, therefore, has been to give more responsibility to able students, both in handling the materials of the course and in presenting their own ideas to the group. As a sound guiding principle, we feel that "the superior student should be given as much freedom to do independent work as is consistent with his initiative and sense of personal responsbility."

During the past five years ten members of our Humanities staff have taught honors sections. An initial policy adopted by the staff specified that the chairman should give this assignment to as many different instructors as possible so long as continuity in the program was maintained. The policy has proved a sound one. Not only has the diversity of staff participation provided a richness of ideas and experience in shaping the program itself, but in part at least this practice has also met one of the serious staff problems in large general education programs where staff members frequently do not have the opportunity to offer advanced courses in their own fields of specialization and miss the stimulus that this affords.   An honors assignment enables, indeed forces, a staff member to escape the monotony and boredom that is often apparent when one gives full time to four or five identical sections of a general course.   There is general agreement among our staff that teaching a Humanities honors section is both more challenging and more rewarding than teaching an introductory upper division departmental course.   Experience has also made it clear, however, that instructors who are successful with regular sections do not always do well with honors sections.   The selection of staff is certainly as important a problem in the success of an honors program as the selection of students.

In addition to these special honors sections, it has also seemed desirable to make available to the abler students in the regular sections of our course a somewhat similar opportunity.   We have just this year (1959) inaugurated an honors program open to all interested students of superior ability in our regular sections.   Such honors work involves an independent essay, an oral examination before our honors committee, and a series of honors seminars throughout the semester, each conducted by several staff members. As yet it is too early to draw any valid conclusions from this undertaking.   A number of students are participating this semester, however, and showing the kind of enthusiasm we anticipated.

III

The third significant change in our program during the past decade has grown out of our concern with the larger world responsibilities which face our nation, and its citizens, today.   When general Humanities courses were inaugurated fifteen to twenty-five years ago, they were quite naturally limited to a consideration of the ideals and values of our Western culture.   The philosophy and the civilization of the Orient, however, is becoming increasingly important in the world in which our students today live.   The very existence of our Western culture may depend indeed upon the attitudes and decisions of American men and women with regard to the Orient.   This presents American citizens with a responsibility that the colleges and universities are not preparing their students to face in intelligent and informed fashion — unless one is willing to adopt the position that our task is simply to train students to think in the abstract, and they will then be able to deal intelligently and objectively with any concrete problem that may arise.

This position, as far as we can see, is not borne out by the facts of college and post-college life — despite the body of reputable authority that can be found to support it. Hence in considering the content of a sound program of general education we cannot avoid the conclusion that we have a responsibility to provide somewhere in this program an introduction to the philosophy and civilization of the Orient together with some understanding of the sharp divergence between the ideals and values of the East and West that makes our present world situation so tense, explosive and precarious.

We would all prefer, of course, to set up a new area in the general education program concerned especially with this problem. More forward-looking and experimentally-minded institutions are moving in this direction. But where this is impossible because of administrative or faculty conservatism and the vested interests that always oppose a change in the *status quo,* then we are faced with the responsibility of finding a place in the established general education program for some treatment of the philosophy and civilization of the Orient. This has been our situation at Florida.

About four years ago, therefore, we began some experimentation in our Humanities program with this in mind. In the off-semester, when enrollment in the course dealing with "Our Cultural Heritage" was relatively light (between 400 and 500), and the staff teaching this course relatively small (about ten or twelve), we introduced some material dealing with the philosophy, literature, religion and art of the Orient. Two obvious but very real difficulties were immediately apparent. The initial one was caused by the difficulty of finding suitable materials for our purpose. The whole spirit and outlook of the Orient is so different from our own that typical freshmen and sophomores in a state university are simply baffled by the religious philosophy and literature of India or China, especially if their first contact with it is in the great classics of the East. To insist that they read such books under these circumstances simply defeats the purpose of general education — no matter how defensible this attitude may be in a departmental course in Oriental religion or literature. It is easy, therefore, to become discouraged and give up the whole undertaking as an impossible one.

This outcome is made more probable by the reaction of an appreciable number of able but conservative staff members in every Humanities program who insist immediately upon two obvious facts. First, there is just too much good material in our own Western heritage that should be included in a basic Humanities course but cannot because of lack of time. Our primary responsibility to our students, such critics insist, is to provide for them meaningful insights into the ideals and values that have shaped our own Western culture. This requires more time than we have at our disposal anyhow, and to take some of this time for Oriental literature, art or religion — which the students can't understand — is obviously unwise and unjuistified. Second, most of us in the Humanities are quite unprepared to deal with these Oriental materials with any academic competence. We are simply misleading our students instead of educating them, and until we get trained Orientalists we have no business attempting to "teach" materials such as these.

These are impressive objections — and are usually ably stated by those with scholarly achievements to their credit. Hence they always carry weight, and should not be lightly disregarded. On the other hand, anyone who has had the experience of setting up a general education program and dealing with the opposition to it from departmental-minded specialists, will at once recognize that these are exactly the same arguments that were used initially to oppose all general education courses, now risen from the grave to haunt us once more. It was for just these reasons that we could not hope to build a general Humanities course in the first place. And for these reasons a number of colleges never tried to do so. But in quite a number of others — well represented by the institutions discussed in the present volume — faculty members and administrators convinced that general education was both desirable and possible went ahead to develop very successful general Humanities courses and thus to demonstrate pragmatically the fallacy of such objections as those noted above.

It is our feeling at Florida that a comparable achievement is both possible and necessary in dealing with Oriental ideals and values. We have still not found the kind of materials we need.

Of all the books we have used, the *Bhagavad-Gita* has proved most successful.   Other Oriental classics in literature and religious philosophy, both Chinese and Hindu, have thus far proved too remote in spirit or approach to contribute greatly to the insights and understanding of our students.   But we are making encouraging progress in revealing the basic contrast between the ideals and values of the East and the West.   And we find a growing recognition among our students of the importance of this undertaking, together with a more evident student concern to develop greater understanding in this whole area — especially in those classes where the instructors are sympathetic.   Naturally where the instructor himself is opposed to such an undertaking, it is doomed to failure among his students.   This fact must be taken into consideration in any experiment of the kind we are making.

IV

In concluding this comment on developments during the past ten years, two final activities should be noted.   The first is an enterprise upon which we are just preparing to embark in the fall — the use of educational television in our Humanities program. The general interest at present in this field needs no emphasis.   At Florida as elsewhere faculty members are concerned to see what educational TV will do to the ordinary classroom procedures and to the role of the instructor in general education, and many are interested also in participating in some experimentation to help find the answers to these questions.

For some time we have been discussing with our School of Journalism and Communications the possibility of putting our Humanities course on the local educational TV channel which is programmed by that school.   As the result of a grant from the Ford Foundation, we are now able to go ahead with this plan. In the fall we will set up a limited number of experimental sections of the course to be taught on a closed TV circuit.   Two members of our staff will handle these sections, working with the program director and staff at our educational TV station.   These classes will meet three mornings a week just as other sections do, and will also devote a fourth hour each week to class discussion, with two instructors who put on the TV program meeting the sections in person to conduct this discussion.

These experimental sections will be given exactly the same tests as the regular sections in the course; they will be responsible for the same body of materials, and their achievement will be evaluated in the same way as that of the other students.   This appeals to us as a significant and quite promising undertaking. We are particularly interested in the kind of information we can secure about method and effectiveness of instruction, about maximum use of staff resources and ability, and about handling large numbers of students — all problems that will become increasingly acute in the next five or six years.

The final matter to be mentioned, and certainly one of the most important, is the question of evaluation.   One of the concerns that gave initial impetus to the general education movement stemmed from a recognition of the inadequate methods of evaluating achievement then being used in most typical departmental courses. This has been a continuing concern in our program.   The Cooperative Study of Evaluation in General Education, sponsored by the American Council on Education and directed by Paul Dressel at Michigan State University, was one of the significant undertakings in the field of general education during the past ten years. Our participation in this study, along with that of many of the other institutions represented in this volume, was one of our more stimulating and helpful activities during this period.   Visits to our campus by both the director and the associate director of the Study provided the kind of stimulus that every general education program must have periodically, if it is to avoid losing its vitality and effectiveness.   This Cooperative Study of Evaluation helped us clarify our objectives, and see more clearly the nature and importance of those achievements in the Humanities that cannot be measured in terms of information alone.   It brought a renewed vitality and interest on the part of a number of staff members.   However it did not fundamentally alter the nature of our program, nor the methods of instruction and evaluation used in it.

From our point of view, by far the most significant single event at the University of Florida during recent years was the evaluation of our total general education program during the spring and summer of 1957.   Eight of the ablest men in this field in the country participated in the study.   Among the consultants who worked with us were such men as Harry C. Carman, Earl McGrath,

Sidney French, Paul Dressel, Hugh Stickler and Lennox Grey. Although Professor Grey was directly responsible for the study of the Humanities program, all the other men mentioned spent some time on our campus, examined what we were doing in the Humanities, met with us to discuss aspects of our work that were of some interest to them, and considered and approved the final Consultants' Report. The evaluation covered such things as course objectives, materials and methods being used, staff competence, methods of testing, general staff morale, student attitude and reaction, administration policy and procedures — by and large, of course, the general sort of thing one would expect in such a study. On the other hand, the broad values of this kind of evaluation, conducted by men of such professional stature, cannot be overestimated.

In our situation the general education program has been an established aspect of the University curriculum for twenty-five years. Our most serious problems at present may well be caused by the lack of flexibility, of interest in imaginative experimentation, the satisfaction with the *status quo,* the tendency to resist all change, which in time come to characterize every successful institutional development. It was this attitude so obvious in the traditional liberal arts curriculum a generation ago that made the general education movement itself necessary and desirable. It is this perhaps that now constitutes the most serious threat to the continued vitality and success of our own general education program, and I am inclined to believe for a good many others in comparable situations.

Under such circumstances, I cannot stress too strongly the importance to us of the kind of honest and intelligent evaluation undertaken here in 1957 by the group of consultants I mentioned. It is perhaps worth noting that this was not an evaluation to see whether general education was a good thing or not. Studies of this kind were made in abundance fifteen or twenty years ago, and the outcome was established plainly enough for any to see who cared to do so. Ours was rather an evaluation of the effectiveness of our own specific program of general education: to determine the extent to which it was doing the job that needed to be done here; where its major weaknesses lay; what specific improvements were needed; how these could be accomplished.

The chief fault of the Consultants' Report, as I see it, was simply that it was not critical enough of our Humanities program.

The study was of great value to us in calling for a broad re-examination of practices and objectives, of focusing attention upon weaknesses of which we were pretty much aware, and providing the necessary situation in which some desirable improvements could be undertaken.   Among other things, we improved our testing program, made the class experience more important by giving the individual staff members a larger share in determining the student's final grade, and set up a more adequate counseling program.   But the consultants, with one or two exceptions I must admit, did not expose the weaknesses of our Humanities program with the vigor that might have forced us to more significant achievement.

chapter 12

THE HUMANITIES AT WESLEYAN UNIVERSITY

*Fred B. Millett**

The article by Professor Norman O. Brown in the 1949 edition of *The Humanities in General Education,* edited by Earl J. McGrath, not only traced the history of the Humanities courses at Wesleyan University but also set forth the objectives, the organization and staffing, and the content of the courses at the time that the article appeared. The purpose of this article is to give some account of the history of the Humanities courses in the decade from 1949 to 1959. Professor Brown's survey was so substantial that this article may limit itself to indicating the respects in which the Humanities courses have remained unchanged and the respects in which they have changed.

Humanities 1-2

The objectives, the organization and staffing, and the organization of the content of this course have been substantially unchanged. With respect to the original objectives of the course, it may be of interest to quote a hitherto unpublished memorandum prepared in the spring of 1943 by Nathan M. Pusey, then Professor of Classics at Wesleyan, for the guidance of those involved in the establishment of the course and for the information of the faculty. Professor Pusey conceived the objectives of the course to be the following:

*Emeritus Professor of English, former Chairman of Humanities 1-2 and, more recently, of Humanities 3-4, Wesleyan University.

1. to stimulate interest in intellectual activity;
2. to develop powers of analytical and sensitive reading; 3. to develop accurate and effective oral and written expression; 4. to provide a preview of the nature and significance of liberal studies; 5. to introduce the student to the departmental structure of the college and to a large number of teachers at Wesleyan; 6. to foster an awareness of the unified nature of knowledge; 7. to stimulate reflection about the nature of man and of society; 8. to introduce the student to major aspects of human culture; 9. to try especially to foster an awareness of the arts and an appreciation of their role in the lives of individuals and societies; 10. to quicken the faculty of critical thinking and to set the student on the way to develop an intelligent personal philosophy.

The staff of Humanities 1-2 is still drawn from as large a number of departments as possible, since the required Freshman course is a college responsibility and not a departmental responsibility. In the spring of the year, the dean, the current chairman of the course, and the Humanities advisory committee make up a list of the members of the faculty whom they would like to have serve as discussion-group leaders. Then, the chairman of the course attempts to win the consent of the various departmental chairmen to the release of a third of some of the members' teaching time for devotion to the required Freshman course. In the main, the departments that contribute personnel most heavily are English, Philosophy, Religion, and Classics. In addition, the modern language departments are usually represented, as well as Psychology and the natural sciences, particularly Biology. Regrettably, it has never been possible to win recruits from Economics, Government, or History. In the earlier years of Humanities 1-2, these departments, to be sure, had the responsibility for staffing the Social Science 1-2 course; in more recent years, although Western Civilization 1-2 has replaced Social Science 1-2 and the Department of History has staffed the course, the members of the Departments of Economics and Government, despite their freedom from the responsibility for Social Science 1-2, have not found it in their hearts to contribute to the staffing of Humanities 1-2. In the interests of flexibility, the Humanities advisory committee has voted that no member of the faculty shall teach Humanities 1-2

for more than two consecutive years.   In the main, too, the instructor assigned to a section retains his section throughout the
college year.   I regret this practice, although there are arguments
in favor of it.   The argument in favor of a shift of instructors is
that the Freshmen in a particular section would get at least two
views of the material discussed.   They would not find themselves
in the position of the Freshman who once told me that what he
got out of the course was the Oedipus complex; apparently, his
year-long instructor had been a psychologist.

The chief change in the operation of the course has been the
disappearance of the lectures that in earlier years had marked major
turns in the cultural history from which the great works studied
had aisen.   The reason for the abandonment of occasional lectures,
usually by experts in the subject covered, was that the Freshmen
did not get enough out of the lectures to warrant the expenditure
of faculty time and energy.   I recognize that the lecture is a me-
diaeval pedagogical device, although its vogue seems likely to increase as mass-education becomes more spectacularly massive.   I
believe, however, that the lecture, if properly conceived and effectively given, can be a valuable and illuminating synthesizing device,
even for Freshmen.   I regret the disappearance of lectures from
the Humanities 1-2 program.

The major change in Humanities 1-2 has been in the works
chosen for discussion and examination.   As Professor Brown indicated, the Humanities staff elects a revisions committee each year;
its recommendations are presented to the staff and are either accepted
or rejected.   In the earlier part of the decade, for personnel reasons,
there was an almost yearly change in the chairmanship of the course,
and the resultant alterations in the reading list were sometimes
spectacular.   In the latter part of the decade, the chairmanship has
been more stable, and the persistent influence of the chairman may
have made for a greater continuity from year to year in the reading assignments.   The choice of texts for such a course is, to be
sure, a matter of trial and error; there is also the need for introducing sufficient new material to prevent the teachers in the course
from getting bored.   In my association with Humanities 1-2 and
3-4, however, I tried to adhere to the policy of keeping a text in
the course unless it had proved to be unteachable.

It may be of some interest to compare the list of readings in 1948-49 with the list of readings in 1958-59. Such a comparison shows the following results. Of the texts read in 1948-49, the following still appear in the assignment sheets for 1958-59: Sophocles, *Oedipus Rex;* Plato, *Symposium, Crito,* and *Phaedo;* the Old Testament: Genesis, Exodus, Job; the New Testament: John; Augustine, *Confessions;* Dante, *Inferno;* Marlowe, *Dr. Faustus;* Voltaire, *Candide.* For purposes of clarification, it may be well to present in two columns the changes as between 1948-49 and 1958-59. It should, however, be kept in mind that the changes, though numerous and striking, were not sudden and catastrophic, but took place gradually over a period of years.

Texts dropped	Texts added
Aeschylus, *Prometheus Unbound*	Hesiod, *Theogony*
Euripides, *Medea*	Homer, *Odyssey*
Aristotle, *Poetics*	Aeschylus, *Oresteia*
Aristotle, *De Anima* (selections)	Sophocles, *Antigone, Oedipus at Colonus*
Aristotle, *Ethics* (four books)	Euripides, *Hippolytus*
The Old Testament: Amos, Isaiah	Gide, *Theseus*
The New Testament: Luke, Matthew, Romans	Plato, *Apology*
Luther, *Christian Liberty*	Lucretius, *On the Nature of the Universe*
Bunyan, *Pilgrim's Progress*	Apuleius, *The Golden Ass*
Montaigne, *Essays*	Cellini, *Autobiography*
Shakespeare, *Hamlet*	Shakespeare, *King Lear*
Descartes, *Discourse on Method*	Twain, *Huckleberry Finn*
Goethe, *Faust*	Dostoevski, *The Brothers Karamazov*
Mill, *Autobiography*	Kafka, *Short Stories*
Whitehead, *Science and the Modern World*	Marx, *The Communist Manifesto*

Texts added, continued
Lenin, *State and Revolution*
Malraux, *Man's Fate*
Wiener, *The Human Use of Human Beings*

The Humanities Laboratory

The required Humanities Laboratory has always been an unusual feature of the Humanities program at Wesleyan. The germinal idea out of which the Laboratory program grew was Professor Pusey's, and it might be well to quote the words he chose to express his conception of the role of the Laboratory work. In 1944, shortly after the initiation of the Humanities 1-2 course, he wrote:

Our belief is that the traditional college education has been too exclusively verbal and has failed therefore to exercise and develop all of the student's mental capacity, specifically perhaps, his imagination and general awareness. In seeking to correct this oversight we have established a laboratory program to accompany the Humanities course, in which it is required that each student spend several hours each week in the practice of some art. The possibilities open to the students are in music, chiefly participation in the choir, though instrumental work and even composition can be provided for; the fine arts in the narrow sense of the word such as drawing, painting, sculpture, engraving, printing, wood-carving and the like; imaginative writing and play production."

The rationale for the required Humanities Laboratory is subtle and elusive, and certainly few of the Freshmen who now participate in the work for a semester grasp or retain its theoretical justification. The problem of the correlation of the great books portion of the course and the laboratory work has been considered and re-considered repeatedly. The obvious solution to the problem would have been the abandonment of the laboratory and the substitution of lectures on the fine arts to coordinate chronologically with the reading and discussion of great books. This solution, however, would have meant the complete negation of the purposes stated by Professor Pusey. To a degree, the problem has been simplified since 1952 by the reduction of the options, namely, "music, graphic arts, theater, and verbal expression," to the single requirement of laboratory work in the graphic arts, directed by members of the Department of Art. On occasion, instructors have attempted to work out some chronological correlation between the reading and discussion portion of the course and the laboratory work. Essentially, however, the Humanities Laboratory, or the Humanities Workshop, as it has come to be called, has become a practical introduction to the problems that the graphic artist faces, the elements in visual design, the choice and use of materials. Despite the difficulty or impossibility of establishing any meaningful relation between the reading and discussion course and the laboratory work, the persons concerned with the course still feel that the laboratory work is valuable in and of itself, whether or not it is relevant to the rest of the required course.

The Integrated Program for Freshmen

In 1952, an integrated program for thirty or forty selected Freshmen was initiated that involved a basic modification of the required Humanities 1-2 course for this group. A number of the faculty who had long been associated with the Freshman Humanities course had come to feel that something more might be done to make the freshman program coherent and significant. The normal Freshman program comprised the required Humanities 1-2 course, the required Freshman English course and three electives, one of which was usually a modern language and another a laboratory science. (Pre-medical students usually had two science courses among their electives.) English 1-2 was a fairly conventional reading and writing course, with one or two research papers. The normal Freshman program, therefore, involved five different intellectual enterprises, no one of which had any obvious relationship to any other; the centrifugal effect made for incoherence and meaninglessness. Permission was obtained from the Curriculum Committee to initiate an integrated program which would, it was hoped, give a greater coherence to the Freshman's intellectual experience. The students who were chosen to participate in this program, in addition to two electives, usually a modern language and a laboratory science, took a special variety of the Humanities 1-2 course, which consisted of readings in philosophy, from the Greeks to Whitehead. These students also took a special variety of English course; at least it was called an English course, for the simple reason that the literary reading and teaching were done in English. The content of this course consisted of selections — usually whole books — from Greek to contemporary European literature. In the first semester, the reading included Greek tragedy and comedy, Dante's *Purgatorio,* and three plays of Shakespeare. In the second semester, the reading included three neoclassical French plays, an eighteenth-century English novel, works of Keats, Dostoevski's *Crime and Punishment,* (or Thomas Mann's *The Magic Mountain*) and Gide's *Theseus.* The theme-writing done in this course took the form of critical essays based on the books discussed. The students in this program, moreover, were required to take Western Civilization 1-2, a course tracing in outline the development of Western Europe from the Greeks to the present time. This course was required in order to furnish the students in this program an historical frame-work for their readings in philosophy and literature. Finally, the students in the integrated program were required to take the Humanities laboratory throughout the year, and not merely for one semester.

Students were chosen for this program on the basis of their prospective interest in it and on the recommendation of their advisors. The program was announced, but not featured, in the material sent to entering Freshmen and they were permitted to sign up for this program tentatively before meeting with their advisors. The program, however, got such excellent word-of-mouth publicity from students who had already taken it that it was always necessary to eliminate some of the less promising applicants, since only two sections of the special courses in Humanities and English could be manned. In the main, the interest of the entering Freshmen and the judgment of their advisors proved reliable guides in the selection of students. The major criterion for selecting students was their potential ability to handle a year's reading in philosophy fruitfully. If, by the end of the first semester, a student (or his instructor) felt that he was not going to be able to profit from the exacting philosophical reading, it was possible for the student to revert to the usual English and Humanities sections.

The faculty for this program was chosen in much the same way as that of the regular Humanities 1-2 course, that is to say, it was not inevitable that the philosophy sections should be taught by members of the Department of Philosophy or the literature sections by members of the Department of English. It was necessary, however, that the faculty involved in this program should believe in it or should want to try their hands at it; the attitude of the faculty-member was, therefore, the primary consideration.

The members of the faculty who have been involved in the program would agree, I believe, that it has been singularly successful. They believe, for instance, that the Integrated Program does give at least a degree of coherence and significance to the Freshmen's intellectual experience. A very large majority of the students who, perhaps naturally, tend to be the better students in the Freshmen class, at least of those oriented towards the Humanities, have also been enthusiastic about the program. One member of the Philosophy Department said repeatedly that his experience with the special Humanities course had been one of the most rewarding that he had ever had. The members of the faculty, to be sure, were always concerned as to whether or not integration was taking place. They felt, of course, that integration, if it did take place, must occur in the student's mind and not in the mind of a member of the faculty. They did, however, experiment with various devices to encourage integration. On some occasions, all or nearly all the members of the faculty teaching the Humanities, English, and Western Civilization sections of the program met with all the students in the program to discuss some work or some concept — like the Renaissance — from their diverse points of view. The most exciting session I ever attended, however, was one in which students assumed all the responsibility. Five students read short papers interpreting some aspect of Thomas Mann's *The Magic Mountain*. The papers struck me as amazing productions for Freshmen, and they induced a lively and extended discussion from students on the floor.

Humanities 3-4

The most significant change in the Humanities program at Wesleyan in the past decade has been the basic alteration in the content of Humanities 3-4. The initial conception of Humanities 3-4 was that it should be an elective that would complement the offerings in the required Humanities 1-2 course by giving the students who elected it the opportunity to read and discuss additional major works in the literature, philosophy, religion, and science of the Western tradition. The contemplated change in the content of Humanities 3-4 was initiated by Professor Brown's suggestion to me that the course might be made more challenging and more broadly educative if a portion of it at least were to be devoted to works from outside the Western tradition. He also made some specific suggestions as to works that might be considered for inclusion in the course. At the time, I was the chairman of Humanities 3-4 and, on consulting with my colleagues in the course, I found that they were prepared to experiment with the suggestion made by Professor Brown. Accordingly, we announced that the first semester of the Humanities 3-4 course in 1954-55 would consist of readings in the literature, philosophy, and religion of the Far East, and I spent a considerable time during the summer of 1954 rounding up suitable and available texts.

Here, inevitably, a more difficult problem presented itself than that of obtaining suitable texts for a course in great books from the Western tradition. We had decided to build the first semester course out of three units: China, Japan, and India, and each of these units offered slightly different problems when it came to the selection of texts. Of the three units, China presented the least difficulty, in the first place because of the work that Lin Yutang had done as a mediator between the culture of the East and of the West, and, in the second place, because of the number of translations that have been made from the rich stores of Chinese poetry. Japan presented a somewhat more difficult problem at the time, since there were far fewer available translations from Japanese poetry and prose. Fortunately, a paper-covered edition of the first volume of Arthur Waley's translation of Lady Murasaki's *The Tale of Genji* appeared. The selection of works representing Indian culture was somewhat more simple. Readings in the Upanishads, in the translation by William Butler Yeats and Shree Pruohit Swami, to be sure, had to be imported, but in the Liberal Arts Press "Library of Religion" there was available Clarence H. Hamilton's excellent anthology, *Buddhism, a religion of infinite compassion* and in "Everyman's Library," Romesh H. Dutt's condensed translation of the *Ramayana* and the *Mahabharata*. The nature of these translations, however, points up one of the crying problems of inter-cultural communication. These two great semi-sacred books of India have never been satisfactorily translated. Dutt's translations not only are in the trying metre of "Locksley Hall" but reduce their great originals to a tenth of their original size! Certainly, from these translations the English reader can get only a very imperfect impression of epics that are a part of the living culture of India.

Our experience with the Far Eastern course was so exciting and stimulating that in 1955-56 we dropped the readings from Western civilization almost completely and devoted the first semester to the Far East and the second semester to the Near East. Thus, with the exception of Homer's *Odyssey* and the Bible, the content of the course had been changed completely. In the Near Eastern course, the problem of suitable and available texts was somewhat simpler than in the case of the Far Eastern course, although the epic again presented a problem.   Since there is no satisfactory available translation of Firdausi's *Shah Namah* (*Book of Kings*), the very existence of which most Western readers are quite unaware, we were forced to limit our readings in this epic to the brief selections in A. J. Arberry's anthology of translations, *Persian Poems*, which "Everyman's Library" had, fortunately for us, brought out in 1954.   For Babylonian and Assyrian culture, the Library of Religion again furnished us a useful book, Isaac Mendelsohn's *Religions of the Ancient New East*.   For Egyptian culture, there was the charming, but rather scrappy, anthology, *Never to Die*, edited by Josephine Mayer and T. Prideaux.   Homer's *Odyssey* was chosen to be read against the background of the Indian epics and as a precursor to Firdausi's *Shah Namah*, and the Bible gave us what we wanted for early Jewish and Christian culture. Arabic culture was satisfactorily represented by the *Persian Poems* already mentioned and by a selection from Sir Richard Burton's translation of the *Arabian Nights Entertainments*, although its pretence to being unexpurgated cannot be sustained when it is compared with the great Madrus-Mathers translation.

The operation of the new Humanities 3-4 course does not differ significantly from that of the old course.   Most of the meetings are group-dicussions; there are a few lectures, primarily in the visual arts produced by the cultures considered.   We have found it profitable to combine the discussion-groups at the end of each unit of the course and devote an hour to a general discussion in which all the instructors and students have a chance to participate.   This discussion ranges freely over the readings that have been considered previously in the smaller groups.   Grades are determined by the student's role in the discussions and their performance on hour-examinations at the end of each unit and on a three-hour final examination.

The problem of discovering suitable teaching personnel for a Far and Near East course is, to be sure, much more acute than that of selecting a teaching-staff for a course in the great books of the Western tradition.   Here, at least in a small college, there are no experts to be called on, except for certain lectures in the visual arts, and sometimes these had to be imported.   If faculty members hesitate to play the role of the intelligent amateur in a course in which Homer, Dante, Shakespeare, Voltaire, Marx, and Whitehead are discussed, how much more audacity is required to tackle works from completely alien cultures! Fortunately, however, a considerable number of the Wesleyan faculty had through their experience in the required Freshman course habituated themselves to the concept of an intelligent reader discussing strange works with less experienced student-readers; fortunately, too, it was not impossible to find adventuresome souls who were not daunted by the bold experiment.

The new Humanities course, it must be admitted, did not attract so substantial a portion of the student-body as the earlier Humanities course had. It called for adventuresome students as well as faculty. About forty students elected the course each year, and, of these, two discussion-groups were formed. In a way, this greater selectivity on the part of the students simplified the choice of teachers, since it was possible to run the course with two discussion-group leaders and a chairman, who prepared the assignment sheets, sat in on the general discussions, and participated in the preparation of the hour-examinations and the final examination.

It can be asserted without question, however, that the new Far and Near Eastern course has proved to be a very exciting experience for both the faculty and the students who participate. I found it the most intellectually and aesthetically rewarding experience of my later years of teaching. I felt that until I taught this course I had been living in a magnificently designed hall with huge picture-windows on one of its long sides opening out on the landscapes that the great books in the Western tradition present to one. Then, suddenly, hitherto almost unsuspected windows were opened up through the opposite wall, and strange and wonderful new landscapes — Chinese, Japanese, Indian, Arabic — were enchantingly revealed. And even though my enthusiasm for the course may not have been shared by all who have participated in it in recent years, there would seem to be ample justification for its existence in a period when the world has shrunken to an unbelievable smallness and international relations have become so complicated that the fate of America is intimately involved and may ultimately be decided by its relationship with what have seemed to be extremely remote and almost inaccessibly alien cultures.

Conclusions

Since I was intimately involved with the initiation of the required Freshman Humanities course and served as its chairman in some of its earlier years and ultimately became the chairman of Humanities 3-4, I may be permitted perhaps to suggest here some of the results, unfavorable and favorable, of the presence of these courses in the Wesleyan curriculum.   Any honest person would be forced to admit that in every Freshman class there are a considerable number of students who are not fired with intellectual excitement by their enforced contact with the great works of the Western tradition or by their practical experience with the methods and materials of the visual arts in the Humanities Laboratory, but the degree of failure, whatever it may be, would hold for almost any course the student was required or elected to take.   Certainly, almost everyone who has taught the Humanities courses would agree that bringing Freshmen into contact with major writers and thinkers is in and of itself a defensible enterprise and that it has added a great deal to the significance of the Freshmen Program at Wesleyan.   Certainly, too, the best of the Freshmen have demonstrated the creative intellectual excitement that can result from these contacts.   Members of the faculty — especially members of the Department of Philosophy — have testified that, since the initiation of the required Humanities course, students bring to their later studies a richness of intellectual background — what used to be called a more complex "apperception-mass" — than they did before the creation of this course.

In my judgment, the work that the Freshmen have been required to do in the Humanities Laboratory, especially since its restriction to the visual arts, has had a great deal to do with the increasing interest that students now manifest in these arts.   This interest, of course, has been aided by the presence on the faculty of creative artists whose ways of working and whose productions the students can observe.   Objectively, another result of the Humanities Laboratory has been the discovery by students themselves of hitherto unsuspected creative gifts.   To me, personally, one of the most exciting indirect results of the Humanities Laboratory requirement has been the excellent creative work produced by a few students whose first practical contact with the visual arts may have occurred in the Humanities Laboratory.

But perhaps the most important result of the establishment and persistence of the Humanities courses has been their educative effect on the members of the faculty who have taught the course. This effect derives, primarily, from the contact of the faculty, in the process of teaching the course, with major thinkers and writers outside their field of specialization. The effect has been enhanced by the weekly discussion-meetings of the Freshmen Humanities staff, occasions that encourage an intellectual interchange among members from very different departments, an interchange that would never have taken place, even in a small college, had it not been for this course and these occasions. One can hardly expect the humanistic spirit to permeate a student-body until it has permeated the faculty that teach the student-body. I personally feel that my own liberal education began with my association with the Humanities course for Freshmen; that education began a little late — I was fifty-three at the time — but, in this case as in others, it was better late than never.

Humanities 1

Texts

Hesiod	Theogony, tr. Brown, Lib. Arts
Homer	Odyssey, tr. Rieu, Penguin
Aeschylus	Oresteia, tr. Vellacott, Penguin
Sophocles	Three Theban Plays, tr. Banks, Oxford
Euripides	Alcestis and Other Plays, tr. Vellacott, Penguin
Geist, ed.	French Stories and Tales, Pocket Library
Plato	Great Dialogues of Plato, Mentor
Lucretius	On the Nature of the Universe, tr. Latham, Penguin
The Bible	King James or Revised Standard
Apuleius	The Golden Ass, tr. Graves, Pocket Books
Augustine	Confessions, tr. Sheed, Sheed and Ward

Meetings	Assignments	Meetings	Assignments
1-2	Theogony	24-26	On the Nature of the Universe
3-7	Odyssey		
8-10	Oresteia	27-29	Genesis
11-15	Theban Plays	30-32	Job
16	Hippolytus	33-34	Golden Ass
17	Gide Theseus	35-37	St. John
18-23	Plato, Dialogues	38-40	Augustine, Confessions

Humanities 2

1958-9

Dante, Inferno, Ciardi, tr. Mentor
Cellini, Autobiography
Marlowe, Dr. Faustus, Crofts Classics

Shakespeare, King Lear, Crofts Classics
The Poetry of Pope, Crofts Classics
Voltaire, Candide, Crofts Classics
Twain, Huckleberry Finn, Rinehart
Dostoyevsky, The Brothers Karamazov, Modern Library, College ed.
Kafka, Short Stories, Modern Library
Marx, Communist Manifesto, Little Marx Library
Lenin, The State and Revolution, Little Marx Library
Malraux, Man's Fate, Modern Library
Wiener, The Human Use of Human Beings, Anchor

Meetings	Assignments	Meetings	Assignments
1-7	Dante	22-31	Dostoyevsky
8-9	Cellini	32-35	Kafka
10-11	Marlowe	36	Marx
12-15	Shakespeare	37	Lenin
16	Pope	38-41	Malraux
17-18	Voltaire	42-43	Wiener
19-21	Twain		

Humanities 3

1958-9

Texts

The Ten Principal Upanishads. Yeats & Shree Purohit Swami, N.Y., Macmillan, 1938.

Buddhism, A Religion of Infinite Compassion ed. by Clarence H. Hamilton, Liberal Arts Press, N.Y., 1952.

The Ramayana and Mahabharata ed. R. Dutt, Everymans, N.Y., 1953.

The Song of God: Bhagavad-Gita tr. by Swami Prabhavananda and Christopher Isherwood, Mentor, N.Y., 1954.

The Wisdom of Confucius, ed. by Lin Yutang, Modern Lib., N.Y., 1938.

From the Chinese ed. by R. C. Trevelyan, Oxford, London, 1945.

The Way of Life According to Lao Tzu tr. Witter Bynner, John Day, N.Y., 1944.

The Tale of Genji by Lady Murasaki tr. by Arthur Waley, Doubleday Anchor, N.Y., 1955.

Anthology of Japanese Literature ed. by Donald Keene, Grove Press, N.Y., 1955.

Meetings	Assignments	Meetings	Assignments
1-5	Upanishads	23-24	Lao Tzu
6-9	Buddhism	26	Lecture: "Chinese Art and Culture"
10	Lecture: "Hindu and Buddhist Art"	27	Hour Examination
11-13	The Ramayana	28-29	The Tale of Genji
14-17	Bhagavad-Gita	30-32	Japanese Anthology
18-20	Wisdom of Confucius	33	Lecture: Chinese and Japanese Culture as Seen in Their Music
21	From the Chinese Early Chinese Poems	34-36	Japanese Anthology
22	From the Chinese Later Chinese Poems	37	Lecture: "Japanese Art"

Humanities 4
1958-9

Texts

Religions of the Ancient Near .East, ed. by Isaac Mendelsohn. "The Library of Religion." The Liberal Arts Press.

Never to Die, the Egyptians in their own words, selected and arranged with commentary by Josephine Mayer and T. Prodeaux.

Seven Odes, ed. A. H. Arberry. Macmillan, 1957.

Euripides, *The Bacchae*. Oxford.

The Meaning of the Glorious Koran, trans. by Mohammed Marmaduke Pickthall. "Mentor Books."

The Living Talmud, the wisdom of the fathers, tr. by Judah Goldin. "Mentor Books."

Persian Poems, ed. A. J. Arberry. "Everyman's Library."

Tales from the Arabian Nights, tr. by Sir Richard Burton. "Pocket Library."

Meet-ings	Assign-ments	Meet-ings	Assign-ments
1-8	*Religions of the Ancient Near East*	20-22	Euripides *The Bacchae*
		23	Lecture "The Koran."
9	*The Bible*: Genesis Books 1-9, 37-47	24-28	*The Koran*
		29-32	*The Living Talmud*
10-13	*Never to Die*	33-37	*Persian Poems*
14	Hour examination	38-41	*Tales from the Arabian Nights*
15-19	*The Seven Odes*		

chapter **13**

HUMANITIES IN GENERAL EDUCATION AT MASSACHUSETTS INSTITUTE OF TECHNOLOGY

*Howard R. Bartlett**

The humanities have been a part of education at M.I.T. since its founding. The first catalogue (1865-1866) stated as the second objective of the new institution: "To furnish such general education, founded upon the Mathematical, Physical, and Natural Sciences, English and other Modern Languages, and Mental and Political Science, as shall form a fitting preparation for any of the departments of active life."

Just over thirty years later President Walker reminded the alumni that one of the four fundamental and far-reaching beliefs upon which M.I.T. was founded was "a belief that, in addition to scientific and technical studies and exercises, which tend to make men resolute, exact and strong, there should be given in every such school, at least a moderate amount of those philosophical and cultural studies and exercises which tend to make man also broad and liberal." He continued with an opinion which unfortunately has not always found support in the faculties of schools of engineering and science; namely, that "liberal studies should be severely pursued; and that, for the highest results, the more liberalizing the tendency of any intellectual exercise, the more it is to be desired that it should be followed with energy, with closeness of application, with punctiliousness of performance, with careful scrutiny of the results obtained."

---

*Head, Department of Humanities.

These expressions of support for the liberal studies have been implemented over the subsequent years in many different ways. On the whole, however, the major emphasis for much of the time has been on subjects which were clearly and directly useful to the engineer — English composition, public speaking, report writing, and economics. The less utilitarian subjects — literature, history, philosophy –– received modest attention, but they were justified on the grounds that they would help the engineer to understand and handle people more effectively and would also make him socially more acceptable.

Within the last twenty years a significant change has taken place in the attitude toward and the role assigned to the liberal studies. As engineers and scientists have become increasingly involved in decisions which affect our conduct of national and international affairs they have realized that technical competence alone is not sufficient. They recognize that without awareness, knowledge, and understanding of the human and social dimensions of our culture future engineers and scientists will be unprepared to make their maximum contribution to society. As a result the utilitarian subjects are still available, but they do not constitute the core of liberal studies.

The question is no longer whether scientific studies or liberal studies are more important; it is rather how within a necessarily limited time can we make the humanities and social sciences an integral and rigorous part of engineering education? How can we achieve the most effective balance between two indispensable components?

The present answers to these questions at M.I.T. stem from a two-year educational survey completed in 1949 by a faculty-appointed committee aided by an auxiliary committee on General Education. A substantial majority of the members of the latter committee was engineers and scientists.

Although the committee recommended an increase in the humanities and social science requirement from eight semester subjects to ten, the faculty voted to retain the eight-semester requirement which had existed for many years. At the same time, however, it permitted students for the first time to elect two additional subjects in these areas in place of two engineering or science electives.

To assure some measure of breadth and depth in the minimum program of eight semesters, the first four are devoted to a general introduction to the humanities. The student has no choice in his first year; in his second year he may elect to continue his studies with the focus primarily on western Europe or he may shift his attention to developments in the United States.

At the end of the second year the student must elect a field for further study. Ten fields are now available to him: history, philosophy, literature, modern languages (literature courses in either French or German), music, economics, political science, labor relations, psychology, and visual arts. Within one of these areas the student elects three semester subjects during his junior and senior years. The remaining subject (to complete the eight-term requirement) is usually selected from a second area. The only limitation upon the choice of field is that students in most of the engineering departments must take one term of economic principles.

This program provides certain things which we believe are highly desirable in a school of science and engineering:

1. It calls for continued study in the humanities or social sciences through the four undergraduate years.

2. It is clearly humanistic in content and spirit except perhaps for one or two debatable areas in the junior-senior elective program. Even the first three terms of study of a foreign language may not be counted toward fulfilling the eight-term requirement.

3. It provides for some study above the introductory level in at least one area of the humanities or social sciences.

4. It brings every student in contact with a substantial number of the great literary, philosophical, and historical works which have helped to mold western ideas and values.

5. It is flexible and allows a student wide choice in his last two years as to area of study and the subjects within that area.

This four-year program in the humanities and social sciences *together with* the basic subjects in mathematics, physics, and chemistry constitute the general education of the M.I.T. student. The only component which requires more detailed attention for this volume is the two-year introductory course in the humanities.

Like many general education courses this one began as an experiment with one or two sections. It was gradually extended until it replaced a conventional course in freshmen composition and a sophomore course in history. Originally we attempted to lay a foundation for later study in both the humanities and social sciences, but the difficulties proved insurmountable within the class hours at our disposal, and we regretfully limited its scope to the humanities. Since that major change the course has been altered from year to year only by minor revisions in the assigned readings.

The following outlines are those for 1958-59. They indicate the major divisions of the course, the items read by all students, and an abbreviated but representative list of optional items which each instructor draws upon as he wishes to meet the needs and interests of his students. The longer works, such as Thucydides, *The Peloponnesian War,* are not necessarily read in their entirety, but the assignments are sufficiently inclusive to give the student a reliable impression of the work as a whole.

FIRST YEAR
First Term

Topic I: Greek Ideas and Values

    Required:

        Sophocles, *Antigone*
        Thucydides, *The Peloponnesian War*
        Plato, *Republic*

    Optional:

        Aeschylus, *Oresteia*
        Euripides, *The Bacchae*
        Aristophanes, *The Clouds* or *Lysistrata*
        Aristotle, *The Poetics,* or selections from the *Ethics*

Topic: II.   Christian Ideas and Values of the Middle Ages

    Required:

        St. Augustine, *Confessions*
        Dante, *The Divine Comedy*

    Optional:

        Selections from the *Gospels,* morality plays, and the philosophy of St. Thomas Aquinas
        Tristan and Iseult
        St. Bonaventura, *The Mind's Road to God*

Second Term

Topic I: The Sixteenth Century

    Required:

        Machiavelli, *The Prince*
        Selections from Calvin's *Institutes*
        Luther, *Christian Liberty*
        Shakespeare, *King Lear*

Optional:
> Sir Thomas More, *Utopia*
> Marlowe, *Dr. Faustus*
> Rabelais, *Gargantua*
> Other Shakespeare plays and sixteenth-century English poetry

Topic II: The Seventeenth Century

Required:
> Galileo, *Dialogue on Great World Systems*
> Hobbes, *Leviathan*
> Locke, *Second Treatise on Civil Government*

Optional:
> Descartes, *Discourse on Method*
> Pascal, *Pensees*
> Spinoza, *Ethics* and *Improvement of the Understanding*
> Selections from Milton

SECOND YEAR — Option A: Modern Western Ideas and Values

First Term

Topic I: Enlightenment

Required:
> Voltaire, *Candide*
> Hume, *Inquiry Concerning Human Understanding*
> Rousseau, *Confessions* and *Social Contract*
> Kant, *Prolegomena* or *Fundamental Principles of the
>   Metaphysic of Morals* or *Critique of Practical Reason*

Optional:
> Smith, *Wealth of Nations*
> Hume, *An Inquiry Concerning the Principles of Morality*

Topic II: Romanticism

Required:
> Burke, *Reflections*
> Hegel, *Reason in History*
> English Romantic Poets in *Immortal Poems of the English
>   Language*
> Stendhal, *Scarlet and Black* or *Charterhouse of Parma*

Optional:
> Bronte, *Wuthering Heights*
> Flaubert, *Madame Bovary*
> Turgenev, *Fathers and Children*

Topic III: Liberalism

Required:
> Mill, *On Liberty* or *Autobiography* or *Utilitarianism*

Optional:
> Dickens, *Hard Times*

Second Term

Topic I: Transvaluation of "Traditional" Values

Required:
> Ibsen, "An Enemy of the People" in *Six Plays by Ibsen*
> Nietzsche, *Beyond Good and Evil*
> Marx, *Communst Manifesto*

Optional:
>   Hitler, *Mein Kampf*
>   Stalin, *Foundations of Leninism*
>   Koestler, *Darkness at Noon*
>   Lenin, *The State and Revolution*

Topic II: Evolution and the Unconscious Mind

Required:
>   Darwin, *Origin of Species*
>   Freud, *General Introduction to Psychoanalysis*

Optional:
>   T. H. Huxley, *Essays*
>   Readings in some of the Social Darwinists

Topic III: New Types of Consciousness — The Meaning of Meaning

Required:
>   James, *Essays in Pragmatism*
>   Ayer, *Language, Truth, and Logic*
>   Langer, *Philosophy in a New Key*

Topic IV: New Types of Consciousness — New Views of the Human Condition

Required:
>   Kaufman, *Existentialism*
>   Cassirer, *Essay on Man*
>   Jaspers, *Man in the Modern World*

Optional:
>   Kierkegaard, *Fear and Trembling; The Sickness Unto Death*
>   Buber, *The Writings of Martin Buber*
>   Maritain, *Existence and the Existent*
>   Niebuhr, *An Interpretation of Christian Ethics*

Topic V: New Types of Consciousness — New Form and Consciousness in the Arts

Required:
>   Joyce, *Portait of the Artist as a Young Man*
>   Mann, *Death in Venice*
>   Hemingway, *The Sun Also Rises*
>   Lawrence, *Sons and Lovers*
>   Gide, *The Immoralist* and *Lafcadio's Adventures*
>   Camus, *The Stranger*
>   Eliot, *The Waste Land and Other Poems*

SECOND YEAR — Option B: The United States: Men and Issues

First Term

Topic I: The Making of the Constitution

Required:
>   Locke, *Essay Concerning Human Understanding*
>   Franklin, *Autobiography*
>   Koch and Peden, *The Life and Selected Writings of Jefferson*
>   *Federalist Papers*

> Birley, *Speeches and Documents in American History*
> *Pamphlet* (Prepared by members of the staff)
>> Selections from writings of John Adams, Alexander Hamilton, John Calhoun, and George Fitzhugh

Optional:
> Becker, *Declaration of Independence*
> *Old South Leaflets*, "Stamp Act Congress", Washington's "Letters on the Constitution"
> Commager, *Documents*, "McCullough v. Maryland", "Gibbon v. Ogden", "Trustees of Dartmouth College v. Woodward"

Topic II: The Coming of the Civil War

Required:
> Emerson, "The Over-Soul", "Self-Reliance", "The American Scholar", "The Fugitive Slave Law"
> *Old South Leaflets*, Parker, "Dangers from Slavery", "First Lincoln-Douglas Debate"
> Olmstead, *Cotton Kingdom* (selections)
> Rozwenc, *The Compromise of 1850*, (Selections by Benton, Clay, Calhoun, Webster, and Seward)
> Lincoln, *Selected Speeches, Messages and Letters*

Optional:
> Twain, *The Adventures of Huckleberry Finn*
> Whitman, *Leaves of Grass* (Selections)
> Thoreau, "Walden", "Civil Disobedience"
> Melville, "Poems of the Civil War"
> Turner, "The Significance of the Frontier"

Second Term

Topic I: The Challenge of the New Industrial Society

Required:
> *Pamphlet* (Compiled by the staff), Jones, "Railroad Transportation", Jenks, "The Michigan Salt Association"
> *Roosevelt, Wilson and the Trusts* (Amherst Pamphlet), Jones, "United States Steel"
> *Democracy and the Gospel of Wealth* (Amherst Pamphlet), essays by Carnegie, Lawrence, Clark, Sumner, Pierce, Ghent, and Veblen

Optional:
> Selections from: Darwin, *Origin of Species*, Hofstadter, *Social Darwinism*, James, *Essays in Pragmatism*
> Norris, *The Octopus*
> Howells, *The Rise of Silas Lapham*
> Dreiser, *The Titan*
> Sinclair, The Jungle
> Steinbeck, *The Grapes of Wrath*
> Odets, *Waiting for Lefty*

Topic II: The Challenge of the New World Order

Required:
> *Pamphlet* (Compiled by the Staff), selections on the growth and regulation of the corporation, Congressional hearings and debates on the question of unemployment, on the Employment Act of 1946 and on Lend-Lease.

Langer and Gleason, *The Undeclared War*
Kissinger, *Nuclear Weapons and Foreign Policy*
Optional:
Selected chapters from Rae and Mahoney, *United States in World History*, or Link, *American Epoch*, or Pratt, *History of United States Foreign Policy*

As the reading lists clearly indicate the course makes no pretense of being a survey of western civilization or an introductory course in any academic discipline. It is one plan for bringing students in contact with some of the great minds of the past as they have dealt with the fundamental problems of human existence.

The goal of the first two years is not "coverage" or the acquisition of factual knowledge, although a substantial amount of both is a result of the experience. The primary objective is understanding of the human being's relation to religion, society, politics, and science. The continual search is for self-knowledge through a close examination of what men of great intellectual power have said about human beings and the range of possibilities inherent in human existence. Through an examination of the bases on which men make and have made responsible moral, philosophical, historical, and aesthetic judgments, the student develops some awareness of his potentialities and limitations. By examining ideas in action at particularly significant periods in man's history he enlarges his perspective and increases his understanding of some of the forces which have created the society in which his life and personality are being shaped.

In addition to this general goal the course has more specific objectives. The first is to teach the student to read analytically, to think clearly, and to ask penetrating questions about his reading. Rather than accept as truthful and relevant or reject as false and meaningless what any particular author has to say, the student is urged to look for the underlying assumptions on which the author has built his case. The search is again for understanding of what the author is saying and why he is saying it.

A second objective is to train the student to write clear, orderly, convincing prose. Since we have no required course in composition, the written problems in the humanities course are of great importance. They are an integral part of the work of the first two years, and the quality of a student's written work is an important factor in determining his standing at the end of each semester. Students seriously deficient in their knowledge of the mechanics of composition are strongly urged to attend a composition workshop which is conducted by the department. In cases of exceptionally poor performance a student receives a composition deficiency at the end of his second year. Unless this is removed in a manner specified by the department, a student's degree may be withheld.

A third objective is to introduce the student to materials drawn from several disciplines in order that he may have a better basis for his choice of area for more concentrated study in his third and fourth years. If he elects a field in the humanities he has a substantial foundation upon which to build; if he elects one of the social sciences, he is unfortunately less directly prepared for more specialized study.

In both options of the second year the general objectives remain the same. Because of the character of the content, however, and the fact that the students have had the experience of a general approach, the emphases shift somewhat. The option designated as "Western Ideas and Values" gives increased attention to the distinct disciplines represented and to the way men think in those disciplines. The student looks at the ideas and values *per se;* he examines them critically, weighs and evaluates them in an effort to assess their validity and to understand the power of ideas and values in man's life.

The second option, "The United States: Men and Issues," not only examine ideas and values in terms of their intrinsic worth but also as motivations of men in specific historical situations. The greater emphasis upon the latter constitutes the major distinction in approach in the two options.

Although the visual arts do not play a large role in our approach to general education, they are not ignored. Carefully prepared exhibits on Greece, The Middle Ages, and the Renaissance are placed in the exhibition gallery to coincide with the classroom discussion of the periods. Each instructor takes his students to the gallery and discusses the exhibit with them. If he wishes the aid of specialists in the fine arts for these gallery talks, it is available to him. Eventually we shall prepare exhibits for the later periods covered by the course and also provide the instructors with reproductions and sets of slides which may conveniently be used in the regular classrooms.

Instruction in the course takes place three hours a week in sections of about twenty-five students. There are no formal lectures and so far as possible the discussion procedure prevails. Although the staff receives frequent memoranda suggesting ways in which readings can be used effectively, we make no effort to achieve uniformity. Each instructor has full responsibility for the conduct of his sections, and the fact that historians, philosophers, and men trained in literature participate in the course assures a variety of approaches which we feel is wholly desirable. Since the staff are with one exception all members of the Department of Humanities, they are in close association with one another and meet both formally and informally to discuss their experiences and suggest new approaches.

The exception is a member of the Department of Modern Languages who teaches a special section of the course in French for students who have had adequate preparation in the language before entering M.I.T. and wish to obtain greater mastery of it. About twenty students each year elect this special section, and with few exceptions continue through the two years.

We base our evaluation of the student on four items: the quality of his writing; his contribution to the class discussion; his performance on one or more hour examinations; and a three-hour final examination at the end of each semester. Our examinations are all of the essay type.

The academic program in the humanities is supplemented by a very strong extracurricular program in music and the drama and by an extraordinarily successful lecture series administered wholly by a student organization.

chapter 14

THE HUMANITIES AT THE CALIFORNIA INSTITUTE OF TECHNOLOGY*

Hallett D. Smith**

I. *The Quality of the Students.*

Since the last report, the quality of the students entering the California Institute of Technology has increased very markedly. The reasons for this increase are that the size of the entering class has remained stable while the number of applicants has gone up sharply, and also the current emphasis on science in our culture generally seems to have drawn brighter boys in larger numbers into science. The easiest measurement to use, and probably the most reliable one, is the scores on the College Entrance Examination Board aptitude and achievement tests. Taking only the five-year period 1954-1959, we find that the mean *Verbal* Aptitude score of all applicants to Caltech in 1954 was at the 73rd percentile on a nation-wide basis; in 1959 it was at the 90th percentile nationally. These are scores for the whole body of applicants (1000 in 1954, 1484 in 1959). When the highly selective admissions process has taken place, the resulting freshman class shows of course even higher scores. The mean *Verbal* Aptitude score for the class entering in 1954 was at the 88th percentile; in 1959 it is at the 97th percentile nationally. The Verbal Aptitude test is supposed

---

*Note: This account will take for granted the description of the place of the Humanities in a scientific and engineering curriculum, particularly the version of it presented by Clinton K. Judy in the first edition of this book. Emphasis will be given here only to changes and developments in the Humanities program at the California Institute of Technology in the last ten years.

**Chairman Division of the Humanities.

to measure general intelligence and is commonly taken to be a good indicator of capacity to do college work in the liberal arts.

It seems evident that Caltech students, even though they are primarily oriented toward science or engineering and are working toward a B. S. degree in one of these areas, have a very high capacity for work in the Humanities. But capacity and performance do not always coincide, so we should look at the scores on College Board achievement tests, specifically the one in English. The mean score in English for the whole body of applicants was at the 59th percentile in 1954 and at the 71st percentile in 1959. The mean scores for the freshman class in the English achievement test were at the 82nd percentile in 1954 and the 88th percentile in 1959. These scores are still more impressive if we remember that the national norms are for boys *and girls* taking the CEEB test in that year, that girls generally do better on Verbal Aptitude and English than boys, and that the Caltech students are all boys.

II. *New Developments in the curriculum.*

The implications of the rise in quality of our students to the highest level have of course affected the attitude of the staff responsible for planning the Humanities curriculum. Professor Judy remarked in his earlier report that "the time allocated to the humanities is insufficient for more than introductory courses," and in a certain sense this is still true, for the amount of time is unchanged (if we consider requirements only), and in no humanistic subject does Caltech have the equivalent of an undergraduate major. But the introduction can take place at a more mature level if the students are extremely able, and the introduction can go further into the area of familiarity and competence.

For several years Caltech offered an advanced course in English to those freshmen with the highest qualifications (Verbal aptitude of over 700 or an average Verbal aptitude and English of over 675). The number of students so qualified kept growing, until finally in 1959 it was decided to put the entire freshman class into this advanced course. Accordingly, the old freshman course which Professor Judy described as "like the first-year course found in American colleges everywhere" has been dropped, and the required freshman course now is substantially equivalent to the one that was taken in junior year at the time of the earlier report.

(There is no required course in English in the sophomore year.) The required junor course in literature will accordingly be revised upward so that it will be far beyond anything that could be called an "introductory course."

As Mr. Judy remarked in his earlier report, the Humanities Division of the California Institute offers no courses called "Humanities" in which literature, history, philosophy and the fine arts are combined.   But there are certain bridges between the various liberal disciplines.   Twice a year freshmen write papers which are submitted in both their English and History courses.   More significantly, courses have been placed in the curriculum which are taught jointly by professors from different fields: a course in The Political Novel, taught by a political scientist and an English professor; a course in Modern America taught by an economist and a historian; a course in Current World Affairs, required of all seniors, taught by specialists from various areas.   The planning and teaching of the American History course required of all sophomores is done by a political scientist, a professor of American literature, a historian of ideas and an American historian.   A new course is being offered this year in the literature and art of eighteenth-century England; it will utilize some of the treasures of the neighboring Huntington Library and Art Gallery.

A significant change in the perspective of our curriculum has come about as the result of America's world interests since the end of World War II.   The California Institute was a founding member of the American Universities Field Staff, and we use its visiting staff members as lecturers in a number of courses.   A seminar for seniors and graduate students in Foreign Area Problems is largely taught by AUFS experts, and others are brought in to assist the Institute staff in a course in Economic Problems of Underdeveloped Areas.   The special capabilities of new members of the Humanities Division itself have made it possible to offer courses in India and Pakistan, Medieval England, the Dynamics of Political Behavior, Political Parties and Pressure Groups, International Law and Organization, Human Relations, American Political Ideas, American Religions and Social Ideas, and Contemporary European Philosophy.   Compared to the courses at present offered, the humanities curriculum of ten years ago looks somewhat provincial.

III. *Expanded Opportunities*

There has been no expansion of the 25 per cent of the student's curriculum which must be spent in the Humanities, and none is visualized. Very considerable improvements have been made in the way that amount of time is utilized, not only by acceleration of able students and enlargement of the horizon of subject matter, but also by concentration and added depth in already existing courses. Furthermore, several of the science options (majors) have liberalized their requirements to allow free electives. Many students in these options choose some of their electives from the Humanities offerings, so that a significant number of our students graduate with about a third of their work in liberal arts.

Candidates for the master's degree must take a year's work in one of the advanced Humanities courses, and candidates for the Ph.D. in science or engineering are required to take work outside their own field which may be in the Humanities. Some Ph.D. candidates complete a minor in the Humanities by taking two year courses at the advanced level and passing an oral examination in the minor field. Pressure is being brought on the Division to offer more courses at the advanced level; when the faculty is available to offer additional courses, graduate student enrollment in Humanities is expected to increase.

chapter 15

THE HUMANITIES IN GENERAL EDUCATION AT CHATHAM COLLEGE

*Robert L. Zetler**

When the original article on "The Humanities in General Education at Pennsylvania College for Women" (now Chatham College) appeared in 1949, it was confessedly a report on an experiment which the faculty and administration thought to be noble in purpose, certainly, but it was likewise a report which could not be buttressed by the objective facts and the graphs and charts so beloved of the practictioners of the art of education. We were "able to assess the value of the program only through faculty and student reaction." In the years that have passed between then and now, we have been able to gather data which clearly show the teaching of the humanities at our college has been more successful than we hoped for in our most sanguine moments in 1949.

As a part of a standard philosophic approach, it is well to define the term "humanities." At Chatham College, we consider our courses in the Arts, Philosophy of Life, English Composition, and Speech to be the core of our disciplines in the humanities. History, ordinarily placed in this category, is instead treated as one of the social sciences.

The Arts course is one which concerns itself with man's achievements in the fields of esthetics; Philosophy of Life examines his methods of organizing his experience, as, to a more limited extent, does English Composition. Our course in speech, although correlated to one of the social sciences, is also an excursion into an

---

*Professor of English, Chatham College. Pittsburgh, Pa., with Professors Arnett, LeClair, Ferguson, Hayes.

esthetic field. To a large extent indeed, these definitions were valid at the beginning of our experiment in General Education: they still seem valid. We have, however, concluded that the impact of scientific thought has had far-reaching effects on the field of the humanities, and because of this, some consideration will be given in the course of this paper to a comparatively new course, the History and Philosophy of Science.

When the new curriculum based upon the framework of General Education was first introduced at the College, it was obvious that there was general agreement on the essential aims of the new courses, for without this the school would have foundered. Yet even with such an agreement, it became apparent there would be a thousand minor rubs and little irritations. Almost every thoughtful faculty member had developed his own course, his own subject material, his own points of emphasis, and often these had to be changed. To paraphrase James Thurber, everyone is crazy about the way he lives — and what he teaches. The rather sudden change from our former ways, the necessity of integrating one of our pet pieces of subject matter to which we had formerly devoted four periods wtih other subject matter, and cutting down the presentation to two class periods; the necessity for accurate scheduling of presentations in the correlated courses such as the Arts — these were harrassing requirements for faculty members accustomed to a much more free hand with their courses. We were all agreed that our major aims were for the greater glory of the college and higher education, but our methods of achieving those aims sometimes led to animated discussion and the extension of committee and faculty meetings into the deep reaches of the night.

Upon looking back, it is apparent that such a catharsis was the healthiest way to introduce the new curriculum. Because everyone had an opportunity to air his views, there were no little groups of dissidents determined upon the promotion of this and the extinction of that. There were no fiats from on high, even if there were extended arguments.

Now that our basic curriculum has been in operation for more than ten years, it is apparent that it has the whole-hearted support of the faculty. It is now generally agreed that any changes in these basic courses are matters which should be approved by the entire faculty as a group, rather than being the business of the particular

course chairmen and his staff.   Proposals for changes are worked
out by the teachers of the basic curriculum courses and forwarded
to the curriculum committee, which, as far as possible, is representative of the major fields of discipline offered by the college.   After
discussion of the proposal by the committee, it is either presented
to the faculty, or returned to the teachers of the course for further
revision.

The attitude with which the administration of the college
views the basic curriculum has apparently changed very little.   From
its inception, the members of the administrative staff have given
it their full backing, and they continue to do so.   This is not to
say that they have regarded it as a sacrosanct thing or a perfect
instrument of education ; to the contrary, they have welcomed
suggestions intended for its betterment and have advanced many
of their own.

Within the basic course in the humanities, there have, of course,
been changes in content and methods of approach, yet the basic
aims of these courses remain essentially unchanged.   To show what
changes have occurred, however, it may be best to examine the
courses in detail.

With changes in the staff, it is natural that the course in
Philosophy of Life has undergone shifts in emphasis, although it
is now as it was in the beginning, primarily an attempt to help
the student to integrate the various elements of her educational
experience, both curricular and extra-curricular, into a more coherent pattern of knowledge and values.   The course has perhaps
become more traditional in that it is now organized around certain important philosophical writings in their sequence.   But the
primary purpose of the course is not to inform the student *about*
philosophical systems or the content of philosophical literature;
rather, its aim is to stimulate philosophical thought about certain
enduring problems by considering various divergent ideas and attitudes in the stream of our intellectual heritage.   The course emphasizes that there are certain problems which man faces as man,
in contrast to those problems which he faces as citizen, business
man, scientist or artist, and that his decisions and resolutions about
such problems affect significantly his values and judgments in all
these other areas.   The course is concerned, for example, with how
man's concept of man affects his evaluation of science, the arts, the

religion, and how a certain view of science, or the arts, or on religion may deeply affect one's ideas about the ultimate nature and destiny of man. Socrates' devotion to inquiry even in the face of death, Aristotle's concern with the intricate relationship between morals and politics, Augustine's vision of the sovereignity of God, Hobbes' systematic materialism, Nietzsche's ideal of a world without moral judgments, and Buber's concept of dialogue between God and man are a few of the general themes pursued in the Philosophy of Life course.

Care is taken to avoid the impertinence of offering the student a ready-made philosophy upon which to base her life. The student instead is asked to read the work of philosophers who are widely divergent in their views, interests and attitudes; she is encouraged to reflect upon these differences in relation to each other, and in relation to her own interests, values, and attitudes.

Generally, the purpose of the Philosophy of Life course is to help the student pull together the intellectual accumulation of her life into a more or less coherent philosophy, allowing her to give precedence to whatever aspects of experience seem most important to her, but insisting that in some measure at least, she make the attempt to see man as man and to see the other aspects of life and understand their relationship to her own major interests. For example, the student who is primarily interested in the sciences will be required (insofar as such things can be required) to reflect seriously on the relation of art, religion, and the needs of society to her particular interests. The student who is primarily interested in the arts will be asked to do the same from her point of major concern.

In other words, the Philosophy of Life course assumes that almost everything is important, and that the liberally educated person is distinguished by her knowledge of the degree of importance of many things as well as the relationship existing between them.

A most serious question now perplexing the staff of the Philosophy of Life course is whether or not the process of philosophical integration and criticism should not be formally undertaken earlier in the student's career, perhaps in the sophomore or junior year. Although it is true that an effort to deduce a working philosophy must be founded on a reasonably large basis of facts, it seems very possible that a student would derive considerable benefit from an earlier introduction into the realm of philosophical thought.

Within the Arts course, which correlates material from the visual arts, drama, prose, poetry, music and the dance, there have been a number of changes of method and course organization. When the course was originated, two lectures were presented each week, followed by one seminar for discussion of the material of the lectures. This has now been shifted to one lecture a week and two seminars, with a consequent greater emphasis on class discussion; student participation has now become the core of the course. Naturally, the body of knowledge presented has decreased somewhat, but the staff of the course are convinced that this is more than counterbalanced by a fuller understanding of the material and a greater student interest and participation.

The Arts course now culminates in a unit on the evaluation of the arts. After some preliminary readings in the field of esthetics, the student is asked to set down in a paper about thirty-five hundred words her personal philosophy of the arts and her tentative standards of judgment about them. For most students, this is the most difficult task in the entire four semesters of the course, yet it is usually the most rewarding, for its requires her to draw together into a systematic organization the materials she has examined, to give thought to them, and to deduce major principles of esthetic criticism.

Originally, the Arts course was intended for freshmen and sophomores. As time passed, it became more and more apparent that it should be directed toward sophomores and juniors. Such a change would allow the instructors to draw upon the students' experience in the History of Western Civilization and their training in English Composition. Further, it would allow a better integration of the basic curriculum, for the students would pass directly from their writing of the "philosophy of art" paper into the Philosophy of Life course. With these advantages in view, it was decided to schedule the four semesters of the course essentially for sophomores and juniors.

The two "tool" subjects of the basic curriculum, Speech and English composition, were originally two-semester courses of two hours each semester. English composition was, of course, a freshman subject; Speech was required of all sophomores. Speech has now been changed from a four-hour, two-semester course to a three-

hour, one-semester offering.   The change is not, however, necessarily a permanent one, for after two years of the single semester
course, a review will be made to determine the merits of this plan
for the organization of the course.

The material for student speeches is drawn from another of
the basic curriculum courses taken in the sophomore year, Modern
Society.   This correlation has worked well during the time that
Speech was a four-hour course, and there seems no reason to believe
that it will not continue to do so, although the content of the
Speech course will be shortened by the omission of three units of
work.

When the basic English composition course was planned, it
depended to a large extent on personal experience for its subject
matter.   With the continued development of the other basic curriculum courses, there has been a gradual swing to the use of essays,
short stories, novels, and poems as sources for the subject matter
for student writing.   There has also been more emphasis on teaching the organization of subject matter.   The reading requirements
for the course have also been increased markedly.

Although not a part of the humanities as they are defined
at Chatham College, attention should be drawn to the course in
the history and philosophy of science.   Like the Arts course, it is
taught by a group of teachers, — a biologist, an astronomer, a
physicist, a chemist and a philosopher.

History and Philosophy of Science is a four-hour, one-
semester course which is divided into four phases.   The first deals
with Greek science, the second with the scientific efforts of the
sixteenth and seventeenth centuries, the third with modern and
contemporary science, and the last with the implications of science
for industry and government.   Such a course has much more to
offer the student than the usual one in science; for one thing,
the teachers in the course make the basic assumption that the
sciences are a humane discipline.   One of the aims of the course is
to inculcate a more exact sense of the mind's strategy in dealing
with problems; another is to make the student aware of natural
science as an historical heritage.

One of the obstacles which existed at the inception of Chatham College's basic curriculum, our inability to evaluate our efforts
save by student and faculty reaction, has been overcome by the

mere passage of time.   Students who have been trained under the new disciplines have now been tested by instruments which enable us to assess their achievements.   The Graduate Record Area Tests were given in 1955 and 1957.   In these tests, the approximate rank of Chatham seniors among 132 participating colleges was second or third.   In the class of 1957, two-thirds of our students tested above the 80th percentile.   In the Graduate Record Advanced Examinations in the Field of the Major, given in 1956 and 1958, 53 per cent of the Chatham students tested in the top fourth of the norms for their respective major groups; 85 per cent tested above the average for their major groups.   In the General Education Development test of correctness and effectiveness of expression, more than half the students who completed the course in English Composition tested in the top fifth of the norms for end-of-year freshman, and 75 per cent tested above the average.   It should also be noted that this group does not include the best students, for these are either exempted from the course initially or at the end of the first semester.

A substantial proportion of Chatham students are prospective teachers who are required to take the National Teacher Examination.   In the tests given in 1959, 86 per cent of these students placed above the national average in the section of the examination entitled Social Studies, Literature and Fine Arts.

Another problem which troubled faculty and administration was that of the foreign language requirement.   Before the basic curriculum was devised, the college had a requirement of two years of foreign language.   This requirement was dropped, but as time went on, the faculty began to doubt the wisdom of this step.   After considerable discussion, the Curriculum Committee recommended that the foreign language requirement be reinstated, and the faculty voted to approve this.

Another difficulty which harassed not only the faculty and administration but students as well was the scheduling of the freshman and sophomore year.   Because the natural science and history courses were both four hours a week, and freshmen were also asked to take Physical Education, for one hour's credit, as well as Human Development and Behavior (three hours), and English Composition (two hours), the schedule for the freshman year automatically came to fourteen hours.   To add another three hour course to this could quite possibly be a too heavy load for many students: yet if it were not added, the student would finish her freshman year with fewer credits than she should have. This problem was eventually met by decreasing the hours for the History of Western Civilization from four hours to three each semester.

The admission policies of the college have gradually changed to secure a higher calibre of students. Applicants now must have a high standing in their secondary school class, and must take the College Board examination successfully. Considerable use is also made by the Admissions Office of the interview technique. Perhaps one may summarize the college's admission policy by saying that we will not matriculate any one who we feel is incapable, physically, mentally or emotionally, of completing the requirements of the college.

Although notice has already been taken of some of the evaluation instruments used, the teachers of the basic curriculum courses necessarily use many tests of their own devising. Our techniques in constructing tests have improved, and our own Office of Evaluation Services has been of inestimable benefit.

A few new obstacles have emerged, of which one is a tendency to crowd the freshman and sophomore year with required courses to the almost total exclusion of electives. There is a general feeling among the students that it is well to complete as many of the basic curriculum requirements as possible during these years. As a result, the work in the major field is placed almost entirely in the junior and senior year, and the student has little opportunity to sample fields in which she feels she might have an interest.

Allied to this obstacle is that of class sizes and scheduling. Although the Chatham student-faculty ratio is 8 to 1, this is rarely the case in most of the classes taken during the student's first two years. And because of the required basic curriculum courses which have one large lecture section, no other classes can be scheduled for the same hour as the basic course if they are to draw their membership from students who are required to take the basic course.

There is a continuing obstacle that must be hurdled every year. Basic curriculum courses cannot function effectively unless they are staffed by first-rate teachers. Chatham College has been most successful in this respect, yet there is always a need for teachers of special flexibility and with enthusiasm for these sorts of projects.   There is always an initial force exerted in getting a basic humanities course started that will carry it along for a while.   But to keep it going is another problem and sound objectives and aims are not enough in themselves; there must be the enthusiastic teacher.

chapter 16

THE HUMANITIES AT THE STATE UNIVERSITY OF IOWA

*Victor Harris**

This report deals principally with two major developments in general education at the State University of Iowa during the last ten or twelve years: the new program leading to the B.A. and the M.A. in Humanities, and the establishing of a college-wide honors plan. In less detail two other important activities are described: the steady growth and continued flourishing of the fine arts on this campus, and a cooperative curriculum in foreign studies.

It should be noted, however, that the basic pattern of general education here remains essentially as established in the 1940's. All students are required to take an introductory course in literature and one of several courses in cultural history, as well as similar courses in the sciences.

Experiment, strengthening, and normal evolution have marked these courses. Instead of choosing two of three available semester courses in literature, for example, the student now chooses one of the two year-long sequences which are offered. An entirely new course in the cultural area was first introduced several years ago under the title "Religion in Human Culture." About half of the first semester is spent on preliterate religion, and on Hinduism, Buddhism, and Islam. The second half of the semester is devoted to an historical and systematic study of Judaism and Christianity. The second semester deals with religion in relation to politics, philosophy, the arts and sciences, and to society in general.

---

*Chairman of Humanities, State University of Iowa, Iowa City, Iowa.

A stiffening of admission requirements has tended to weed out most students below the fiftieth-percentile line in their high school standings, and remedial courses in communications and mathematics have been or are being eliminated. Both these changes have helped to raise the level at which the core courses can be given.

Yet the past decade has witnessed also a considerable relaxation at this university of the basic concept that a common "core" of studies should be required of all students. Alternative core courses were available even at the outset of the program. More recently further options, usually the introductory courses in the various disciplines, have also been approved. At present approximately half the students meet their requirement in the cultural area by taking the course in Western Civilization, and the other half are divided among the core courses in Art, Music, Theatre, Religion, and History of Ideas. In the area of the Natural Sciences, about half the students take one of the three alternative core courses, and the other half elect departmental courses instead. In the Social Sciences, only about a fourth of the students take the core course; the others take a combination of departmental courses.

Furthermore, a student ordinarily need not take a core course in the area of his major, so that if he majors in Art, Speech, or Music, for example, he may ask to be excused from the course in Western Civilization and from the other alternatives in the cultural area. A student may also discharge any of his core requirements by examination without taking the courses, though only a few students at present apply to take these examinations.

Increases in enrollment, together with the rising cost of every phase of the educational process, have necessarily resulted in budgetary pressures. Specialized training continues to become more complex, demanding, and competitive. By and large the program in general education here has lent itself better to techniques of mass production than has been the case with more specialized work.

In the face of these pressures, and in part to fill a need created by them, two new programs of considerable importance to the intellectual life of the college have been developed. First, the interdepartmental courses and curriculum culminating in the B.A. and the M.A. in Humanities have been gradually taking shape through the last decade. Secondly, this university in 1958 instituted its first college-wide honors program.

I.

Degrees and Courses in Humanities

From a single experimental course a dozen years ago, work in Humanities at Iowa has developed into a substantial program leading to the B.A. and M.A. degrees in Humanities, engaging the cooperation of many departments, and offering a wide selection of upper-level seminar courses. A student majoring in Humanities, either as undergraduate or graduate, takes a series of related courses in several disciplines, plus a sequence of integrative Humanities seminars (open also to qualified upperclassmen and graduate students from other departments).

This program was launched in 1947 with a course taught by professors of English, History, and Classics. A year later a new undergraduate major, and several new courses, were offered under the label of "European Literature and Thought." In this form the work prospered modestly for several years. The courses attracted superior students with many different interests; additional departments took active part in the teaching; a handful of majors received their degrees in European Literature and Thought each year.

In 1956 the name and organization of the program were changed to accord with what it was gradually becoming — a truly interdepartmental curriculum in the Humanities. The fine arts, including imaginative writing and dramatic arts, were formally incorporated into the design. Liaison with the social sciences was improved. The student was given a wider range of options within which to arrange a concentrated and coherent schedule of courses. Graduate degrees in Humanities were offered, either for terminal study or linked with the M.F.A. or Ph.D. in one of the departments associated in this enterprise. Some of the original courses were retained as courses in European Literature and Thought; others were made part of the broader program in Humanities.

In the three years since its expansion, the program has continued to grow steadily in the richness of its offerings and in its appeal to able students in search of a challenging elective or of an entire course of study. If the academic disciplines of this university are grouped into those with the largest number of majors (such as English, Chemistry, or History), those with the smallest (such as German, Classics, or Philosophy), and those in between (such as Geography, French, or Botany), it is into this middle group that the present Humanities program, in its third year of operation, would fall.

Since 1947 perhaps 1500 students have enrolled in the seminar courses. This is, in itself, not an impressive figure in a large state university where as many students will take some of the introductory or core courses in a single year. But the courses in Humanities are all at the upperclass level, and, except for Humanities majors, all of the courses are chosen as electives. Certain prerequisites are also imposed, in Literature and in historical and cultural studies. As a result, and because the staff is made up of senior faculty members who are not only expert in their fields but who have proved their skill as teachers, the work in Humanities has regularly attracted a cross-section of the best students on campus. An interesting index of student abilities, and the only one uniformly applicable throughout the university, is the composite entrance test score, by which, beginning in 1953, student registrations in the various departments have been measured. From 1953 through 1955, according to this index, students in Humanities courses ranked second among all the academic departments, and from 1956 until the present they have ranked first.

Thus the questions raised in the Humanities program can be serious questions, and they can be treated imaginatively and systematically. In such a context the Humanities can be properly defined as the domain of responsibility and choice in Human affairs, of standards of conduct and taste, of faiths and loyalties, and of the search for excellence, self-knowledge, and self-expression. Convinced that the search for excellence is among the first casualties where the choice is made without understanding, men trained in many intellectual disciplines have put this curriculum together in order to encourage students to keep weighing the evidence, facing up to the facts, evaluating, and choosing.

Courses

Each course is taught jointly by two instructors from different fields of study. The instructors divide the responsibility for introducing the various works, and for directing the discussion, but both are present throughout and share the give and take of classroom analysis.   Within the last three years the staff members have been drawn from the following areas: English, Art, Religion, Political Science, French, Psychiatry, History, Anthropology, Philosophy, Journalism, Oriental Studies, and Classics.   The juxtaposing of men trained in different disciplines has invited and stimulated a rethinking of old patterns, not only for the students but for their teachers.

These are not "great books courses," if by that term is meant a course in which the various works are treated in isolation from each other and from their settings.   Each Humanities course explores a single issue of major importance in our culture.   The books studied in any given course are significant expressions, often great ones, of interest in the particular issue to which the course is devoted — the place of science in today's world, for example, the core of irrationality in our natures, the challenge to democratic ideals, the range of sanctions for moral conduct, and the like.   Though the titles of the courses remain constant, the readings vary from year to year as different faculty combinations unite to study one or another pertinent problem, and the authors named in the course descriptions constitute a characteristic rather than a fixed list.

Liberal use of these original sources brings the student into close and sustained contact with many works of great insight.   Some lecturing may be part of the class schedule, in order to sketch in background or provide links from one work to the next, but the classes ordinarily proceed as colloquia or seminars, and are kept small enough to make such procedure possible.   Term papers are regularly assigned. A student may register for two, three, or four hours' credit in each course, depending on the extent of the independent work he undertakes.

The courses are open to all juniors, seniors, and graduate students, and to sophomores who have completed the core courses in literature and in the historical-cultural area.   Enrollment is usually about equally divided between graduate and undergraduate sudents. In addition to special projects, reading courses, and other forms of individual study such as the work for Honors, the following courses will be offered in 1959-60:

Values in the Contemporary World: The modern conflict over the definition and choice of values, examined through the writings of Riesman, Silone, Santayana, Maritain, Dewey, Pasternak, Morris and Brecht.

Science and the Nature of Man: Aspects of the relations of scientific to social and humanistic thought. This year two periods are examined: the seventeenth and the twentieh centuries. Reading centers on works by Galileo, Descartes, Pascal, Donne, Montaigne, Oppenheimer, Fry, Proust, Freud, and Bowen.

Form and Milieu in the Arts: The interplay between art forms and other patterns, rituals, and institutions in a culture. Principal illustrations are drawn this year from the literature and art of the Middle Ages and of the modern period. Works studied are by Muller, Dante, Celine, Tate, Ozenfant, Adams, and Faulkner; specific works of music and of graphic art are also considered.

Cultural Ideals of East and West: Social, philosophical, and religious ideals of East and West examined in relation to their respective cultures. Course list includes works by Bodde, Cassirer, Murasaki, Plato, Lin Yutang, Rabelais, and Russell.

The Human Condition: An examination of man as he faces some fundamental situations of his life. Reading includes works of Greene, Benedict, Dostoyevski, Camus, Kierkegaard, Malraux, Whyte, and Tillich.

Romanticism and the Democratic Spirit: The interaction of art and ideology — the relationship of the Romantic concepts of art and society to the development of the democratic ethos. Works by Byron, Goethe, Mazzini, Rousseau, Stendhal, Whitman, Wolfe, and others are considered.

The B.A. in Humanities

The B.A. in Humanities is set up on the premise that the best liberal education is also the best training for a career. A pre-professional education need not be narrowly technical but must be concerned with fundamental principles and methods in the professional and cognate areas, and with the whole intellectual and social context in which the profession is to be practised. A course in Reformation History, for example, may be the vocational concern only of students in History and Religion; but it is the proper province of any student with serious intellectual interests. The same kind of thing may be said of a course in Political Theory, Calculus, or Modern Art. Such courses, with their counterparts in Psychology, Literature, Economics, Philosophy, Languages, Geography, Humanities, and many other areas — such courses, rather than the necessary introductory surveys or technical specialities, are thought of as the real heart of liberal education.

Confirmation of this view comes from any sources. Two instances may be cited — the official positions of the Colleges of Law and of Medicine — from the 1959 Catalogue of the State University of Iowa:

> Traditionally the men who have attained distinction at the American bar are men who have brought to it a broad cultural background. Recently, the Association of American Law Schools, through its committee on pre-legal education, emphasized the fact that education of students for a full life through a liberal education is far more important than education directed too pointedly for later professional training and practice . . . It is ordinarily wise for the student who expects to study law to acquire a broad rather than a narrow base in filling out academic requirements for admission to the College of Law.
>
> Students planning to study medicine should bear in mind that the college work is required because in addition to prerequisite sciences it offers an opportunity to secure a well-rounded education, which is of special importance to those entering the medical profession. In the selection of applicants preference will be given to those who give evidence of having obtained such a broad education.

The B.A. in Humanities is designed to help prepare the student for an active, informed, and responsible life. By its breadth of background it can help him also to discover the subject area of greatest interest to him, and equip him for further work in that area. Students who have earned this degree have gone on to advanced study in Philosophy, Literature, Religion, History, and various other special fields. Those who do not wait too long to begin planning their schedules can usually satisfy the requirements for a double major — in Humanities and in one of the cooperating departments. The most frequent choice for such a combined major has been either English or History, but other alternatives are open and have been selected. The B.A. in Humanities has been recognized as useful also for students entering such fields as law, government, and the social sciences in general. The plan for the degree is flexible enough to anticipate and adapt to a wide range of practical applications. Students seem more and more aware that among professional groups and in management — in business, engineering, medicine, social work, and in almost every other field — there is an increasing tendency to look for men and women educated to understand the human factors in their work.

In addition, a student majoring in Humanities may earn a teaching certificate by taking the appropriate professional courses in Education. The work needed to qualify for teaching the specialized subjects becomes part of the major program; most Humanities majors who seek certification choose from English, History, and a language, though a number of other options are also available. These graduates are prepared also to teach the core or Humanities courses which are widely offered. The teacher, surely no less than anyone else, needs to study a wide range of human experience.

Undergraduate Requirements

The following outline represents the distribution of work toward the B.A. degree, beyond the core courses in general education required of all Liberal Arts students. Each student's program is planned in consultation with his adviser.

Fields of study: 42 semester hours. The student selects two of the following four fields for major emphasis (15 hours or more of work in each) and gives minor emphasis to the other two (6 hours or more in each): Literature; History and Social Sciences; Fine Arts; Philosophy and Religion.

Integrative courses: 12 semester hours from the seminar courses in Humanities. Other appropriate courses may be used to fulfill this requirement, with consent of the adviser.

Language: command of a language other than English, as represented by at least one semester of work at the third-year level of college study. French or German has been the usual choice, but almost all other languages taught here (including Russian, Greek, and Latin) have been used to meet this requirement. Humanities majors have been encouraged to continue their work in language throughout their four years; many have been able also to add a second language. Courses in foreign literature may serve toward satisfying the requirement in Literature.

Concentration: a student majoring in Humanities is expected to balance the breadth of his training by building his program around a single topic which he then approaches in the context of each of his fields of study.　This is a unique and important part of his preparation, providing him with an interdepartmental field of specialization equal in thoroughness to that of a departmental major.　If he chooses, for example, the topic of Renaissance Culture, he would elect courses in Early Modern History, English Renaissance Literature, Renaissance Literature of the language he is pursuing, the Reformation and Counter-Reformation in Religion, Plato and the Renaissance Neoplatonists, the beginnings of modern scientific philosophy, and Renaissance art and architecture.　The area of concentration will ordinarily be developed in at least half of his required courses.　Various suitable topics are suggested as follows, but the student is encouraged to substitute a similar organizing principle of his own: Civilization of a period (Classical Culture, the Middle Ages, Renaissance and Reformation, the Age of Enlightment, the Nineteenth Century, Modern Culture); a national culture (England, France, Germany, Russia, Spain, Spanish-America, etc.); Literature and the Stage; Religion in Western Culture; Language and Comparative Literature; Aesthetics, Criticism, and the Arts.

The B.A. with Honors

The degree of B.A. with Honors may be earned by a superior student who undertakes a further program of independent study beyond the requirements for the major in Humanities.　To be admitted as a candidate for Honors, and then to be certified for the degree with Honors, he must have the endorsement of the Honors supervisor in Humanities.　Criteria for this endorsement will be the student's capacity for independent work, his intellectual range and alertness, and evidence of a good mind well disciplined.

In addition to other courses that may be recommended by the supervisor, the student must complete two special projects with distinction.　The first is an Honors Essay — an historical, analytical, or imaginative paper on a subject to be chosen through consultation with the supervisor.　The second is an examination over a reading list constructed on the basis of the student's area

of concentration (as described above, in the outline of undergraduate requirements).

The M.A. in Humanities

The M.A. in Humanities may serve as the terminus of a
broad program in liberal arts, as a professional degree for teachers
of humanistic subjects, or as an intermediate step toward the Ph.D.
in one of the related departments.

To be admitted to candidacy, a student will ordinarily have
a humanistic undergraduate major — either in such form as is prescribed for this B.A. degree, or in one of the departmental fields
of the Humanities. Other preparation, however, may be acceptable,
where the M.A. course of study can be sufficiently expanded to
make up any deficiency. Somewhat to the surprise of the founders
of the program, a number of students have enrolled for the M.A.
in Humanities after undergraduate concentration in Business Administration, Mathematics, Nursing, Engineering, and other areas
equally remote from the usual humanistic subjects.

Graduate assistantships, fellowships, and other graduate awards
are available to qualified applicants. These have ordinarily been
held either by candidates for the M.A. in Humanities, or by students who have a degree in Humanities but are working for the
Ph.D. in a related department.

The M.A. can be taken with 30 semester hours in courses
if the student as an undergraduate earned 12 semester hours of
credit in each of two humanistic fields outside his major, or if he
has a B.A. in Humanities. Otherwise a more extensive course of
study may be required. If the degree is taken without thesis, 38
hours or more will be required.

Fields of Study: The student works primarily in two of the
following fields: Literature, History, Philosophy and Religion,
Language, Fine Arts. Work in one of these categories may be
reduced in scope if relevant courses in Education are elected.

Integrative work: The student takes nine hours of work in
the Humanities courses, which serve as integrative seminars. Other
courses similar in their interdisciplinary design may be used to
satisfy part of this requirement.

Concentration: The student chooses an area of concentration
to serve as a guide in the selection of courses and of a thesis topic,

and as the basis for his M.A. examination. The areas suggested as part of the undergraduate requirements may be useful here also, though usually the topic chosen for the M.A. will be somewhat more precisely centered and correspondingly more fully treated.

Thesis: Students taking the degree with fewer than 38 hours of course work must submit a thesis. The thesis may be undertaken under direction of a faculty member in any of the participating departments, though it will usually reflect the interdepartmental nature of this program. It may be a piece of historical research, a critical study, or a piece of imaginative work in writing or in the fine arts. Typical recent topics have dealt with the backgrounds of T. S. Eliot's critical theory, the origin of a philosophy of social work, and the relation of form and ideology in the writings of Katherine Anne Porter. Where the thesis is a piece of creative writing, or studio work in the fine arts, it is to be judged by the same standards as prevail when such work is submitted in the separate department, and the studio or workshop instructor will be the chairman of the thesis committee.

Examination: Each candidate will stand an examination which reflects his particular pattern of study. By the beginning of his final semester he should submit for approval a reading list over his topic of concentration. The examination will then be given on the basis of this list.

The Combined M.A. and M.F.A. Degrees

A student may earn the M.A. in Humanities and the M.F.A. in one of the creative arts by following an integrated program of 60 hours' work. The selection of courses is made on an individual basis upon consultation with the two advisers. In general, the emphasis in the M.A. curriculum would be upon areas other than that in which the M.F.A. is taken. If the student elects to come up for the M.A. without thesis, he must have a total of 68 hours for the two degrees. As of this date, the combined program has already been chosen by candidates for the M.F.A. in Art and for the M.F.A. in English (creative writing).

The Graduate Minor

A candidate for the Ph.D. in one of the departments in this area can qualify for the minor in Humanities. To do so he must work primarily in a field other than that in which the major thesis is taken, with subordinate study in a second. In addition, he takes nine hours of work in the Humanities courses.

Since the aim of the minor is to provide a competence in a broad and related area, the number and distribution of hours may differ for each candidate. A student who already has the M.A. degree may apply toward the completion of this minor any pertinent courses from his work for the M. A. The selection of courses is made with the candidate's entire program in mind, and must be approved both by the adviser and the adviser in Humanities.

II.

The Honors Program

The following statement by the President of the University accompanied the launching of the Honors program in 1958:

> The Honors Program in the College of Liberal Arts quite appropriately emphasizes the need for excellence in our society. We have accepted the principle of equality of educational opportunity for all American youth. This has as an integral part the education of our youth to the highest level of their respective abilities. Thus we have provided much aid and counseling for the marginal youth. We are equally obliged under the principle to provide exceptional opportunities for unusually able students. The Honors Program is designed to meet this need. I am happy to welcome it as an added service of the State University of Iowa to meet the educational needs of our people.

Scope and Purposes

Honors work at the State University of Iowa is offered under a college-wide plan, adopted by the Liberal Arts faculty in April, 1958, which aims at the early identification of superior students and the increasing of their educational opportunities throughout their undergraduate years. Under this plan, students who exhibit special promise will be accorded Honors status and assisted in a number of ways to take full advantage, commensurate with their abilities, of the educational resources of the college. In planning their work they will receive careful individual counseling. Their general studies will be enriched by instruction in special sections.

In their major fields, in all departments which offer an Honors curriculum, they will be able to earn a baccalaureate degree "with Honors," signifying a calibre of work which can be accomplished only by good minds properly challenged. The intended outcome is the sort of education which, apart from its inherent value to the superior student, will provide a solid basis for subsequent high achievement in the professions, in postgraduate study, or in public life.

Eligibility

Demonstrated ability is the only criterion for admission.

At the beginning of their work in the college, Freshmen who make exceptionally high scores on the entrance examinations will be immediately admitted to Honors status, allowing them to participate in the program. It is anticipated that the top five to fifteen per cent of entering freshmen each year will possess abilities qualifying them for Honors study.

Other students, including transfers, may be admitted to Honors status on recommendation by instructors or on their own application to the Director of Honors, provided that their academic records meet prescribed standards.

A student admitted to Honors status will continue to hold this status in succeeding semesters if his interest and academic progress justify it. He may withdraw from Honors at his own request. Honors status will be noted each semester as part of the student's permanent academic record.

Privileges and Responsibilties

Though their curriculum will be in part a special one, it is intended that Honors students shall participate in worthwhile activities of the student body as a whole rather than constitute a closed or self-sufficient group. Honors status will, however, entitle students to certain special benefits appropriate to their educational goals. The University Libraries will provide special facilities for study. An Honors Reading Room is planned. Faculty members connected with the program will help and encourage students to take advantage of particular opportunities as they arise, whether to compete for prizes and scholarships or to meet for informal discussion with distinguished visitors. Though Honors students should have little trouble in satisfying the academic requirements of the college, the Honors Council will recommend special curricular adjustments where these appear to be in the genuine interest of the student.

Honors students, for their part, must be prepared to assume a relatively large responsibility for the use of their opportunities. They must view their college work in terms of real values rather than the mere performance of assignments and the accumulation of academic credits. They must possess broad intellectual curiosity and be willing to indulge it. In their special fields they must be ambitious to excel. They must be intolerant of the second-rate in themselves or in their education.

Faculty Sponsorship

In order to enhance the effectiveness of the advisory program for superior students, a student admitted to Honors status will be assigned to a member of the faculty who will act as his Sponsor. It is intended that Sponsors shall come to know Honors students well personally and thus be able the more advantageously to give friendly assistance and guide them into activities, curricular and extracurricular, which will promote intellectual growth.

Special Courses and Sections

So far as feasible, students with Honors status will be admitted to special sections of core courses and language courses required by the college, and of introductory departmental courses which may be taken in lieu of core work.

At a more advanced level, each department which offers a program leading to an Honors degree will provide certain required Honors courses for its own majors. Some departments will also offer special courses which Honors students majoring in other departments may take on an elective basis.

Special course work for Honors students will vary in nature with the different departments and fields of study. Some Honors courses will be organized as discussion groups or seminars; others will center on individual projects, readings, reports, or theses. Usually there will be some combination of these. Honors work will often involve more individual study and carry correspondingly larger credit than regular courses. Grades assigned will be the same as the work would merit if done in regular courses. In general, Honors courses and sections represent an effort to provide a more stimulating situation for learning than otherwise might exist for the superior student — they are meant to encourage greater student initiative in college work and to promote a more vigorous exchange of ideas with fellow-students and instructors.

Requirements for the Honors Degree

It is assumed that most students admitted to Honors status will desire to complete work for an Honors degree in one of the many available fields of concentration. At the initiation of the program in September, 1958, departments and interdepartmental programs offering Honors work, or making plans to offer such work at an early date, include American Civilization, Art, Bacteriology, Botany, Chemistry, Classics, Elementary Education, English, Geography, German, Geology, History, Home Economics, Humanities, Journalism, Mathematics and Astronomy, Music, Philosophy, Physics, Physical Education, Political Science, Psychology, Religion, Romance Languages, Sociology and Anthropology, and Speech and Dramatic Art. It is expected that still other departments will be prepared to offer honors work in due time.

Students will be admitted to work in candidacy for an Honors degree, normally not later than the beginning of their junior year, upon application to and approval by the Director of Honors and acceptance by the department. The candidate must complete six semester hours or more of Honors work as part of the departmental major; at the option of the department, this work may be prescribed either as an addition to the regular requirements for the major or in substitution for some part of these requirements. In his final semester the student will take an examination based on his departmental Honors work, and will be awarded the appropriate degree (e.g., B.A. with Honors in Physics) on a basis of this examination and his total academic record.

Minimal academic standards for admission to departmental Honors work, and for the award of Honors, are set by the Honors Council. Individual departments are empowered to set higher standards if they find it advisable. A student whose work is judged not to merit the designation of Honors, but who is otherwise qualified, will be graduated without such a designation in the ordinary manner.

III.

The Fine Arts

The State University of Iowa has long been noted for its work in the fine arts. Courses and workshops of distinction have prospered in various fields. Students may get practical experience and guidance, and in many departments they may offer as a Master's or Doctor's thesis an original creative contribution in the arts — whether in musical composition or performance, acting or playwriting, graphic art or sculpture, the writing of poetry or fiction. In recent years the strength and vitality of this program has made itself felt more and more widely throughout the university. A few signs of such vitality are seen in this incomplete list of new projects in the general area.

For each of the last four years the Department of Music has sponsored an annual Contemporary Composer's Festival. The men honored have been William Schumann, Samuel Barber, Aaron Copeland, and Wallingford Riegger. New works have been commissioned for the occasion. Lectures and concerts have been regular features.

In 1958 a Studio Theatre was established to augment the other offerings of the Dramatic Arts Department. It is intended for experimental plays that could not be produced in the main theatre, for plays written by students here, and for plays of various sorts directed by students.

An annual Seminar on New Plays was set up in 1958, featuring the production of an original script, readings of other original scripts, and appraisals by several professional critics.

In 1958, also, a student conference on the theatre was undertaken as an annual event. Delegates were invited from 60 midwestern colleges and universities. The two days of the conference were given over to panel discussions, demonstrations of directing and acting, and the performance of six student-directed one-act plays.

Still in the planning stage is a comprehensive plan for further strengthening the fine arts program. Resident fellowships are proposed for established artists — in the fields of musical composition, playwriting, the graphic arts, poetry and fiction. A week of demonstrations in these various fields would be held on campus, and a briefer but representative series of exhibitions and performances would be presented at other points throughout the state.

IV.

Program of Foreign Studies

An integrated program has been established for study in each of five areas: France, Spain and Latin America, Germany and Austria, Russia, and China. Cooperating in setting up the curriculum are the departments of History, Modern Foreign Languages, Oriental Studies, Economics, Geography, Political Science, and the School of Journalism.

A student in the program studies courses outlined for a specfiic area, along with those in his major department. With the successful completion of the area courses, he receives a Foreign Studies Certificate indicating his special background for assignment as a military or civilian worker in the particular area of his specialization. The program ordinarily consists of 24-26 semester hours of area study. It may be completed in about two years along with a major in any other field of study, and is open to graduate and undergraduate students.

The program in the Russian area, for example, consists of the following courses: Russian language (3 semesters), Soviet Geography, History of Russia to 1800, History of Russia 1800 to the Present, Modern Russian Intellectual History (1860-1917), Government of Russia, Soviet-American Relations. Recommended in addition are: Modern Russian Intellectual History (1725-1860), Russian Literature (2 semesters), further work in the Russian language, and Comparative Economic Systems.

chapter 17

HUMANITIES PROGRAMS IN 15 ARKANSAS COLLEGES

*Hoyt Trowbridge**

I

In a survey of changes in humanistic teaching during the past decade, the fifteen public and private colleges of Arkansas are particularly interesting because of their participation in the Arkansas Experiment in Teacher Education, a statewide cooperative project sponsored by the Fund for the Advancement of Education. The largest of some two dozen similar programs supported by the foundation, the experiment was designed to test a pattern of preparation for elementary and secondary teaching which included a four-year liberal education followed by a fifth year, specifically professional, which was devoted partly to theoretical studies and partly to practical experience in the classroom. During the five years, 1952-57, grants totaling more than two million dollars were made to the colleges for the improvement of undergraduate liberal curricula, especially for general education.

Although some innovations had been introduced as early as 1934 at Hendrix College, a Methodist school with a fine liberal tradition at Conway, most of the Arkansas institutions scarcely felt the impact of the general-education movement until after World War II. A new required program was approved at Agricultural, Mechanical, and Normal College (AM&N) in 1946, and at the University of Arkansas a year later. Henderson State Teachers

---

*Mr. Trowbridge, who is chairman of the department of English at the University of New Mexico, served as consultant to the Arkansas Experiment in Teacher Education during the two years, 1954-56.

College undertook a major reorganization in 1949, and in 1950 the faculty of Arkansas Polytechnic College (Tech) voted to revise its degree requirements and introduced a series of new courses. The coming of the Arkansas Experiment gave an opportunity for further and more rapid advances at the colleges which had already revised their programs, and an occasion for the others to attack the problem with new energy and confidence. The years from 1952 to 1956 were a period of extraordinary activity throughout the state, a time of rapid and revolutionary changes.

Changes in the humanities were influenced, of course, by the overall pattern of degree requirements, modified at most of the colleges during the same fruitful years. The number of hours assigned to general education as a whole ranges from 34 to 72; the median for the state is 49 hours and the mean 53.5. Within this total, the relative weights allowed to the three basic fields are as follows:

HOURS REQUIRED IN THREE BASIC FIELDS

	Natural Science	Social Science	Humanities
Mean	12.2	13.5	9.1
Median	12	15	9
Mode	12	15	10

The commonest pattern assigns the equivalent of three one-semester courses (four hours each) to science and mathematics, five semester courses (three hours each) to history, the empirical social sciences, and psychology, and three semester courses (three hours each) to literature, art, and music.

In their humanities requirements the Arkansas Colleges can be divided into three groups, with programs of two, three, and five semesters respectively:

(1) Hendrix College, Ouachita Baptist College, and Henderson State Teachers College have one-year required courses (six course hours at Hendrix, eight at the other two), which include literature, varying amounts of visual arts and music, and some philosophical material. Arkansas State Teachers College and John Brown University require some study of art or music (three hours, at ASTC, four at JBU), allowing a choice between the two; six hours in English are required,

in addition to the freshman course in composition or communication, but three or more of these may be elected in speech or journalism. The commonest pattern at both schools is a semester of literature and a semester of art or music, totaling six hours at ASTC and seven at John Brown.

(2) More than half the Arkansas colleges, eight in all, require three semesters in the humanities, or the equivalent in two semesters. Four of them (Arkansas College, Arkansas State, Harding, and Southern State) offer a year of literature and the equivalent of one semester of art, music, or both. College of the Ozarks covers the same ground in two five-hour courses. At Arkansas A & M and Philander Smith College, literature and fine art are not taught separately but are combined in both a six-hour basic course and a second course of three hours. AM&N offers introductory courses in literature and in general humanities (three hours each), with an additional four hours to be elected at a more advanced level. At all these colleges the humanities requirement totals either nine or ten hours.

(3) The two remaining colleges, Arkansas Tech and the University of Arkansas, require 13 and 15 hours respectively. The humanities program at the University is similar to those at the institutions in the second group, except that the course in fine arts runs for a full year and includes architecture, drama, and the dance as well as painting and music. Six hours are required in world literature, and three additional hours may be selected from a variety of humanistic fields and courses. The Tech program includes an eight-hour sophomore course in American history, literature, art, and music (of which five hours are credited to humanities, three to the social studies), and two junior courses, one in European literature and thought (six hours), the other in European art and music (two hours).

At the colleges in the first two groups, instruction in the humanities is constricted within very narrow limits. In a single one-year course it is hardly possible to do justice to one of the main components — literature, the other arts, or philosophy — to say nothing of covering all three. The three-semester pattern at the colleges in the second group, though more defensible, is mini-

mal at best. The chief defects of this plan — a year of literature
and a semester of art or music — are the thinness of the work in
the fine arts and the total or partial omission of philosophy. In
general, the underweighting of philosophy is most serious at the
state-supported schools, for the requirements in Bible study at the
church-related colleges compensate to some extent for the relative
neglect of intellectual history and moral ideas in their humanities
courses. Courses in religion are not always taught humanistically,
but where they are not conceived in a dogmatic or narrowly sec-
tarian spirit such courses can do much for general education. At
the state colleges, however, both religion and philosophy are commonly slighted, if not altogether omitted from the general-education
program.

    Two changes which are everywhere characteristic of the general-
education movement — its identifying marks, one might say —
are the reduction or elimination of elective freedom in this part of
the college curriculum and the effort toward interdisciplinary synthesis, especially through the development of courses covering two
or more of the traditional specialized fields. The influence of both
tendencies is manifest in Arkansas.

    John Brown and ASTC still maintain the older system of
group electives, with students making their own choices from a list
of possibilities in each field; in form at least, degree requirements
at these two colleges do not differ much from those which prevailed
in most American colleges in 1920. On other Arkansas campuses,
four-fifths of the total requirement in general education, on the
average, must be met by courses specifically prescribed, less than
20 per cent being elective.

    Commitment to interdepartmental courses is less complete and
widespread. In the state as a whole, departmental courses in all
fields of general education are favored by a ratio of about five to
four, which is also the proportion in the humanities; combined
courses are somewhat less common in the social studies (5:2), more
so in the sciences (5:9). Five colleges — Tech, Henderson, Hendrix, Ouachita, and Philander Smith — favor interdepartmental
courses by ratios of more than two to one, but ASTC, Harding,
John Brown, and the University come close to reversing this proportion. These variations seem to have no connection with institutional type: the four regional state schools are fairly close together,

except for Tech's high proportion of interdepartmental courses, but the independent colleges are scattered between the extremes, and the two teachers colleges are at opposite poles.   Yet all offer a substantial number of interdepartmental courses.

In the broad outline of their programs, the patterns and trends briefly sketched above, the Arkansas colleges represent a typical cross-section of the general-education movement as it has developed throughout the country.   Most of their individual courses are also similar in design and method to those offered elsewhere, but several have unique or unusual features and all show a thoughtful and imaginative concern both for the needs of students and for the larger values of humanistic teaching.   These courses will be described in the rest of this chapter.

II

In the last chapter of McGrath's report ten years ago, Robert F. Davidson distinguished three main points of view underlying the programs and courses summarized in the body of the book. The governing purpose most common at that time was "to provide for the student some broader understanding of his cultural heritage," a point of view which led to a central emphasis on cultural history.   The other two aims, correlated with a primary emphasis on philosophy and the arts respectively, were to develop intellectual maturity through the study of great books, issues, and ideas, and to foster aesthetic understanding and appreciation.

Following Davidson's classification, we may separate the Arkansas humanities courses into three groups: those limited to or centered on literature, those in which literature is combined with other humanistic studies, and those which are concerned primarily with painting, music, or other non-verbal arts.   The points of view defined by Davidson are still current in Arkansas, though often in mixed form and with some drift away from the cultural or historical conception and toward the second and third aims.

McGrath included one or two courses in "History of Civilization" or "Greek and Roman Culture" in his report on the humanities, and similar courses are offered under various titles at most of the Arkansas schools.   Though all are committed in some degree to the "cultural heritage" philosophy, the courses at Hendrix and the University — both influenced by the famous Columbia orientation course, "Contemporary Civilization" — are the only ones in the state which give much emphasis to cultural or intellectual history; the others deal chiefly with politics and economics, international relations, and the growth of social institutions. Such courses are usually considered, in Arkansas as at Columbia, to be part of the program in the social studies, and they have been so counted in my summary of degree requirements in the preceding section. It is in literature rather in history proper that Davidson's first purpose is most clearly illustrated.

Literature courses accepted as meeting general-education requirements include traditional surveys of English literature, departmental "appreciation" courses, and courses in world literature. The latter have become increasingly dominant.

Where students are allowed to choose among several alternatives in meeting part or all of the humanities requirement, as at AM&N, John Brown, and Southern State, surveys of English literature may be elected as part of the program in general education. In general, however, they are conceived as primarily intended for students specializing in the department. Only at ASTC is a course of this kind the standard means of fulfilling the degree requirement. Most students take either the first or second semester of "English Literature I and II," filling out the rest of the requirement (12 hours in English, including six in composition) with a course in speech or journalism. The course is a good one, but as a pattern of studies in the humanities the scheme leaves much to be desired.

Departmental "appreciation" courses, frequent elsewhere, are rare in Arkansas. The clearest example is "Introduction to Literature," a three-hour one-semester course at AM&N. It is described in the catalogue as "Reading in imaginative literature to provide materials for careful analysis and subject matter for critical writing." The main purpose, as in all such courses, is to develop the student's powers of interpretation and judgment; the material is not chronologically organized, but is selected and arranged to include a variety of literary forms, raising interpretive problems of several kinds and degrees of difficulty. Although this kind of course can degenerate into a series of exercises in remedial reading, with nothing poetic about it, "appreciation" courses have several notable advantages: their clarity of purpose, the instructor's freedom to select the readings from any period and arrange them in any order, and above all the likelihood of a carry-over or transfer of the skills developed in the course to the reading of other literature. A teacher who reads well himself can do a great deal with such a course if the material taught is of first-class literary quality and the standard is kept high.

Seven of the fifteen institutions include courses in world literature in their programs of general education. They are taught under a variety of titles, including "Introduction to Literature" (Arkansas College), "Humanistic Literature" (Southern State), "World Classics" (John Brown), and "Our Western Heritage" (Harding). Most are six-hour courses at the freshman or sophomore level, but at Philander Smith a three-hour course, Humanities 473: "Masterpieces of World Literature," is required of all seniors. Most of these courses are taught by instructors in English, though at two of the larger institutions, Arkansas State and the University, the staffs include teachers of ancient and modern languages.

The original germinal idea underlying all such courses is perhaps most clearly shown in English 223, 224 at Arkansas College, described as "Masterpieces of world literature from the Homeric epics to the present day which have value in western culture." To this basic conception the Harding and Southern State instructors add a secondary emphasis on the history of thought. Though mainly literary, the works studied at Southern State are "read in the perspective of the related disciplines of philosophy and the arts," while at Harding the cousre is centered on "ideas regarding the nature of man and his place in the world." Both have something in common with "Man's Search for Values" at Hendrix and "World of Literature, Philosophy, and Religion" at Arkansas State, to be discussed later. The University's world literature course, on the other hand, has some of the characteristics of an appreciation course, especially in its first semester. In a history dating back to 1940, World Literature 103 has been organized at various times not only according to historical epochs (the usual pattern in such courses), but also by literary types, by problems or themes, and by the languages in which the works studied were originally written. At present it is taught in some sections as an introduction to literature, organized by forms; the second semester then becomes an abbreviated survey of ancient and modern literature. In most sections the whole course is historically organized.

The characteristic defect of courses like these, it has seemed to me, is a vagueness or multiplicity of purpose. The original intention was to trace the development of "Our Western Heritage" through its major epochs or phases. In actual practice, this conception is seldom applied in a consistent, thorough-going way. The works are presented in chronological order, and the usual historical periods are recognized; something is said about Greek religion and the city-state, about feudalism and the medieval church, about the Renaissance, Enlightenment, Romanticism, industrialization, and the conflict between science and religion. But the discussion in class from day to day often has little to do with cultural history; instead a great many questions are raised about the work under discussion — the ideals and values it embodies, the human problems it so vividly dramatizes, its form, technique, and power over the emotions. As if reluctant to sacrifice any of the potentialities of his material, the instructor seems to be trying to do everything at once. The result is a dispersion of effort and attention which is likely to leave the student without any clear idea of what he has been doing.

This problem is seen in an extreme form in the University's course, a large one with ten or more sections each semester. Its sister-courses, "Western Civilization" and "Basic Course in the Arts," follow well-defined plans, made clear to staff and students by syllabi and other devices. In "World Literature," however, there has been little effort to reach agreement on purposes and procedures. There is no syllabus, no common examination; each instructor is free to follow his own bent. The course as a whole is not committed to anything more specific than a list of works to read.

At the smaller colleges, where only one or two instructors are involved, the courses in world literature usually have a more definite shape. At Arkansas College, for example, the instructor has tried to direct his teaching primarily toward the development of his student's interpretive and critical capacities; the works are treated as literary masterpieces of enduring interest, illustrating a variety of forms, rather than as historical documents. Yet here, too, there is a mixture of other motives. In the anthology which is used as a textbook, the various writings are grouped by periods, each new section being prefaced by an essay summarizing the main characteristics of the era.   The instructor also touches in passing on the history of ideas, literary biography, and other themes or background materials.

Such a course is perhaps not excessively eclectic.   The instructor knows what he is trying to do; he has decided on the purpose and point of view which is to dominate his teaching, and other approaches may be introduced from time to time without confusion or dispersion of attention.   And yet the text and the chronological arrangement create a constant subtle tension between the purpose of the course and its design, which was first invented for different purposes, now abandoned — to introduce the student to a cultural heritage, not to give training in perceptive reading.   How much freer the teacher would be if he could forget about temporal sequence and cultural epochs, choosing as materials the works that best illustrate his own kind of points and arranging them in an order determined by the logic of his own aims and values!   Courses governed by the historical point of view will and should continue to be taught, either in the humanistic or in the social-studies part of the general-education program.   In the long run, however, I believe that the shift of purpose which has been going on for some years will lead to the emergence of new course-designs, more directly adapted to a non-historical philosophy of literary teaching.

III

Ten of the fifteen Arkansas colleges offer some form of broader course, in which literature is combined with philosophy, with music and the visual arts, or with all three.   At four colleges (Ozarks, Henderson, Hendrix, and Ouachita) a course of this kind is the only one required in the humanities.   At Arkansas State the integrated course is supplemented by a separate course in fine arts, at Philander Smith by a course in literature, while at the University two three-hour integrated courses are included among the alternatives from which students may choose a final, more advanced course after fulfilling the basic requirements in world literature and fine arts.   Arkansas A&M has two integrated courses at the sophomore and senior levels (the first being an alternative to world literature), and Tech requires sophomore and junior courses in general humanities in addition to a two-hour course in art and music.

As a class, these combined courses are more like those in literature than those in the fine arts. In only one of them, at College of the Ozarks, are the component studies presented separately and in series. At Ouachita and Arkansas Tech the different subjects are handled by different instructors, as in most of the fine-art courses, but all the others are taught by the same instructors throughout. Most of them are staffed wholly or chiefly by teachers of English. The most basic problem for these integrated courses, as for those in literature, has been to come to terms with the historical approach to the humanities — to find a way to bring out the non-temporal values in literature, the arts, and philosophy without completely isolating them from the stream of history.

The course at Ouachita is particularly interesting as an attempt to find a middle ground on almost all the issues which have confused and complicated the development of integrated courses in the humanities. One of the major possibilities has been rejected: the course is not organized as a history of ideas. On other problems the instructors have sought to achieve a compromise or balance: the method is partly lecture, partly discussion, partly free listening and viewing; one instructor teaches literature and music, but art is taught by another; the organization of materials is largely chronological, but the treatment is primarily aesthetic.

The course is directed by a member of the department of English, assisted by an instructor in art. The lecture periods, twice a week, are about equally divided between them, though without a systematic pattern of alternation. On the two remaining days, which are entirely concerned with literature, the students meet in smaller groups for discussion. The distribution of time among the component studies is approximately half for literature, one-fourth each for art and music; two-thirds of the teaching is done by one instructor. This arrangement helps to provide a consistency and continuity which is usually difficult to achieve where a course is taught by more than one instructor.

The most notable feature of the course is its first six weeks, in which chronological sequence is disregarded. The lectures are on the subject-matter, elements, media, and organizing principles of music and visual art; analogous points are illustrated from literature in the discussion sections. Although the rest of the year is historically organized, the course does not attempt to present a complete history of the arts.   The intention throughout is to treat the works studied as individual masterpieces, to be analyzed for their instrinsic value and as illustrating basic principles of art; the concepts and terms developed in the first six weeks provide the tools of interpretation and judgment.

If the Ouachita course is an effort to escape from history, the sophomore integrated course at Tech is an unqualified endorsement of the historical approach in humanistic teaching.   Its purpose and content are accurately suggested by the catalogue title, "Our American Heritage."   The aim is to define the culture or way of life inherited by Americans, and the method is that of cultural history — to study the origin and growth of political and social institutions in close coordination with national literature, music, painting, and architecture.

The course meets five days a week, the first three periods being devoted to lectures, the Thursday hours to "laboratory" periods (mainly used for viewing and listening to supplement the lectures on art and music), and the Friday meetings to discussion and examinations.   It is taught cooperatively by four instructors, each handling the material in his own field.   Three of the eight hours' credit for the course are assigned to social science in the college requirements, the remaining five being counted under the humanities.   Approximately three-fourths of the course content is divided between literature and history; the remaining quarter is devoted to art and music in roughly equal amounts.

In spite of its diversity of materials, the course is closely knit. The basic structure is laid down in the lectures on social and political history; the literary material elaborates and develops the basic themes, while the discussion of music, painting, and architecture supplies additional detail and concrete documentation.   In its total impact, "Our American Heritage" is a synthesis of the social science and the humanities, dominated by the historical point of view.

If it were the only course offered by the college in these basic fields, it would doubtless be open to some criticism.   Although the whole of it contributes to the student's understanding of society, it would not be sufficient to provide the comprehensive grasp of social institutions and mechanisms, nor of the techniques of investigation employed by students of society, which sound general education requires.   On the humanistic side, too, the course is incomplete and partial.   While five-eigths of the content falls within the humanities, social and political history is the dominant element, the controlling idea.   Questions of aesthetic form and technique, central in the Ouachita course, would be out of place here, at odds with the spirit, method, and educational purpose of the course. But the general-education program at Tech is an elaborate design, in which this course is only one piece.   It is flanked on one side by year courses in the history of western civilization and in human growth and development, in which missing aspects of society and the social sciences are solidly represented; on the other side it is supplemented by later courses in "Western Ideas and Values" and "Western Art and Music," in which philosophy, literature, and the fine arts are further developed and shown in a different light. Within this larger pattern, the sophomore humanities course is intended to fulfill a specific function, which its content and plan are well adapted to achieve.   Being well taught, too, it seems to me one of the most interesting and effective general-education courses in the state.

The humanities courses at Hendrix and Arkansas State are closer to Davidson's second category, being designed like a number of those in the 1949 survey to bring their students "face to face with the great issues of living that man has had to confront in the past and must face today."   The material is presented chronologically in one, while in the other it is organized around large general themes.   But in both the central purpose is to engage the students in a struggle with the "big questions" which have concerned thoughtful men over the centuries.

The Arkansas State course, "World of Literature, Philosophy, and Religion," begins with a nine-week unit on Greek and Christian ideas, considered as "foundations of our common thought." The reading materials include the *Iliad*, some Greek plays, several Platonic dialogues and brief selections from Aristotle's *Ethics*, and more extended readings in Genesis, Proverbs, and Ecclesiastes.   The rest of the course — the second half of the first semester and the whole of the second — is devoted to an exploration of three main problems: man's relationship to society, to the political state, and to God.   The writings chosen to illustrate these themes include much the same variety of philosophical and literary forms as those read in the opening unit, but they are not always taken up in chronological order. The primary emphasis is on ideas, organized around a few central themes which provide a dialectical framework for the whole. The historical setting ("the unique social and political climate which produced the writing and gave it meaning," as the course syllabus says) is usually sketched in by way of preparation, and questions of literary artistry may be touched upon occasionally. But the main concern is with patterns of thought which "transcend historical limitations and become the natural heritage of all men in all times." The concept underlying the course is that of the "cultural heritage," with major emphasis on philosophy, but it has been dissociated to some degree from the usual historical and chronological implications of that view.

Like other parts of the present program of general education at Hendrix, "Man's Search for Values" is contemporary with the Arkansas Experiment. First offered in 1952, it is now taught in five sections under two instructors, with a normal enrollment of some 125 students. The instructor and his class are seated around a circular table, so that everyone's face is visible to the whole group, and the method is almost entirely discussion. It is the only course in the humanities which is required of all students.

The aims of the course are to acquaint the student with the history of ideas in the western world and to assist him in forming his own philosophy of life. The plan follows the narrative sequence presented in Crane Brinton's *Ideas and Men*, which is used as a text; a syllabus prepared by the staff includes a detailed set of questions, based on Brinton, which are designed to help the student in reading the assigned material and to provide a point of departure for class discussion. There are also required and optional readings in literary and philosophical classics, but little is done with art or music. In the last six weeks — probably the high point of this fine course — the students work together in pairs to read and report on important books in which some of the great questions debated in earlier months are arised again in contemporary form. The first half of each hour is allowed for the report, which is followed by a barrage of searching questions and lively argument. How much these freshmen have learned about reading a book dealing with general ideas, how significant and vital these great issues have become to them, and the advance they have made toward maturity of mind cannot be doubted by anyone who has had the pleasure of observing these discussions.

IV

The natural and social sciences can be clearly identified by their objects of study, the natural and social worlds, but the humanities are not concerned with any analogous aspect of reality. If they have a definite subject-matter, it is the whole body of philosophic, literary, historical, and artistic works which have been created by human thought and skill for the pleasure and profit of mankind. These materials are so rich and many-sided that they can be turned to almost any educational use. Literature and art, as well as philosophy itself, can be taught philosophically, as an expression of ideas and values; they may also be studied historically, for they not only have their own internal sequence and continuity of aesthetic development but also reflect the larger story of cultural change. What is unique in humanistic study, however, is an interest in individual works considered as artistic constructions, and the methods of inquiry peculiar to the humanities are the techniques of analysis, interpretation, and evaluation.

A complete and balanced program in the humanities should include all the possible ways of teaching the material admits — though not necessarily all at once or within a single course — and several of the courses reviewed in the preceding sections attempt to develop the student's interpretive and critical faculties. Courses in the fine arts, however, are most likely to give central emphasis to that aim, the third of Davidson's governing purposes.

All fifteen of the Arkansas colleges include some work in the fine arts, especially painting and music, among their prescribed or alternative requirements in general education. Some of the courses meeting these requirments have already been described — those in which study of the arts is combined with a more substantial presentation of literary and philosophical works. Of the programs not yet considered here, three teach art and music separately, in one-semester departmental courses, three teach them together in a combined course, but under different instructors, and three offer courses of wider scope, though still without a complete integration with a single instructor throughout.

At State Teachers College, students are allowed to choose among four alternatives, all departmental: "Art Appreciation," history of art or history of music, and "Music in the Modern World." All of these semester courses giving three hours' credit. The college has not attempted to develop a combined course. Harding and Arkansas State, both of which originally hoped to integrate the two arts, have reverted to separate courses in music and the visual arts. As presently taught, these are large courses with several sections and total enrollments averaging close to two hundred students; the approach is analytical rather than historical, emphasizing aesthetic structure, basic forms, the media and elements of visual and musical art, and the purpose is to develop the power to see and listen with understanding — as the Arkansas State catalog puts it, "to *observe* as well as to see, to *hear* as well as listen." At both colleges the requirement is four hours, two in each field, so that all students have some experience of both arts.

The obstacles to an integrated treatment of the fine arts are clearly illustrated by the experience at Arkansas State. As originally designed in the summer of 1953, the new general-education program included a one-year combined course in art and music. The staff was committed to a unified presentation, a common syllabus was drawn up, and the course was taught on that basis during the 1953-54 academic year; each instructor continued through the whole course, handling both visual and musical material. But the plan was abandoned after the first year. The two parts of the course are still listed under a common title — "Fine Arts: Visual" and "Fine Arts: Musical" — but they are taught independently, with a semester for each, and they are staffed by different instructors.

The chief obstacle was the feeling of the teachers in the combined course that they lacked sufficient preparation outside their own fields. According to the head of the department of fine arts at Arkansas State, "The music teachers found great difficulty in coping with the visual art, and the art teachers were equally troubled with the music work." Only one member of the staff had had sufficient training in both fields to carry on the teaching with confidence. But there were other difficulties and hazards. Instructors often speak feelingly of the lack of background in the arts among many students; as in mathematics, a considerable proportion comes to college not only ignorant of the subject but hostile to it.   At both colleges, however, the instructors feel that most students shake off these prejudices and begin to find an un-expected interest and enjoyment in art.   It is hard to say how far they advance in the power of analysis and critical judgment, for the staffs both report that they have had great difficulty in estab-lishing satisfactory testing instruments and standards of grading. Textbooks present another problem, although an inexpensive paper-backed book by the composer Aaron Copland, *What to Listen for in Music,* has been used with some success on both campuses.   They also both make extensive use of records, mounted prints, and slides; at Arkansas State, some attempt has been made in "laboratory" periods to involve the students in the performance of music or the making of simple art works — an idea which has been more fully realized in the "Basic Course in the Arts" at the University of Arkansas.

In the three colleges where art and music are taught together, the courses differ considerably both in their present form and in their origin and history.   At John Brown, where students are allowed to choose among several alternatives, a course in "The Visual Arts and Music" was added in the fall of 1955 to the pre-viously existing departmental courses.   A three-hour general-education course in art and music was introduced at Southern State College in 1954.   The staff originally hoped to include a substan-tial amount of studio work, but practical difficulties have limited the laboratory phase to listening hours in music and some simple exercises in pencil drawing, coloring, and elementary perspective. Although an attempt is made to integrate the course, the two arts are presented in sequence and by different instructors; the art section is taught from an historical point of view, while music is treated more analytically, through a study of its basic elements and major forms.   At Arkansas Tech, the equivalent of four hours in art and music was incorporated in the American and European humanities courses, one for sophomores and the other for juniors. Art and music are still coordinated with American literature and history in the sophomore course, already discussed, but they were removed from the junior course in 1955 and are now taught in a separate two-credit course, "Western Art and Music."   It is taught cooperatively by an instructor in art and an instructor in music.   The two subjects are developed simultaneously, rather than in sequence, and are taught in closely parallel fashion.

Three other courses, though broader in scope, belong here because of their primary focus on the fine arts.   One of them, "Music and Fine Arts" at Arkansas College, is not a regular formal course but a series of lectures and demonstrations at the bi-weekly college assembly hour.   It is an interesting effort by a very small college (fewer than 200 students) to use the traditional period to provide some aesthetic background and experience for the students. One-half hour of credit is given each semester, a total of four hours being required for graduation.   A three-hour freshman course at AM&N, Humanities 132, deals not only with music and the graphic and plastic arts but also with literature, philosophy, and religion. Fine Arts 103 and 113 at the University of Arkansas is a six-hour full-year course which introduces students to architecture, visual art, dance, music, and theater.

The humanities course at AM&N, required of all freshmen, meets three times a week in sections of thirty to fifty students and is offered in both the fall and spring semesters; it is taken by some 350 to 400 students each year.   It is coordinated and directed by an instructor whose own major interest is in philosophy and religion; he gives about a third of the forty-eight lectures, the others being divided among instructors from the departments of speech and drama, music, art, foreign languages, and English.   The component subjects are not presented sequentially but in a complex alternating pattern; in the fourth and fifth weeks, for example, the lectures deal with the following subjects, discussed by four different members of the staff:

What the theater is and does
The subject of art
What the musician works with
What philosophy is and does
What the musician works with
Skeletal and organic structure in the arts

Even in the last three weeks of the course, which are devoted to world religions, contemporary philosophy, and "the quest for the good life," two hours are assigned to lectures on architecture.

A procedure of this kind undoubtedly has its dangers. The kaleidoscopic shifting of subjects and instructors is likely to be confusing, and there is little chance to develop any aspect of the material in depth. The student's role is largely passive, and the topics discussed are for the most part highly general and abstract. The instructor in charge has done his best to offset these defects of the course design, particularly through optional laboratory periods which provide more direct experience of the arts, but the course is essentially a lecture series, a sequence of general discussions by several speakers.

The University's "Basic Course in the Arts," with which this rapid survey must be concluded, is an ambitious effort in humanistic education. The first semester is devoted to architecture and the visual arts, the second semester to music, dance, and the theater; the five arts are taught in sequence, each with its own instructional staff, but according to a common plan and under the direction of an interdepartmental committee. The method combines lectures with laboratory or studio work, two hours a week of each.

Although it shows the dispersive tendency of all combined courses in which the different arts retain their separate identities and are taught by different instructors, Fine Arts 103, 113 holds together remarkably well. An essential tool is the two-volume syllabus, one for each semester, which includes not only an outline and schedule of assignments for each unit but a statement of objectives for the course as a whole, a philosophy which animates it throughout. Another interesting device is a chart, bound in with the syllabus, which lists the five arts in parallel columns with an analysis of each under four common headings: purpose and materials, dominant sensual activity, organization, and response of spectators or listeners. The unity of the course in the student's mind is also undoubtedly due in part to the rhythm of the teaching method — the regular alternation of lecture and laboratory every week and the repetition of this pattern in each new unit. Students begin to be at home in the course, to understand the purpose behind the procedures, to anticipate some of the points to be made as they move from art to art. With the great advantages of a splendid Fine Arts Center and continuity of staff from the first beginnings of the course, it has thoroughly established itself as one of the unquestioned successes of the program at the University of Arkansas.

One final point about general education in the fine arts may be illustrated by the University's course. It is an article of faith among a good many college teachers in these fields that students ought to have some experience in the production of art, as well as in observation, interpretation, and judgment. "An ounce of playing is worth a pound of listening," one of the instructors in music at Arkansas has said. In the laboratory periods of the "Basic Course" the staff has had an unusual opportunity to put this conviction to the test of practice.

As the instructors are quick to acknowledge, the results are limited in many respects. Because of differences in the media, the idea is more difficult to apply in some arts than it is in others. In the architecture laboratories the last three meetings have sometimes been devoted to a design exercise, planning a residence, but most of the hours are used to supplement the lectures by additional slides and films. In music, too, the line of least resistance is to fall back upon further listening as the primary function of the studio sessions. In all five arts the students' lack of background is a severe limitation. As at other colleges, most of the students are ignorant of the arts, some of them actively hostile; almost all are embarrassed and ill at ease when asked to perform before a class, or even to sing in a group or dabble with paints at a desk or an easel. In five two-hour laboratory periods for each art — all that are available for music, theater, and dance — it is obviously impossible to carry the students very far; the instructor is doing well if he overcomes the initial inhibitions. At best he cannot expect more than a handful of the students to achieve anything of real artistic merit.

The results, nevertheless, are sometimes astonishingly good. The general level is probably highest in the visual arts, in which the students are taken through a well-designed eight-period sequence of exercises in line, value, color, texture and pattern, ending with a fairly substantial drawing or construction to which the last three laboratory periods are devoted. The most remarkable results, perhaps, are those achieved in the dance laboratory. The instructor, an artist herself as well as a fine teacher, is able to wheedle most of her awkward beginners into a variety of expressive movements, if only a two-minute rhythmical pantomime, accompanied by a drum. She manages to communicate something of her own feeling for the dance, a glimpse at least of its beauty and power. The lectures also contribute to this result, as do the films and demonstrations, but there is much more meaning in a professional performance for students who have actually tried to do such things themselves. The strength of the "Basic Course," I believe, is its combination of studio activity with the study of first-class examples, practice in analysis and criticism, and a well-defined framework of organizing ideas. Few general-education courses in the arts show a more thorough-going and imaginative effort toward the development of aesthetic appreciation.

Teaching in the humanities is harder to describe and evaluate justly than instruction in the natural and social sciences. The more specialized studies included within the field are very different from each other, rich in human interest and educational potentialities; they have a chameleon quality, various and changeable. All liberal teaching is human and personal, but humanistic teaching especially so because of its concern with intangibles and undefinables, with habits of thought and feeling that are usually concealed beneath the surface of the social mask. The effects of such teaching cannot always be guessed from course designs and administrative arrangements, nor measured by the devices of the obective examination. I am sure, however, that nothing can kill the vitality of literature, philosophy, art, and history. Even bad teaching cannot wholly stifle their human meaning, and when taught in a truly humanistic spirit they are what they have always been, the heart of liberal education.

chapter 18

THE HUMANITIES IN GENERAL EDUCATION: 1949-1959

James A. Fisher*

General Education

A modern day Polonius looking over the educational scene might be no less confused in his attempts to classify general education than his forebear was in classifying the drama. Something like general-liberal, liberal-general-rational, instrumental-general-liberal, general-humanistic-liberal and so on might occur to him. Of one thing the observer may be certain — as often as the general education movement has tended to lose dynamism during the last forty years, there has been no loss of vitality in the attempts of educators to define the term.

The purpose of this summary is not to re-define a term which one is almost compelled to feel is indefinable or perhaps ineffable, but rather to indicate some of the trends remarked by the contributing institutions since the appearance of the original volume of this study a decade ago. Let it suffice the reader to make several general comments. In what must be considered a careful and studied analysis of general education made in 1952, the 51st Yearbook of the National Society for the Study of Education, *General Education,* two definitions of general education are quoted as typical. The first is that of Clarence Faust. Speaking of general education, he says:

> Its function is not to prepare young people . . . to deal with the special problems parceled out in our society

---
*Chairman, Division of Humanities, Boston University College of Basic Studies.

to the members of the various occupations and professions
— to the chemist and the carpenter, the architect and the
accountant, the merchant and the housewife — but with
the problems which confront all members of our society
alike, such problems as our domestic and foreign policies,
our political universe, our personal philosophies. General
education appears from this point of view to be the
preparation of youth to deal with the personal and social
problems with which all men in a democratic society are
confronted.   (Clarence H. Faust, "The Problem of General Education," in *The Idea and Practice of General
Education: An Account of the College of the University
of Chicago*, p. 6.   By Present and Former Members of the
Faculty.   Chicago: University of Chicago Press, 1950).

The second definition is Earl McGrath's.

General Education . . . is that which prepares the
young for the common life of their time and their kind
. . . It is the unifying element of a culture. It prepares
the student for a full and satisfying life as a member of
a family, as a worker, as a citizen — an integrated and
purposeful human being. It does not overlook differences in talent, interest, and purpose; nor does it attempt
to form everyone in a single mental and spiritual mold.
Seeking to make possible the maximum development of
the individual consistent with the general good, it encourages respect for inventive genius and tolerance for variations in opinion, while at the same time it rests on the
principle that deviations in thought or in act must be
based on understanding rather than ignorance of the purposes, values, and standards of society. (Earl J. McGrath,
et al., *Toward General Education*, pp. 8-9. New York:
Macmillan Co., 1948.)

There are probably no real conflicts between the various con-
tributors to this volume and the two definition just given.   The
differences, if they really exist, are in terms of approach, methodology, emphasis.   For the very fact that the many colleges are
engaged in the task of general education indicates a core of agreement.

However, many of us who have been engaged in the field of
general education for the last decade have been aware of a subtle
change in attitude on the part of some of the persons occupying
the higher administrative positions in the field.   This change in

attitude, in what amounted to a bitter struggle between those in the field of general education and those in the traditional liberal arts, is most characterized by the tendency, now, to make the terms "general education" and "liberal education" synonymous. There was a time during the last ten years when these two terms were anathema. Such is not now the case. Dr. Carpenter in her report from Stephens College is sensitive to this shift and seeks to point out once again factors which make liberal education different from general education. She has discovered a series of tendencies which are characteristic of each. Liberal education, she feels,

1. *Tends* to use traditional materials in the hopes that they will "liberate the mind."
2. *Tends* to emphasize mental training in an assumption that everything else is going to get done somewhere.
3. *Tends* to educate the elite, the students whose intellectual capacity is greatest, without too much consideration of the student who has average ability ("ability" *tends* to be identified with verbal ability.)
4. *Tends* to ignore methods of teaching (even, at times, to scorn them), or to choose those methods which are convenient for faculty and administration, regardless of consideration of methods which best suit the student.

On the other hand, Dr. Carpenter states that those who use the term "General Education" must also accept the implications which come from that term. These implications she also sees as a series of tendencies. It is in a comparison of these tendencies that one becomes aware of the real differences between general education and liberal education. Dr. Carpenter lists five important tendencies in general education among "institutions which use the term and attempt to follow through on its implications." These institutions:

1. *Tend* to explore the needs and interests of students, both immediate and future needs, insofar as studies reveal trends which are significant.
2. *Tend* to sift all *Materials* AND *Methods* through consideration of #1, rather than adopting materials which have traditionally been presented in the way in which they have been traditionally presented. This selection of materials and methods may or may not result in curriculum and course changes.

3. *Tend* to consider students of average ability as important as brilliant intellectuals.
4. *Tend* to offer guidance to students to a greater degree than is the case with liberal education.
5. *Tend* to consider the student's total development — emotionally and socially, in and out of the classroom — as part of a good education.

It will be unfortunate, she concludes, if we ignore those differences because it means increased work and study and planning in developing good general education courses, and "because it is not now popular to do more than make our higher education courses as difficult in traditional respectability as the Russian courses in science."

One final observation about general education to be made is that it is a peculiarly American phenomenon. Considering the two definitions cited, it is doubtful whether they could be made by any other than an American educator. General education is democratic education, but it is more than that — it is American-democratic education. Of the democracies throughout the world, only America does not have a heritage of feudalism, caste systems, mass illiteracy, and hereditary nobility. Only America with its strong, dynamic middle class could have provided the appropriate political, economic, social and educational climate for the general education movement. So one may say of general education that whatever else it is, it is peculiar to the democratic context. Such objectives as critical thinking on political, economic, and social issues and effective citizenship are the rightful aims of general education in a democracy, they are not the bona fide aims of education in a totalitarian regime. The whole frame-work and philosophy which gave rise to the general education movement points out its inextricable connection with the desire to preserve and enrich our democratic heritage. That the humanities have a vital role in this movement is unquestionable.

The Problems of Administration

There are two broad methods of administering general education courses. The first method places the responsibility for general education in the hands of the dean of the Arts and Science College and the second method provides for a separate and autonomous college devoted to general education. Proponents of both of these methods are to be found in the present volume.   Professor Robert Davidson of Florida puts his position in favor of the separate college forcefully.

> Since the general education program at the University of Florida was established some twenty-five years ago (1935-36), it has been handled by an independent administrative unit, the University College, and has had strong administrative support during this entire period.
> Our situation with regard to staff is a comparable one.   We have a staff each year of from twenty-five to thirty members.   Twenty of these are on our own Humanities budget; four or five staff members are "borrowed" from the departments of English and philosophy, and four or five from other areas in the University College.   Consequently, the teaching staff as a whole is not only sympathetic to the broad aims of general education but is committed professionally to making a success of the Humanities program.   My experience during twelve years as chairman of the program at Florida confirms an unqualified enthusiasm for this type of organization.

The conflicts involved in the separate administrative organization as opposed to the non-separate are pointed up by Dr. Herndon in her report on the program at Florida State University.   At the present time, the Humanities course together with the whole general education program is under the Dean of the Arts and Science College.   The Dean appoints the various chairmen who then direct each of the courses.

> These chairmen form a committee to recommend general policy.   The Dean is also advised by a General Education Committee of the Council of Deans.   The chairman of Humanities is given a full-time secretary and a budget for equipment and supplies, but he must bargain with department heads for staff.   The system is not as difficult as it sounds, for the various departments strongly support the Humanities course and consider it a part of their responsibility.   We have continued to maintain a competent staff under this administrative arrangement because we have been free to use only those genuinely interested in teaching the course and because the course itself offers a challenge to broadly trained and alert teachers.   In 1949, when it was possible that the general education program might become a separate administrative

unit, there was some uneasiness among the various staff members lest loyalties should be divided between general education and their department.   Now there seems no doubt that in the foreseeable future general education will be the responsibility of the departments contributing and of the Dean of Arts and Sciences.   Staff members then will be appropriately rewarded for their general education teaching by their own department heads and Dean.   More and more department heads are considering qualifications for teaching Humanities in making new appointments. There is a feeling of satisfaction and security in the present arrangement.   The development of our course has always been solidly in the hands of those teaching it and it seems likely that its greatest strength will continue to be the enthusiasm and devotion of the staff.

However this issue is settled at any particular college, it is one which does not admit of indecisive action.   No middle ground where there is no clear-cut responsibility whether it lie with the Dean of the Arts and Science College or whether it rest with the Dean of a separate college devoted to general education is permissible.   This leads to administrative and academic chaos.   It works a particular hardship on the instructors responsible for the course. In the 1949 volume, Robert Miller of Florida State pointed out that, "new instructors are properly concerned with advancement, and they often feel that promotion can be better secured by faithfully discharging departmental duties than those in a course which has no administrative status."   Where there is divided loyalty, whether on the highest administrative level or on the departmental level, maximum effectiveness of teaching and academic security are unobtainable.

Three Approaches to the Humanities

In his summary to the 1949 volume on *The Humanities in General Education,* Professor Davidson saw three major approaches to the Humanities.   He categorized these approaches as (1) the Great Books or Great Issues approach; (2) the history of Western Culture or Western Civilization approach; (3) the approach which seeks to orient the student to the work of art and focuses upon critical judgment of the products which make up the Humanities. After ten years of serious work and thought, the colleges represented in this study continue to find these three emphases satisfactory and defensible.

St. John's College may be considered the classic example in the volume of those institutions who find the aims of general education in the Humanities best served through a study of the Great Books of the Western World. Requiring the same course of all its students and centering as it does around these monuments of western man, the "whole St. John's program is a Humanities program." Dr. Kieffer writes,

> The heart and substance of the St. John's program is reading and talking Great Books of the Western tradition. The program is articulated by having twice weekly discussions of the Great Books (read in chronological sequence) supported by daily classes in language and mathematics, and twice-weekly laboratory periods for the natural sciences. A weekly formal lecture on some topic of the tradition supplies a thread of authoritative commentary, its authoritativeness tempered by requiring the lecturer to submit to questions by the students at the conclusion of his formal presentation.

The criteria used by St. John's for the inclusion of books in the course helps one to form a clear picture of the nature and aim of the course. There are, in essence, three criteria: (1) any book included must be a classic, that is, a lasting treatment of those questions the world poses to those who live in it; (2) the books should cover all of the facets of man's questions, thus the books would include poetry, history, mathematics, science and the several branches of philosophy; (3) the books must come from the context of Western Civilization, "since the world our students will live in is the world of that civilization."

The rationale for the great books program may be summed up in a statement Dr. Kieffer makes about books.

> Books are the highest use of man's distinguishing characteristics of language. Books speak to their audience in the familiar language of their experience to lead them up to unfamiliar levels on which they can transcend the immediacy of the world of personal observation. This happens on the level of plain information, on the level of imaginative sympathy with unknown persons, and on perhaps the higher level, that of flashes of insight into

the reasons of things.   Books do not do this by telling the truth to a passive recipient.   The process of reading requires the active participation of the mind of the reader. Great books are those that do what books do with the greatest artistry and about the greatest questions, those that keep recurring to men no matter how often they think they have them answered.   To go to school is to withdraw from the world.   To go to school to the Great Books is a fruitful withdrawal from the world because the student learns both to build his own world and hence to live in the great world that is the, as yet, un-finished building of the greatest teachers, the great books. The world itself, the cosmos of God's creation, is, of course, the ultimate teacher.   Great Books are a proxi-mate teacher, in that they are immediately intelligible and better ordered than the world as it appears to the child.

In the ten years that have elapsed since that statement there have been no major revisions in aims or approach at St. John's. Changes in details as a result of annual studies of the curriculum made by the Instruction Committee of the Faculty are, of course, to be noted.   As a result of a foundation-sponsored study of the college made in 1955, the most significant result was "the weight given to the necessity of more attention to the art of writing."

Surveying the program of the Great Books at St. John's, Dr. Kieffer can conclude, "St. John's is well satisfied that its decision in 1937 to require a single program of all the liberal arts, linguistic and scientific if the goal of a true program of Humanities was to be pursued was the right decision."

Although in the past the historical-epochal approach to the Humanities in general education was the most popular and widely used structuring of such courses, there has been a significant shift away from the purely historical-Western Civilization aspects to a selected study of important cultural epochs and a chronological study of ideas and masterpieces.   As Bartlet of M.I.T. expresses it, the humanities course makes "no pretense of being a survey of Western Civilization."   The plan is to bring the "students in contact with some of the great minds of the past as they have dealt with the fundamental problems of human existence."   "By examining ideas in action at particular significant periods in man's history he (the student) enlarges his perspective and increases his understanding of some of the forces which have created the society in which his life and personality are being shaped."

So significant in one case was the shift that at the University of Florida which had previously had a historically oriented course the faculty put the second, "contemporary," semester first. The reasons for this shift were dissatisfaction with the traditional course organization which began with the Greeks and concluded "with a hasty survey of important trends during the past hundred years," and the feeling that the traditional approach did not sufficiently motivate students who brought a built-in dislike of Humanities to the course. To start with a past so remote as to be almost meaningless to little but a handful of students resulted in a loss of interest and motivation which could not but impair the reaching of course objectives. As a result of these considerations, the course was simply reversed. The semester is devoted to "The Humanities in Contemporary Life" and the second semester to "Our Cultural Heritage." The results as reported by Professor Davidson are encouraging.

> I am happy to report that . . . the change has proved a most successful one. In "the Humanities in Contemporary Life" we include literature, philosophy, art and music of our own age (the past hundred years being a convenient period), selecting material that makes immediate and effective contact with the experience and vital concern of students such as ours. The general student response to this approach to the Humanities has been quite encouraging — we now "lose" during the early weeks of the semester far fewer practical-minded students who had never been reconciled to this requirement, and we find a growing and very genuine enthusiasm among a majority of our group. But this we had expected. What was not anticipated was the way in which this interest and concern, developing during the first semester, would carry on into the second course dealing with "Our Cultural Heritage." Our students are now better prepared — that is, far readier psychologically — for a study of "the great books," the great ideas, the great art and ideas of the past. They now have, in much greater number certainly, the needed sense of the relevance of this material to their own interests and the needed desire to enlarge their understanding and appreciation. The uncertainty, the confusion and the anti-intellectualism so

widespread in our own age has made them anxious to find in our own cultural heritage ideas and values that will give to human life some greater meaning, stability and purpose.

Another institution devoted in 1949 to the "Western Civilization" orientation which has made a significant shift in emphasis at the expense of the purely historical approach is Florida State University. Because of a loss of three semester hours from the course, a revision was obviously necessary. The earlier course had two objectives centering around western civilization: (1) "To develop understanding and appreciation of the cultural heritage of Western Civilization through the study of representative masterpieces," (2) "To present this cultural heritage through the chronological study of the great periods of Western Civilization." In the revision of the course it is significant that this second objective was abandoned. Dr. Herndon explains:

> Humanities had come to mean to all of us less a study of cultural history and more an understanding of the ideas and concepts which are important in the world today and which are expressed in works that are still significant and valuable to people in the twentieth century. In the revised course, we intended to emphasize *Humanities today*, not only the creative expression of the twentieth century — though we planned to enlarge our section on modern culture — but the ideas and forms of the past which have particular present values and which we believe will be permanently significant.

At Michigan State University a change in the Humanities program has also been effected. In 1952 the two courses, History and Civilization and Literature and Fine Arts, which had previous to that time constituted the Humanities program at the Basic College, were merged into one course. This course because of the college requirements is open only to students of sophomore standing or better. The course consists of three terms of ten weeks each. The titles of the respective terms, "Roots of the Western Tradition," "Medieval Culture and the Dawn of Modern Times," "The Modern world," indicate the historical framework upon which the course is built.

As Professor Hirschfeld points out, "the course examines man's creative expressions in the context of historical reality. It represents the ideas, beliefs, and aesthetic creations of men as rooted in historical culture."

The results of this type of presentation are described by Hirschfeld.

> This thread of historical continuity . . . serves to lift the student's view above the *purely contemporary* so that he may see "the nature of man as reflected in the historical process." The course is basically concerned with the persistent problems that man has faced, . . . the nature of the universe, man's place in it and the meaning of his being, the disparity of man's deserts and rewards, the gap between society's ideal imaginative ends and the means used to realize them, and the inadequacy of language to express ideas and feelings which cry for expression. At the same time, the student is brought to see that each age offers solutions to these constant problems in its own terms. This paradox of permanency amidst change is particularly challenging to the complacent acquiesence in the overwhelming impact of the merely contemporary. Finally this dynamic historical approach provides the basis for the organization of the content of the course.

We see in this statement and that of Professor Davidson describing the shift in the Humanities course at the University of Florida in which the historical approach is sacrificed in the first semester to engage the student's attention with the "purely contemporary," something of a conflict within the historical approach to the Humanities which has not as yet been resolved. The problem may be reduced to the simple question, how can one keep before the student the fabric of history and at the same time show him or make him feel in his own life the overwhelming relevance of the Humanities?

What seems to be happening in these various courses is a shift away from the strict coverage of the History of Western Civilization type of course to a combination of "great issues" of Western Civilization which one might expect to find in the traditional "Great Books" orientation with some of the basic objectives of what might be called the "aesthetic-critical judgment" approach

History remains of great importance as the climate or soil from which spring the great masterpieces of the western world, but the student's ability to make valid aesthetic judgments of art objects and to relate these seemingly disparate objects to his contemporary world has moved up from a secondary objective to a primary one as Dr. Herndon of Florida State has noted. The historical aspect is now, at least at Florida State, given in the Freshman history course which is a survey of Western Civilization.

The third method of organizing Humanities courses is built around the belief that the student is best served by developing certain critical attitudes towards the whole field of artistic endeavor so that he may participate emotionally and intellectually in the world of creativity throughout his continuing adult life. These colleges do not attempt to slight the role of either great ideas or the sweep of history; but they see their objective as one of confronting the student with the art object *qua* art object rather than a monument to the past glories of mankind. To develop a critical and unbiased attitude toward all of the Humanities and an understanding of the vital role they have had and will continue to have in the affairs of men is a major aim in these courses. Not only great books, but great works from the whole realm of artistic endeavor serve as the source for developing the critical attitudes sought.

For example, the primary purpose of the course in philosophy at Chatham is, "not to inform the student *about* philosophical systems or the content of philosophical literature; rather its aim is to stimulate philosophical thought about certain enduring ideas."

Summing up the feelings of the staff at Stephens College after ten years, Dr. Carpenter affirms, "if anything, we are more than ever convinced that the layman needs the arts. We are more than ever aware that the layman has need of experience in judging the arts and in finding in them genuine release from tension." Looking at the other possibilities of structuring Humanities courses at Stephens, Miss Carpenter reports that different approaches from the one presently used at the college have been suggested by the college curriculum committee. The one put forward most often being, "a survey of Western Civilization which concentrates on ideas which have influenced us in the United States." This suggestion has generally been viewed with disapproval, "because of the need for more knowledge about the East and less concentration on the West, and also because there is a pronounced feeling that the arts for our students need to be understood for themselves. We view the arts as living experience, as parts of life. We try very hard not to attach labels to a work of art and then dismiss it."

The University of Chicago has continued through the years to follow the same approach to the arts. As Thomas pointed out, "Our aim . . . was to develop as large an experience of products of the various arts of mankind as time allowed us and to cultivate the understanding and the exercise of the disciplines which lead to an intelligent and cultivated appreciation of art, as *works of art*, and not as documentary evidence of political and social theory or of natural history." The rationale for using what is considered the non-historical approach to the arts is explained by Thomas in the following manner.

> We were concious . . . of the fact that we were planning courses for several hundred students, the majority of whom would not continue formal study of the humanities beyond our courses. It was therefore necessary to consider what, of all the activities which we might legitimately pursue within the sphere of humanistic study, would be most profitable as a comprehensive experience and most useful to these students in the future. We agreed that we could not do justice to the artistic achievements of men if we neglected any one of the three great media of creative expression: music, the visual forms, and literature. We agreed, too, that in each course and at all times the particular work of art ought to be the principal object of study. Each work of any kind should therefore be chosen not merely because it was representative of a type, of a historical period, or of any of the great ideas that have stirred the minds and emotions of man, but because it possessed values which were its own unique achievement.
>
> This is one reason why it was decided not to organize the sequence in a historical framework or around themes and ideas, since there seemed to us to be a tendency to reduce the study of works of art to only one of their many dimensions. The decision was in no way a rejection of the importance of historical knowledge in the appreciation of the arts nor of the contribution of the arts to cultural history. We recognized that where

history would enlighten understanding, historical knowledge should be given, and this was one of the uses which
we made of the lectures (one each week) in the first two
courses. We believed that it would be impossible to read
the *Protagoras, Crime and Punishment, King Lear,* or
the *Decline and Fall of the Roman Empire* without considering significant ideas about public and private virtue;
but it seemed better that students should understand how
each author treated these ideas in his own way for his
own artistic ends whether as philosopher, as dramatist,
as novelist, or as historian.

The course is primarily interested in teaching the students,
"the arts of listening, seeing, and reading thoughtfully and analytically; to hear what the music is saying . . . to see with eyes
trained to see something akin to the visual experiences of artists
so different as Botticelli and Cezanne; to read Thucydides, Shakespeare, Conrad, Plato, and T. S. Eliot in a way appropriate to the
artistic form and purposes of each author."

At Boston University Junior College the Humanities program is also oriented around the need for the students to develop
critical attitudes toward the arts. Little or no attempt is made
to structure the course upon historical lines in the sense that art
works are taken up in a chronological order. As Black and
Richter have pointed out, the course is structured upon four "vectors" which give unity to the two-year core curriculum. Their
description of the structure defines these four vectors.

> The *analytic-systematic* vector governs the study
> of the work of art itself: its parts, its medium and skills,
> and its style. The *retrospective-historical* vector focuses
> the attention of students upon the cultural context in
> which art objects are created and from which they derive
> their unique characteristics. The *creative-innovative* vec-
> tor operates when students are challenged to innovate
> from what they have learned or to re-synthesize what
> they have learned, as for example in the creation of
> short stories, plays, poems, or essays. Finally, the
> *contemplative-speculative* vector induces the student to
> contemplate the ideal ends of the good life and to specu-
> late upon the construction and reconstruction of the older
> forms of social and esthetic order, thereby widening their
> own sense of tradition.

In order to develop the critical attitudes toward the arts which this and other courses centering around the "critical thinking" orientation feel are of primary importance, the program operates upon four "esthetic principles" which are felt to be fundamental to the Humanities.

1. All works of art are artificial constructs dependent for understanding upon the fact that they are expressed in a symbolic language.
2. All works of art are enriched in meaning when they are understood as related to the historical, cultural, or traditional context in which they were created.
3. The significance of a work of art is in no way dependent upon the historical information imparted by it, but rather depends for its significance upon the artist's ability to transcend the limits of his time and to relate the universal aspects of man's experience.
4. Understanding a work of art is in a great measure a matter of awareness, awareness of the possible choices among the language, media, skills and technics of a given civilization and its given view of art.

Thus we see three major approaches with their proponents, still vital after a decade of revisions, questionings, and attacks. It is doubtful whether any real trend can be noted. However, there seems to be a tendency on the part of at least some of the colleges formerly devoted to the historical approach to limit the scope of history and to stress as a primary objective the development of critical attitudes toward the art, what was previously considered a secondary objective. On the other hand, such an institution as Boston University which is committed to the "critical thinking" approach is constantly searching for fresh and original ways of making clear to the students that the arts are part of the great "fabric of history" and do not exist merely in their own contexts.

New Methods of Instruction and Content

Of the new methods of instruction that have been reported by the various colleges, the one that is most reflective of the changes that have taken place in the last ten years is the use of educational television. There is no denying the impact this medium has made upon the life of nearly all of our citizens both children and adult. In spite of the many criticisms that have been directed against the form and content of the medium, it is true that the non-commercial television station has touched upon some of the educational possibilities latent in such a medium. It is not surprising, then, that some of the colleges represented in this volume should have experimented with television as means of bringing education to more people and enriching the curriculum.

Florida State University has used educational television as a possible method of "meeting the wave of increased enrollment." During the academic year 1958-59 the staff in humanities began experimenting with teaching by television. Several advantages to such use of television can be generalized. One major advantage is that superior teachers can be used for greater numbers of students. Visual materials can be shown in far greater detail than can be normally done in the usual classroom. Also, new kinds of graphic aids can be made available for the teaching of literature and philosophy. In addition to these advantages, others such as making the lecture a more personal experience for the student, making use of "on-campus" artists are noted by Dr. Herndon. These advantages are also echoed by Dr. Carpenter describing the course, "Ideas and Living Today," a course given to all beginning students over a closed-circuit television system. In this course,

> each student sits with a group of seventeen or eighteen other students and hears a presentation for about twenty minutes on some topic which she then discusses with her fellow students for thirty minutes, while the impression of the lecturer is fresh in its impact.

The course centers around such topics as "Freedom and Authority," "Principle and Expediency." Such topics are discussed by a group of representative teachers in the various disciplines so that the student in any one series begins to realize how many subject matter areas need to be known before decisions can be reached." When discussions have centered around ideas of particular interest in the Humanities, Dr. Carpenter feels that "these discussions have freed us in the Humanities course for a more detailed study of some of the same principles in class."

As with any new venture into experimental instruction, there are drawbacks. Dr. Herndon sums up the situation at Florida State.

Television also has its disadvantages, and we are not far along enough in our experiment to say whether it will be successful for Humanities classes. *One of the chief disadvantages is the necessity of returning to the lecture method.* We do not expect, however, to eliminate classroom discussion. No more than two-thirds of the course will be taught from the studio. We expect to provide for the television sections quiz or discussion periods in a conventional classroom atmosphere. We do not expect in the foreseeable future to substitute television teaching for classroom teaching. That would be impossible even if we wanted to do it. We will continue to use our regular faculty for sections taught in the conventional way. We have no illusions about the financial advantages of this new technique. *It is considerably more costly than classroom teaching.* It remains to be seen whether it will be more effective.

The University of Florida as the result of a Ford Foundation grant will inaugurate in the fall a limited number of Humanities sections to be taught the course over closed-circuit television. These sections will meet just as the regular sections do with a fourth meeting a week devoted to discussions with the two instructors responsible for putting on the TV program. These sections will be given the same tests, they will be responsible for the same material, and their achievement evaluated just as that in the other sections. Of particular interest to those responsible for this experiment will be the effectiveness of handling large groups of students, a problem of a pressing nature in the next few years.

Of course it is much too soon to judge the success of educational television. However, the expense and the tentative results so far indicate that while it definitely has possibilities in the field of education, it has yet to indicate that it is the solution to educating effectively and inexpensively large numbers of men and women.

One of the difficulties might be that some educators are more interested in the medium as a means to an end — more education for less money — than they are in it as an end in itself. It would appear, now, that the way to solve the teacher shortage is to put more teachers in the classrooms rather than more TV screens.

There are other changes in methods which while lacking the spectacular aspect of TV are of importance to the educator. What can be noted in several institutions is the abandonment to some extent of the use of the large lecture and greater emphasis upon class discussion. This shift in emphasis can be noted at Wesleyan, Stephens, Florida State, and Chatham. At Florida State, the change was necessitated by the change in the content of the course, where the "new emphasis upon ideas and relationships necessitated some abandonment of the formal lecture in favor of class discussion."

At Chatham, the Arts course has shifted from two lectures and one section meeting a week which was the original structure to one lecture a week and two discussion meetings. There has been a resultant emphasis upon student discussion and "student participation has now become the core of the course."

While not a shift in emphasis M.I.T. uses the discussion method to the exclusion of the lecture method completely. The problem of uniformity does not arise because although the staff receives memoranda suggesting uses of assigned readings, "no effort is made to achieve uniformity."

Fred Millett notes a change from the formal lecture at Wesleyan but expresses a different attitude toward its passing.

> The chief change in operation of the course has been the disappearance of the lectures that in the earlier years had marked major turns in cultural history from which the great works studied had arisen. The reason for the abandonment of occasional lectures, usually by experts in the subject covered, was that the Freshmen did not get enough out of the lectures to warrant the expenditure of faculty time and energy. I recognize that the lecture is a medieval pedagogical device, although its vogue seems likely to increase as mass education becomes more spectacularly massive. I believe, however, that the lecture, if properly conceived and effectively given, can be a valuable and illuminating synthesizing device even for Freshmen. I regret the disappearance of lectures from the Humanities 1-2 program.

At Stephens College, on the other hand, greater emphasis has been placed upon the discussion than previously had been the case. It is interesting to remark that the reason for the shift was the success Stephens had in setting up a program of adult education centering around the discussion of important issues in the arts. As a result of comments by the adults, a change in class structure resulted, where now "students work in groups, make judgments and take self-tests to establish their own confidence on articulating opinions and to force a defense of opinions by specific observations."

It is worthwhile to conclude this brief resume of the uses of the discussion method by quoting the "general Gestalt" suggested for all class discussions as described by Gutwirth at Haverford College.

1. The discussion is not non-directive. It ought not to consist solely of an airing of student views, a kind of democratic assemblage of unreconciled but mutually tolerant asseverations. It is the instructor's task to direct the discussion by his questions and comments in such a way that the class may be made aware of elements in the general scheme of the book, or in the issues it raises, which might otherwise have escaped them.

2. As the above suggests, the instructor does not act as an authority (which in most areas of the course he is not) lecturing from special knowledge; nor yet is he to be impartial moderator of a forum. Ideally, he ought to function as the experienced reader who helps the class come to a more focussed awareness of what they may themselves have but dimly perceived in their own reading.

3. Finally, the discussion ought to be a coming to grips with the work as a living thing. It must do away with attitudes — either fawning or condescending — by which the student seeks to evade the sharp point of the book's argument. Neither the worship of greatness nor a misguided sense of the past as radically *other* must be allowed to come between the reader and, say, Pascal's denunciation of him!

In addition to this change from the lecture to the discussion method, a new method of group instruction unknown at the time of the 1949 volume but which has been used extensively by one college since that time should be summarized. This new method is known as the "team system" at Boston University Junior College.

The "team system" was originally started by the faculty members of the Junior Division of the College of General Education in 1949. In 1952 when the Junior College was founded as a separate college within Boston University the system was adopted on a college-wide basis. The team is composed of one instructor from each of the five divisions at the college: Humanities, Social Science, Science, Communications, and Psychology and Guidance. With the exception of the instructor from the Guidance division, these four people share a common office and from 110-125 students. "Each team member teaches the same sections composed of approximately twenty-five students throughout the academic year, meets weekly for team meetings, and, at the end of the year, evaluates each student's academic potential and transfer prospects on the basis of his cumulative progress at the Junior College and his ability to handle occasional electives at other colleges of the University."

The weekly team meetings enable each instructor to report on the progress of his sections, compare results of class work and exams with the other instructors and share ideas and information about particular students. As originally conceived, the team system was to enable the instructors to correlate and integrate the program of instruction on a unit to unit basis, as the college grew and the number of teams expanded and the course became more fixed this kind of integration gave way to integration on a conceptual level as opposed to subject matter integration.

What the team does in the field of teaching is to make available to the student of a large university and college the benefits of close and intimate associations with instructors and students normally thought to be the unique climate of the small college. The somewhat impersonal attitude that tends to permeate some large institutions, especially on the freshman and sophomore level, is easily dispelled through the use of the team system. Another feature which deserves mention is that the team offers a way of in-service training and orientation for the new instructor. Teaching in a core general education course is not like teaching in a more traditional college. The older members of the team are able to help the young instructor in meeting some of the problems that inevitably arise with new people and induct him into the mysteries of the college's traditions and mores. This kind of orientation is good because it is done by members of the new instructor's own team on a faculty member to faculty member basis rather than in an administrator to faculty member situation. Both Black and Richter feel that the team system is one of the chief forces in enabling the Junior College to make what progress toward reaching its obectives that has been made.

New Content

Not only have there been significant changes in methodology at various of the institutions, but in at least one area there has been an important addition in the content of the Humanities courses. This addition is the inclusion of the world of eastern culture within the scope of the Humanities. The significant aspect of this inclusion is that it shows graphically the impact of the world of politics upon the curriculum planning of college educators.

In 1954-55 at Wesleyan University, the first semester of the Humanities 3-4 course was changed so that some of the work centered around readings in the literature, philosophy, and religion of the Far East. In spite of the difficulty of obtaining suitable translations of materials to be used in the course, Professor Millett found the experience so exciting that in 1955-56 all readings concerned with the Western Civilization were dropped from the first semester and the whole time was devoted to a study of the Far East. Although texts were hard to locate and faculty members adventuresome enough to teach in areas outside their specializations equally so, Professor Millett looking back over those years sums up his experience:

> It can be asserted without question, however, that the new Far and Near Eastern course has proved to be a very exciting experience for both the faculty and students who participate. I found it most intellectually and aesthetically rewarding experience of my later years of teaching.
> And even though my enthusiasm for the course may not have been shared by all who have participated in it in recent years, there would seem to be ample justification for its existence in a period when the world has shrunken to an unbelievable smallness and international relations have become so complicated that the fate of America is intimately involved and may ultimately be decided by its relationship with what have seemed to be extremely remote and almost inaccessible alien cultures.

At the University of Florida, "concern with the larger world responsibilities which face our nations and its citizens" has led the faculty of the humanities course to explore the possibilities of including material about the philosophy and civilization of the Orient in the course. The rationale for such consideration is the need for intelligent men and women to make sound and informed judgments in the near future with regard to the Orient. The conclusion Dr. Davidson draws is "that we have a responsibility to provide somewhere in this program an introduction to the philosophy and civilization of the Orient together with some understanding of the sharp divergence between the ideals and values of the East and West that makes our present world situation so tense, explosive and precarious."

When the experimentation on the course began some four years ago, two major obstacles emerged. The first paralleled that at Wesleyan, namely, the difficulty in obtaining materials to be used. The second objection came from members of the staff who pointed out that there was too much material in the Western Culture that has to be omitted because of the press of time to think of including material from Eastern Culture; and that the staff was not adequately trained to teach such material. These members of the staff felt that it would be misleading to the students to attempt to teach the material rather than putting it in the hands of trained scholars in the field.

> These were impressive objections, but, Davidson points out, Anyone who has had the experience of setting up a general education program and dealing with opposition to it from departmental-minded specialists, will at once recognize that these are exactly the same arguments that were used initially to oppose all general education courses, now risen from the grave to haunt us once more.

In spite of opposition, Davidson feels that encouraging progress is being made in "revealing the basic contrast between the ideals and values of the East and the West." And what is more important is the "growing recognition among our students of the importance of this undertaking, together with a more evident student concern to develop a greater understanding in this whole area."

Further evidence of the impact of the contemporary scene upon general education courses is the course in history and philosophy of science at Chatham College.   It is taught by a group of teachers — a biologist, an astronomer, a physicist, a chemist and a philosopher.   Zetler describes this four-hour one-semester course in terms of its phases.

> The first deals with Greek science, the second with the scientific efforts of the sixteenth and seventeenth centuries, the third with modern and contemporary science, and the last with the implications of science for industry and government.   Such a course has much more to offer the student than the usual one in science; for one thing the teachers in the course make the basic assumption that the sciences are a humane discipline.   One of the aims of the course is to inculcate a more exact sense of the mind's strategy in dealing with problems; another is to make the student aware of natural science as an historical heritage.

The Superior Student

Any teacher knows that all students are not created equal, and even if they were they would not all be equally interested in each of the disciplines.   In large required courses in general education such as the courses which are described in this volume, one of the basic problems facing the alert and enthusiastic instructor is the superior student.   He is the student who is genuinely attracted by the subject matter and seeks additional and more penetrating experiences in the field.   By their very nature, required general education courses in large institutions, and even in the smaller colleges as well, must be constructed to challenge but not over-challenge or frustrate the general student.   What can be done so that the teacher does not neglect the desires of the majority of the students nor over-ride the legitimate aspirations of his superior students?

Michigan State University, Stephens College, Wesleyan University, the University of Chicago, the University of Florida and the State University of Iowa have sought answers to this question.

At Stephens College, a prize called The Humanities Award is given to honor students for extra reading and papers.   The award indicates that the student has, in a period of two years, satisfactorily completed extra work in the interrelated arts.

While not, strictly speaking, a program for the gifted student, an experimental integrated program adopted at Wesleyan University in 1952 involved students of greater potential, at least in the field of philosophy. This program sought to give unity and coherence to what was heretofore a somewhat disjointed program. The students, who tended to be the better students in the Freshmen class, responded to the challenge with enthusiasm.

At Michigan State University, Hirschfield describes the efforts of the department to challenge not only the better students but to relieve some of the inevitable monotony that comes with teaching a limited subject matter.

> For the better students it has organized pro-seminars and honors sections which permit the prescribed subject matter to be taken up more intensively and with a higher degree of sophistication . . . The Department also makes it possible, under Basic College regulations, for some superior students to earn credit for the course on the basis of examination only. It has also conducted an experiment on a substantial scale to encourage independent work on the part of the students. Students in some sections of the course have met in class only three times a week and have been assigned the work of the remaining hour to be done independently. The results showed that the better students profited most from this procedure.

At the University of Florida so important was the problem of the superior student that Professor Davidson considers the efforts on the student's behalf the second major development at the University College in the last ten years. Recognizing the problems of lack of interest and motivation on the part of the better student in courses pitched to the level of the average student, the University of Florida established a limited number of honors sections for students who had completed the first semester's work with distinction. The top five per cent are automatically included in the honors program and the Humanities instructors recommend from the top quarter of their classes students who they feel would benefit from the program. The chairman of the Humanities program then extends an invitation to each student to participate in the honors program if he wishes to do so. About two-thirds of those invited have joined the program.

Limited to twenty students (the regular sections have between thirty and forty students), these honor sections are encouraged to participate more actively in the work and to delve more deeply into the subject matter. For, what the instructors found was that what was needed was not more readings but rather more emphasis upon student responsibility to do more than merely attend class and make satisfactory grades. Davidson writes of the past,

> We have given even our best students too little chance to discover what has been called "the first law of learning: Whatever a man learns he must learn for himself." No program for superior students can be defended if it fails in this. One of our chief concerns, therefore, has been to give more responsibility to able students, both in handling materials of the course and in presenting their own ideas to the group. As a sound guiding principle, we feel that 'the superior student should be given as much freedom to do independent work as is consistent with his initiative and sense of personal responsibility.'

The policy of aiding the superior student also aids the faculty. At the University of Florida the policy is to give the honors sections to as many different instructors as possible; this brings freshness into the shaping of the program and also meets a serious problem in any large general education program of boredom and frustration on the part of many staff members who do not have an opportunity to teach upper division courses in their own special fields. "An honors assignment enables, indeed forces, a staff member to escape the monotony and boredom that is often apparent when one gives full time to four or five identical sections of a general course."

In addition to this honors course, Florida has this past year inaugurated what might be called a "sub-honors" program for the abler students in the regular sections. Such work calls for independent essays, and oral examination before an honors committee, and a series of honors seminars throughout the semester.

The results of this work with the superior student are gratifying at Florida. One result, however, is of interest to those planning such a course. "Experience has . . . made it clear, however, that instructors who are successful with regular sections do not always do well with honors sections. The selection of staff is certainly as important a problem in the success of the honors program as the selection of students."

The University of Chicago has also wrestled with the problem of the superior student. The staff at the college has made a proposal which would affect work done in the Spring Quarter of the school year. For those who have made rapid progress in the first two quarters of the humanities course, work would be suspended, "while the remainder of the class, needing to move at a slower pace and needing intensive review, would continue through the third quarter, with more attention to fundamentals of listening." In addition to this plan, a new one-quarter course for the more advanced students has been proposed but it would be deferred until the student had completed the literature course which immediately follows the first course.

Evaluation Procedures

Since the advent of large classes and the IBM answer sheets, there has been a conflict in the minds of many teachers between the undeniable ease of the objective test and feeling that somehow this was not quite sound or that it did violence to the very aims they had set for themselves in their courses. The colleges represented in this presented volume give ready evidence that the resolution to this conflict has not been found. There are several problems which should be noted in this area. This first, as already indicated, is the one of sheer man-hours of work: how does one grade 100 to 150 exams at each examining period if they are of the essay type without spending a disproportionate amount of time in a task that, while certainly vital, is not so vital that it must consume time better spent in seeking new ways to enrich the subject matter and to present the material? Another pressing matter is that of equality of grading practices. In large core Humanities courses the administration is justifiably concerned that some kind of uniformity be preserved in fairness to the student, if for no other reason. They need to be confident that the same quality of work for one instructor will get approximately the same letter grade with another instructor. If such is not the case, student morale and rapport tend to suffer at the expense of achieving legitimate academic aims.

On the other hand when objectives stress: critical thinking and evaluation of art objects; sensitiveness to aesthetic experiences; "concern with the meaning of Humanities-art, literature, music, and thought . . .;" the need "to deepen the degree of his (the student's) intellectual maturity, to enhance his sensitivity to humane values in fields of mans' thought and endeavor . . . to make him intel·

ligently aware of his own worth and dignity, his obligations and responsibilities, as an individual human being;" one is rightfully concerned with the adequacy of teacher-made objective instruments to measure accurately such objectives. Another factor in the conflict is the feeling on the part of some of the members of Humanities' staffs that they are not qualified in the mysteries of test construction nor sufficiently initiated into the matter of statistics to construct objective tests which are little more than word or phrase recognition tests. Also where one has to make tests of the objective nature year in and year out there just seem to be only so many items that can be constructed and then one finds the whole process beginning to repeat itself. Security problems tend to force constant revision which in the end usually ends up as mere rewording of the same old items. Dr. Herndon voices some of the feelings of those opposed to the objective exam when she writes,

> Since 1955 the staff at Florida State University has changed its attitude toward examinations. We had experienced a growing dissatisfaction with the uniform machine-graded test, even though it was combined with an essay for the final, and instructors were free to give tests and quizzes throughout the course . . . we felt that students should be able to discuss intelligently the ideas stimulated by the course instead of merely making marks on an answer sheet. Something seemed wrong when the major effort of the examination came from the faculty's struggle to devise questions. The machine-graded test offered little challenge to the students to review carefully, and they took the test with little mental effort.

As a result, such tests were abandoned in 1956 and the instructors were left free to devise their own test although the essay type was recommended. The final examination in the course is an essay examination based on three kinds of questions: (1) fifteen to twenty brief identification questions; (2) four of five topics for brief discussion covering the various works studied during the course; (3) a general topic for fuller discussion offering the student the opportunity to integrate the material of the course.

Boston University Junior College has also, in the Humanities, found a shift away from the objective exams desirable. Two intra-semester exams and a final exam are given, all of them, essay. To aid the instructor to grade the exams more speedily and to solve, at least partially, the problem of uniformity of grading, "a guide, containing a list of the expected answers or appropriate lines of discussion, is prepared in division meetings prior to the examination. Instructors use this guide at their discretion and are urged to consider it a helpful compendium rather than an absolute directive. At the same time, it helps to give some common basis for subjective evaluation."

Stephens College also uses the essay examination as a major part of student evaluation. At mid-year, the test used is "frankly one of vocabulary so that discussions can be based on common use of terms for the second semester." At the end of the year, however, the student is responsible for three comparative analyses, one in the visual arts, one in music and one in literature; she is evaluated on the basis of her sensitiveness in observations and the relevance of her conclusions.

At the College at the University of Chicago, the gradual transition from reliance on objective testing to greater emphasis upon essay exams is described by Russell Thomas.

> The system of comprehensive examination, a requirement in all general courses, has been one factor which has commanded close staff cooperation. When students are to be prepared for a common examination there must be a clear understanding of common objectives and cooperation in planning the tests . . . Some important changes have occurred in the character of these examinations since they were first introduced. At that time they were wholly objective. Today nearly half of all exinations are essay examinations, and in the case of Humanities III, two-thirds of the grade are on essay assignments. Almost all of these are written under supervised conditions, however. All essays are read by two instructors, who do not know the identity of the students, and if there is more than one grade point difference in their judgments, a third reader is required to give judgment.

Michigan State University through the Office of Evaluation Service of the Basic College continues the use of common objective exams. The evaluation of the students' work is based upon a grade assigned to the student by the instructor who takes into consideration such factors as classroom examinations, quizzes, oral participation, and attitude. This mark is combined equally with the grade received on the large common examination and a final grade for the student is arrived at.

The construction of this common exam is a joint effort with the evaluation office at the college and the Humanities staff. The questions are submitted by the staff to a specially assigned and tarined "Humanities examiner" who does the job of editing and *adding additional* items to insure balance. The test is reviewed by the members of the "Humanities staff" to insure that it samples adequately the materials and reflects the aims of the course. Hirschfeld feels the common objective test tends to equalize variable grading practices, to discourage too much attention to some phase of the course at the expense of other phases, and, by including materials from preceding terms, to "reinforce for the student the view of the course as a unit."

One other type of examination which falls neither in the objective nor essay category should be mentioned. This is the oral examination used by the Division of Humanities at the Boston University Junior College. The oral examination is used as the final evaluation for the sophomores in the second semester of the course. Coming as it does at the conclusion of the "Utopia Unit," it serves as a kind of capstone to the two years' work in the Division and, to a much lesser extent, an opportunity for the student's team of instructors to form an impression of his growth and level of maturity at the end of his work at the college.

The five to seven students who have been working in and out of class for the final seven weeks of the course on their utopia project gather with their team in one of the conference rooms of the college for the oral examination. For an hour in an informal atmosphere amid coffee and smoke fumes, the students present their utopian structure, answer questions from the various members of the team, and defend their vision of the ideal society. Though this is a time-consuming task, sometimes running as high as twenty-two hours of examination, the rewards in terms of student and faculty insight make it an indispensable part of the total project.

Whatever the merits of the case are, a shift seems to be taking place from objective to essay examination.

Teacher Training and Recruitment

Many are the obstacles which still face the General Education movement in the country even though educational institutions in the field are gaining in prestige as a result of the leadership they have given, and even though an academic robe of respectability has fallen gently over the shoulders of those who are engaged in General Education. Some of the problems such as, lack of acceptance and understanding by some of our colleagues in the liberal arts college, lack of adequate evaluation of the total effect of the education given upon our students, "lack of flexibility, of interest in imaginative experimentation," can be met by the individual members acting with vigor and integrity or by the members of the Humanities staffs of the various institutions acting in concert.

There is one obstacle, however, which calls for constant alertness on the part of people in the field and it is the attitude of smugness or self-satisfaction which seems to be an ineluctable part of course stability. As Davidson says, "It was this attitude so obvious in the traditional liberal arts curriculum a generation ago that made the general education movement itself necessary and desirable." For a course to fructify, to continue to be a source of challenge and meaning to the students and teachers alike calls for imagination and vitality from all concerned.

To bring this vitality and imagination to the courses is of paramount interest to administrators, but out of this interest emerges perhaps the most vital problem facing General Education in this country and that is the need for trained teachers to give leadership and direction to the ever-expanding courses. This is a problem that cannot be solved by small colleges without graduate facilities, rather the solution lies in the graduate departments of the large state and private universities. Florida State, Wesleyan and Iowa State University through their graduate programs in the Humanities are moving towards a solution to this problem.

Dr. Herndon sees this need for teachers as, "our greatest problem today." At Florida State University steps are being taken to alleviate to some degree this shortage of teachers. An interdivisional graduate program leading to the Ph.D. in the Humanities was established in 1956. In addition to this program, "a cooperative program with the School of Education leading to a master's degree in the Humanities with certification for junior college teaching," was established. It is too soon to assess results of this effort, although there are four candidates for the Ph.D. degree expected within a year. Dr. Herdon concludes, "The program attracts extremely capable students whose major interest lies in teaching, though they are well qualified to contribute to research and criticism. The unusual demands of the program keep out of it those who wish to avoid an arduous academic discipline."

Without men and women who are dedicated to the ideas of General Education as vigorously as they are to the profession of teaching we cannot look forward to significant growth in Humanities programs.

Conclusion

General education is that education, in terms of content, attitudes, values and tastes developed which results in an honest and imaginative approach to all problems on the part of reasonable and intelligent men and women. Intellectual and moral integrity characterize those who have successfully completed a general education.

The growth of general education in the early twenties and after 1945 seems to suggest that it takes its motivation from and flourishes after a crisis in which our total resources, physical and intellectual, have been called into play. The disillusionment which followed hard upon the wars of the first and middle parts of the century played a large part in the fostering of the general education ideal. In the disillusionment many of the nation turn back to seek fundamental causes and answers and look for new directions in which to move. The present challenge to us is, apparently, not a sufficient enough moral crisis to many people. There is the feeling that the answer to our problems lies quite readily and literally in the hands and minds of the scientists. We as a people are no longer concerned with the *oughtness* of acts only the *how*. Where other disciplines are concerned with helping men answer the *hows*, the *wheres* and the *whens*, the humanities remains focused upon the root of man's activities with the sterner question of *ought*.

In order to remain a vital force in the field of education, the humanities, or more properly those in administrative positions, must strive to bring new teachers into the field. Even those teachers who have been working for the first ten years are perhaps tending towards solidity and conservatism. Without originality, vitality, and spirit a kind of hardening of the intellectual and administrative arteries often sets into a program and eventually buries it under a host of memories of "what we used to do." Constant recruitment of young men and women who are willing to commit their academic lives to general education will assure the continued growth spirit in the humanities.

At a recent meeting on general education at Drake University, Earl McGrath pointed out several forces at work which make for renewed interest in general education. These forces are: increased demand for college education; an awareness on the part of many college graduates that the highly specialized instruction they have received has not adequately prepared them to live in the complex world of today; and the shortage of college teachers. As a result of these forces and the new vitality engendered, Dr. McGrath felt that in general education certain shifts in emphasis will be required.

They are:

1. Selection of subject matter so as to introduce the student to the basic principles, experiments, or key ideas in the major disciplines, making no attempt to lay a complete foundation for the specialist.
2. Stress on methodology employed by those who create new knowledge in the various disciplines.

Dr. McGrath concluded that further developments in general education, sensitive designing of new types of instruction, and the recognition of the importance of general education in our national welfare are matters of dominant concern to the members of our profession. He asked the question, "Can the general education of the people here and abroad be accomplished quickly enough to make democratic government effective in grappling with the issues of our time, and by comparison, more desirable than another system which to those of limited educational advantages may appear to be more successful in meeting their emerging needs?" One can only hope that the answer is in the affirmative.

It is necessary to keep in mind, however, that neither universities, their faculties, nor their curricula should be considered solely or in part instruments of governmental, national or foreign policy. If our education is wise and good, our citizenry should be wise and good, and it is to be hoped that the wisdom and goodness of the people will find expression in their government.